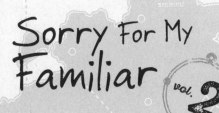

Sorry For My Familiar vol. 2

story & art by
TEKKA YAGURABA

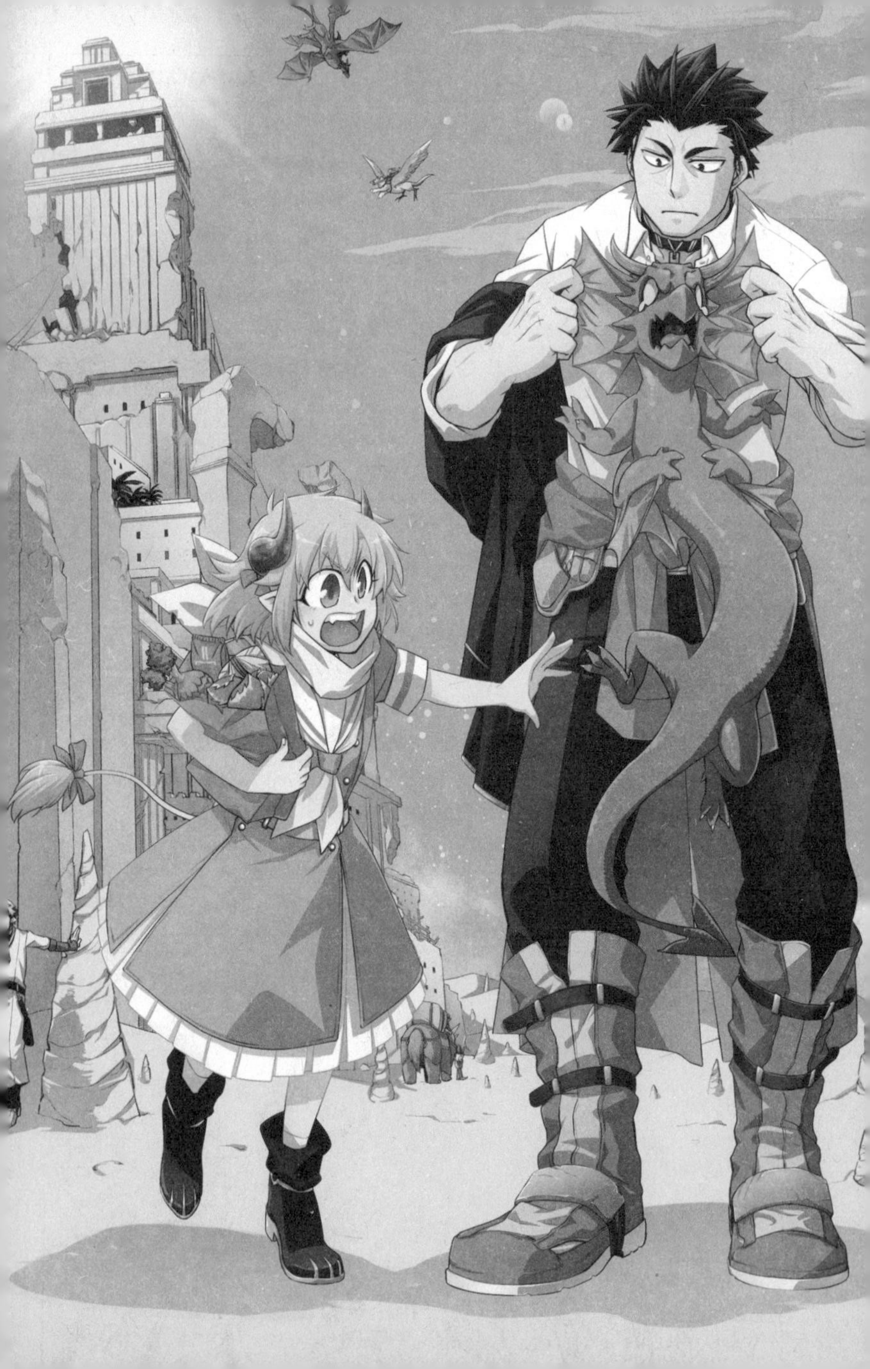

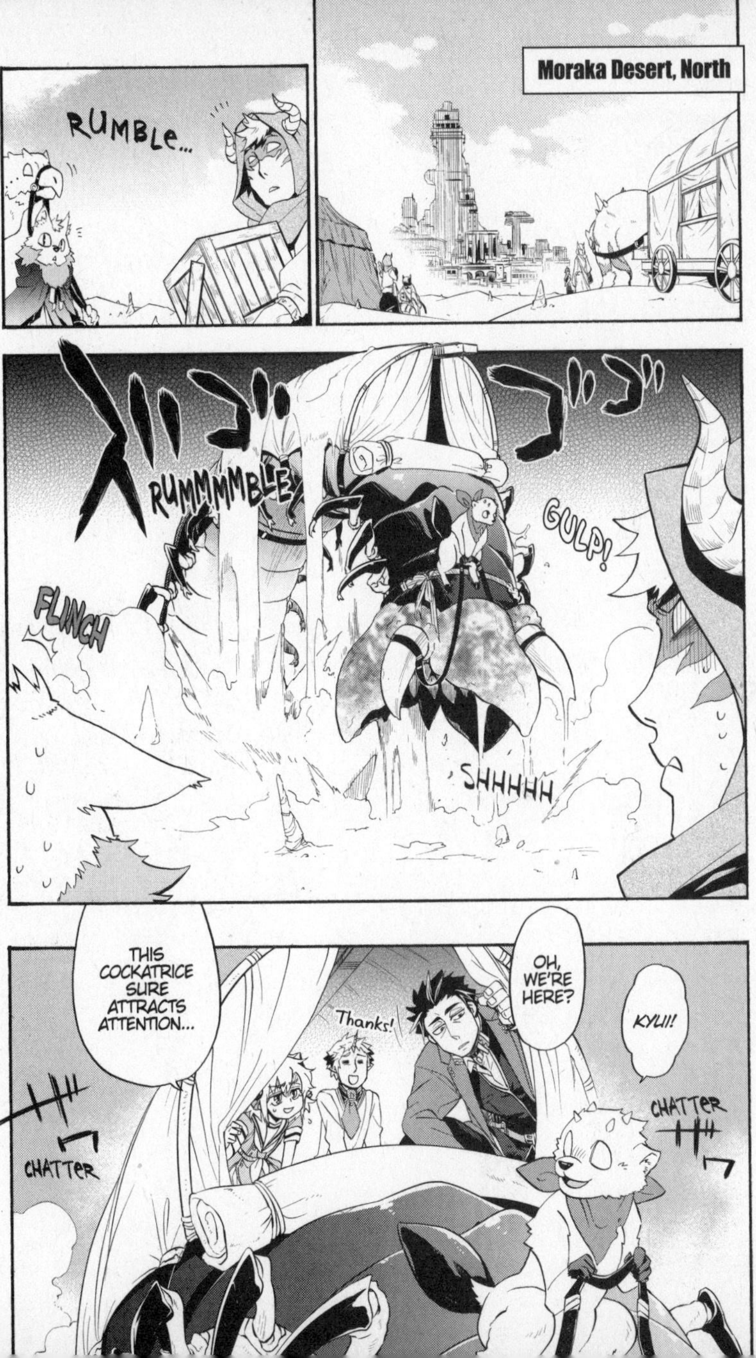
Moraka Desert, North
RUMBLE...
GULP!
RUMMMMBLE
FLINCH
SHHHHH
KYUI!
OH, WE'RE HERE?
Thanks!
THIS COCKATRICE SURE ATTRACTS ATTENTION...
CHATTER
CHATTER

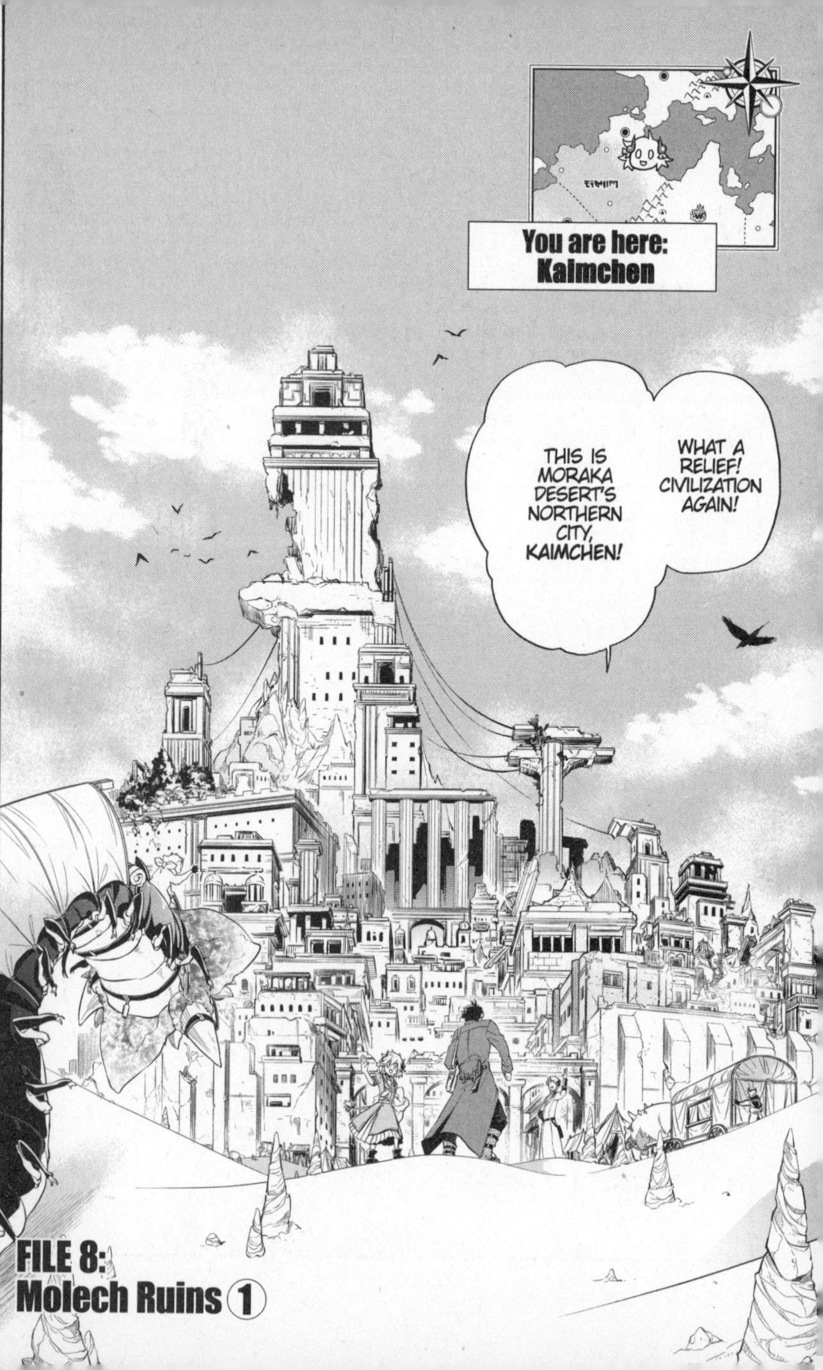
You are here: Kaimchen
WHAT A RELIEF! CIVILIZATION AGAIN!
THIS IS MORAKA DESERT'S NORTHERN CITY, KAIMCHEN!
FILE 8: Molech Ruins ①

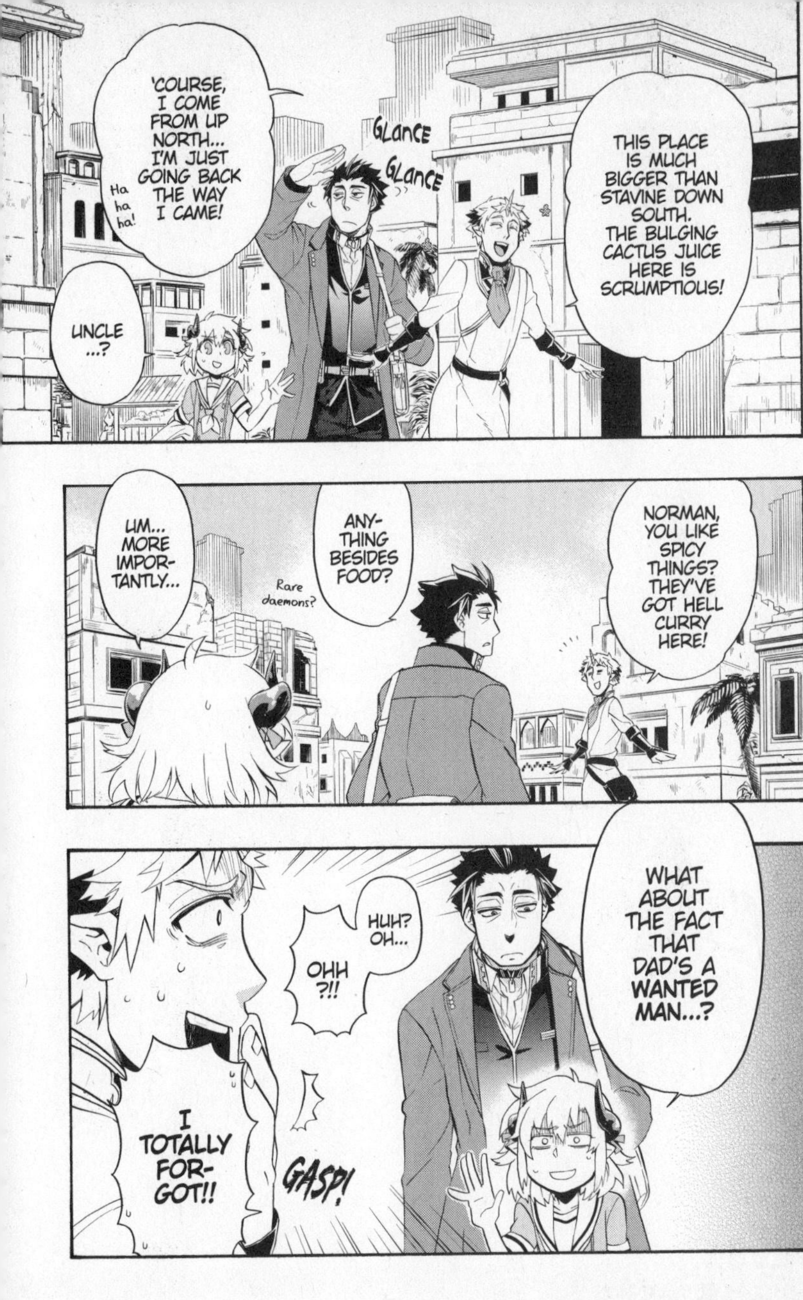
THIS PLACE IS MUCH BIGGER THAN STAVINE DOWN SOUTH. THE BULGING CACTUS JUICE HERE IS SCRUMPTIOUS!
GLANCE
GLANCE
'COURSE, I COME FROM UP NORTH... I'M JUST GOING BACK THE WAY I CAME!
Ha ha ha!
UNCLE ...?
NORMAN, YOU LIKE SPICY THINGS? THEY'VE GOT HELL CURRY HERE!
ANY-THING BESIDES FOOD?
Rare daemons?
UM... MORE IMPOR-TANTLY...
WHAT ABOUT THE FACT THAT DAD'S A WANTED MAN...?
HUH? OH...
OHH ?!!
GASP!
I TOTALLY FOR-GOT!!

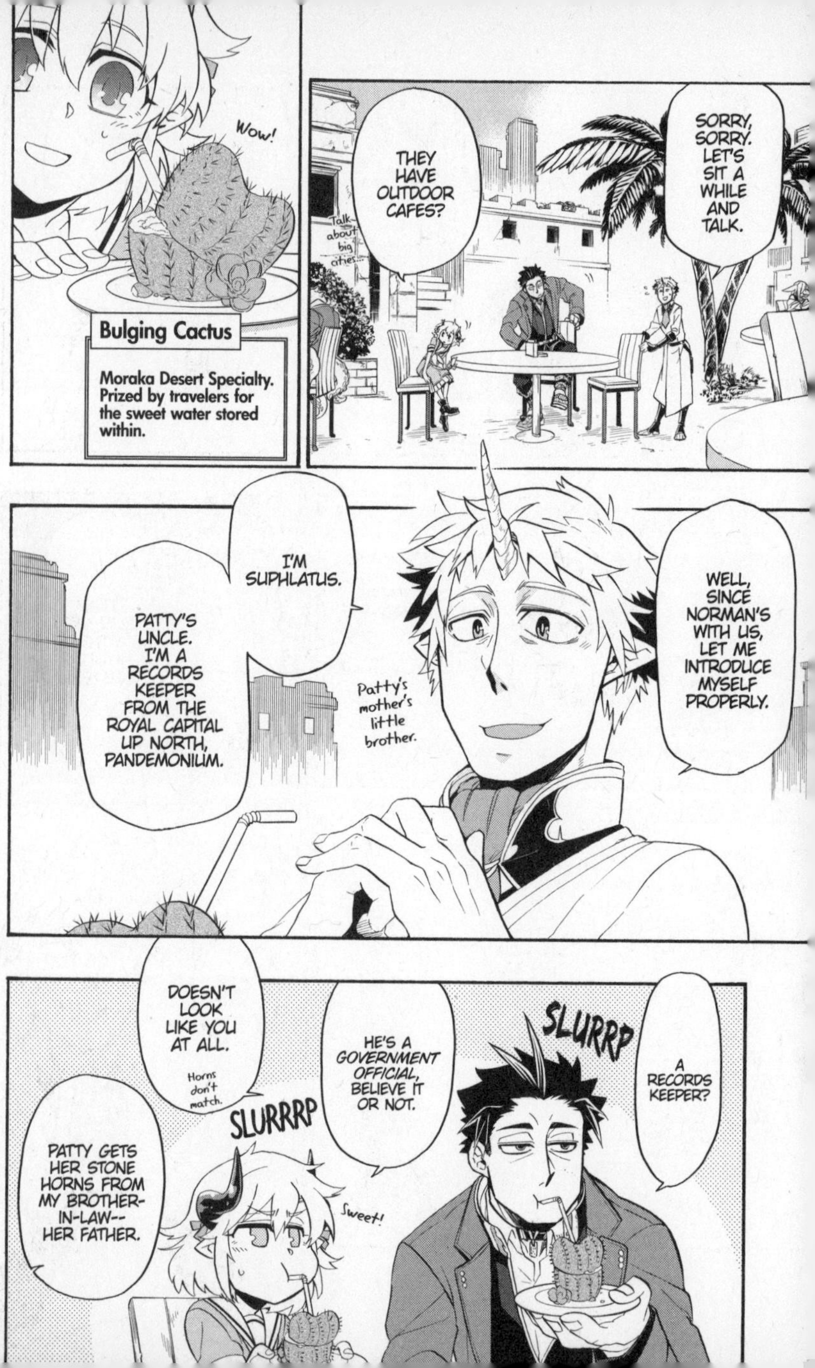
SORRY, SORRY. LET'S SIT A WHILE AND TALK.
THEY HAVE OUTDOOR CAFES?
Talk about big cities...
Wow!
Bulging Cactus
Moraka Desert Specialty. Prized by travelers for the sweet water stored within.
WELL, SINCE NORMAN'S WITH US, LET ME INTRODUCE MYSELF PROPERLY.
I'M SUPHLATUS.
PATTY'S UNCLE. I'M A RECORDS KEEPER FROM THE ROYAL CAPITAL UP NORTH, PANDEMONIUM.
Patty's mother's little brother.
A RECORDS KEEPER?
SLURRP
HE'S A GOVERNMENT OFFICIAL, BELIEVE IT OR NOT.
DOESN'T LOOK LIKE YOU AT ALL.
Horns don't match.
SLURRRP
Sweet!
PATTY GETS HER STONE HORNS FROM MY BROTHER-IN-LAW-- HER FATHER.

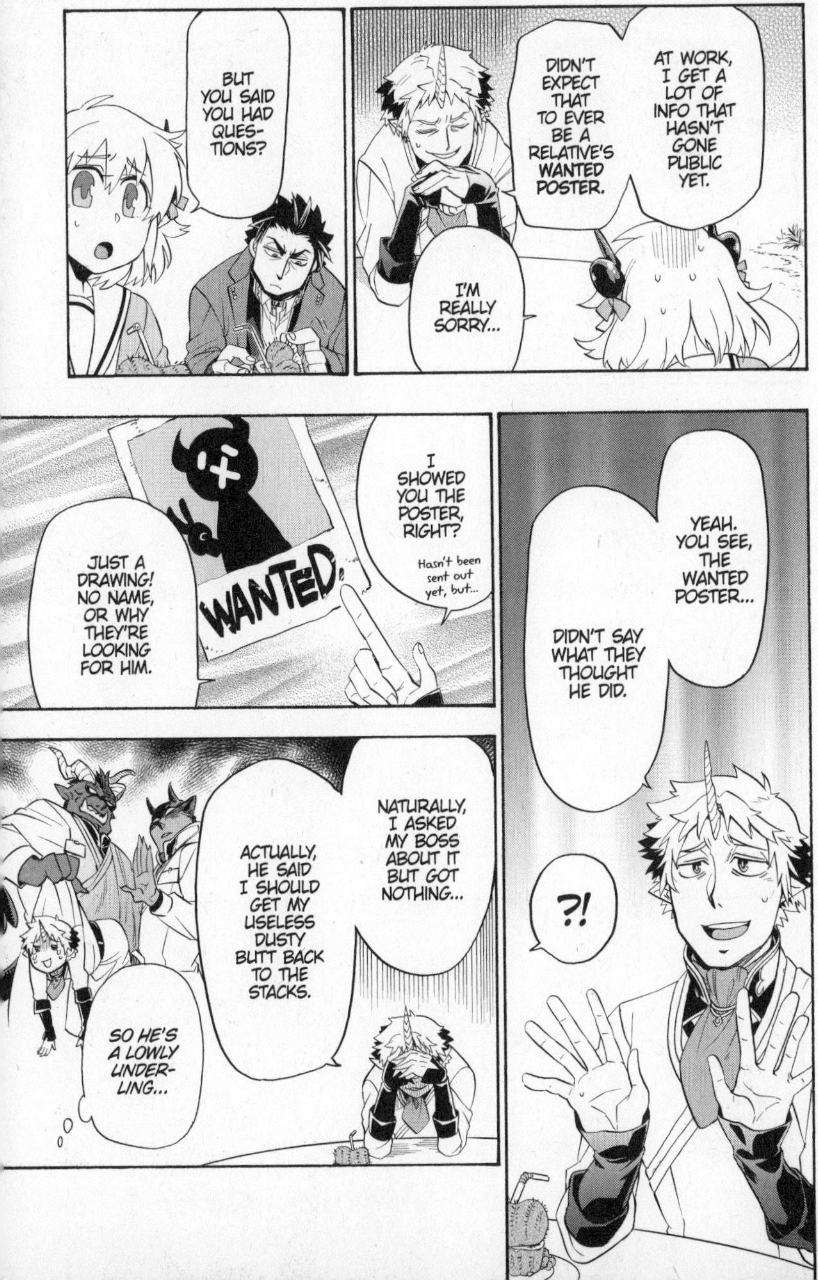
AT WORK, I GET A LOT OF INFO THAT HASN'T GONE PUBLIC YET.
DIDN'T EXPECT THAT TO EVER BE A RELATIVE'S WANTED POSTER.
I'M REALLY SORRY...
BUT YOU SAID YOU HAD QUES-TIONS?
YEAH. YOU SEE, THE WANTED POSTER...
DIDN'T SAY WHAT THEY THOUGHT HE DID.
?!
I SHOWED YOU THE POSTER, RIGHT?
Hasn't been sent out yet, but...
WANTED
JUST A DRAWING! NO NAME, OR WHY THEY'RE LOOKING FOR HIM.
NATURALLY, I ASKED MY BOSS ABOUT IT BUT GOT NOTHING...
ACTUALLY, HE SAID I SHOULD GET MY USELESS DUSTY BUTT BACK TO THE STACKS.
SO HE'S A LOWLY UNDER-LING...

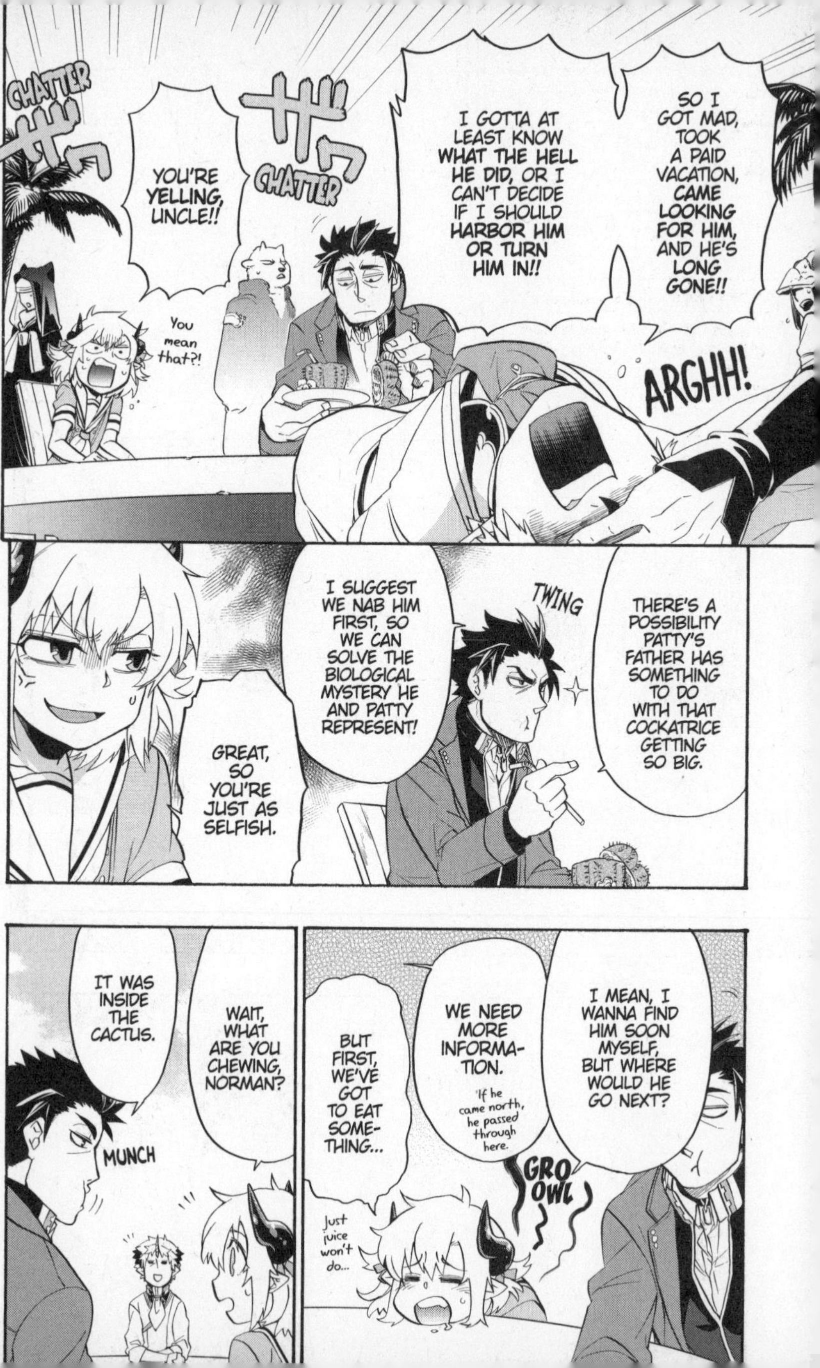
SO I GOT MAD, TOOK A PAID VACATION, CAME LOOKING FOR HIM, AND HE'S LONG GONE!!
ARGHH!
I GOTTA AT LEAST KNOW WHAT THE HELL HE DID, OR I CAN'T DECIDE IF I SHOULD HARBOR HIM OR TURN HIM IN!!
CHATTER
YOU'RE YELLING, UNCLE!!
CHATTER
You mean that?!
THERE'S A POSSIBILITY PATTY'S FATHER HAS SOMETHING TO DO WITH THAT COCKATRICE GETTING SO BIG.
TWING
I SUGGEST WE NAB HIM FIRST, SO WE CAN SOLVE THE BIOLOGICAL MYSTERY HE AND PATTY REPRESENT!
GREAT, SO YOU'RE JUST AS SELFISH.
I MEAN, I WANNA FIND HIM SOON MYSELF, BUT WHERE WOULD HE GO NEXT?
WE NEED MORE INFORMATION.
If he came north, he passed through here.
GROOWL
BUT FIRST, WE'VE GOT TO EAT SOMETHING...
Just juice won't do...
WAIT, WHAT ARE YOU CHEWING, NORMAN?
IT WAS INSIDE THE CACTUS.
MUNCH

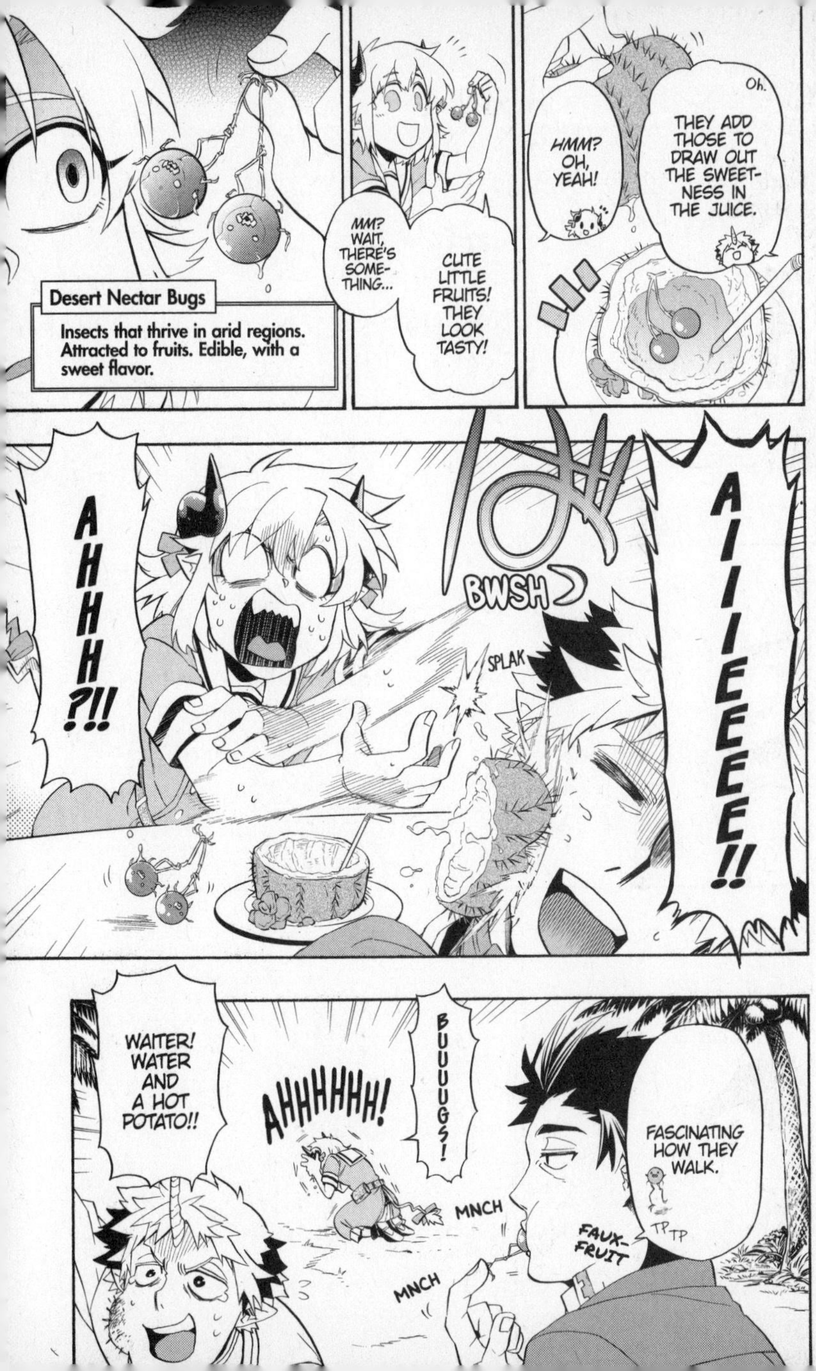
Oh.
THEY ADD THOSE TO DRAW OUT THE SWEETNESS IN THE JUICE.
HMM? OH, YEAH!
CUTE LITTLE FRUITS! THEY LOOK TASTY!
MM? WAIT, THERE'S SOMETHING...
Desert Nectar Bugs
Insects that thrive in arid regions. Attracted to fruits. Edible, with a sweet flavor.
AIIIEEEEE!!
BWSH
SPLAK
AHHHH?!!
FASCINATING HOW THEY WALK.
TP TP
FAUX-FRUIT
MNCH
MNCH
BUUUUGS!
AHHHHHH!
WAITER! WATER AND A HOT POTATO!!

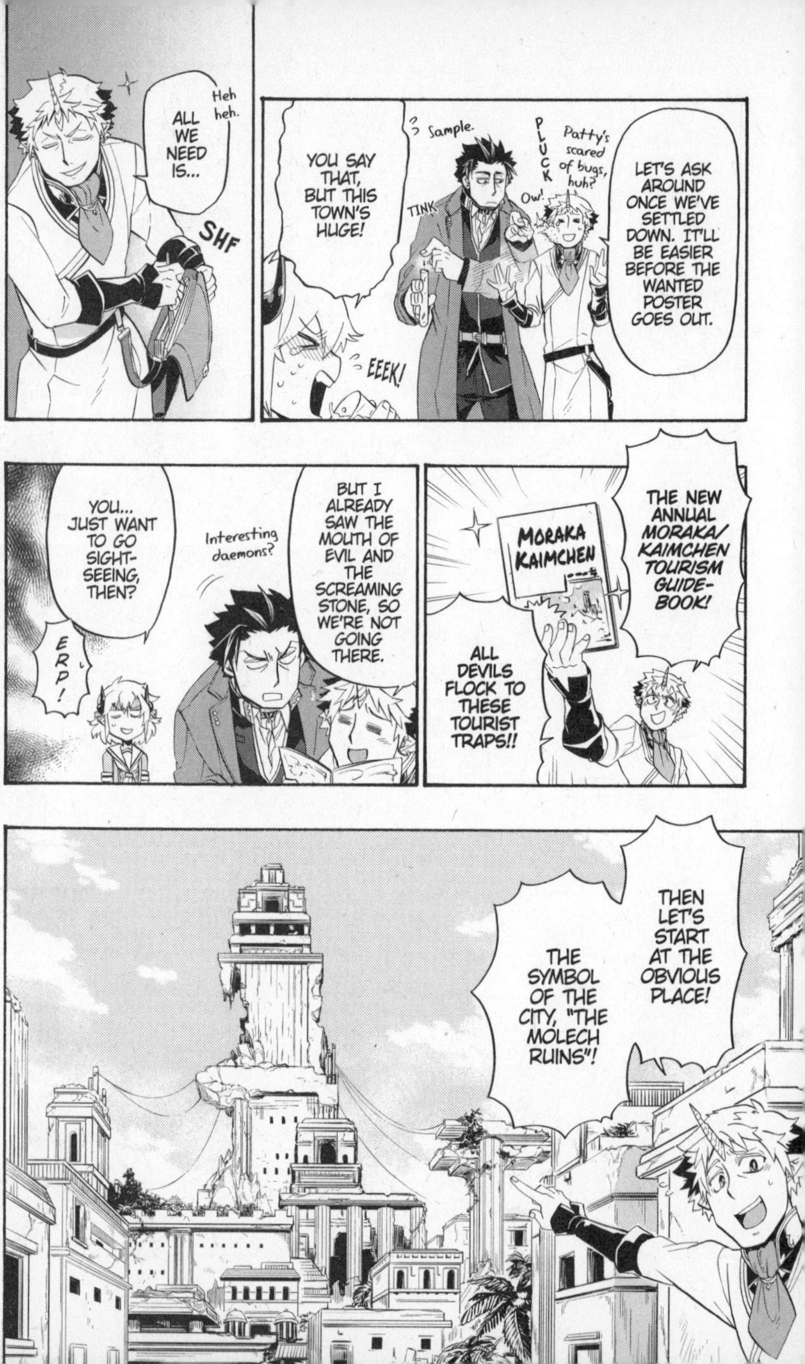
LET'S ASK AROUND ONCE WE'VE SETTLED DOWN. IT'LL BE EASIER BEFORE THE WANTED POSTER GOES OUT.
Patty's scared of bugs, huh?
Ow!
PLUCK
Sample.
TINK
YOU SAY THAT, BUT THIS TOWN'S HUGE!
EEEK!
Heh heh.
ALL WE NEED IS...
SHF
THE NEW ANNUAL MORAKA/KAIMCHEN TOURISM GUIDEBOOK!
MORAKA KAIMCHEN
ALL DEVILS FLOCK TO THESE TOURIST TRAPS!!
BUT I ALREADY SAW THE MOUTH OF EVIL AND THE SCREAMING STONE, SO WE'RE NOT GOING THERE.
Interesting daemons?
YOU... JUST WANT TO GO SIGHT-SEEING, THEN?
ERP!
THEN LET'S START AT THE OBVIOUS PLACE!
THE SYMBOL OF THE CITY, "THE MOLECH RUINS"!

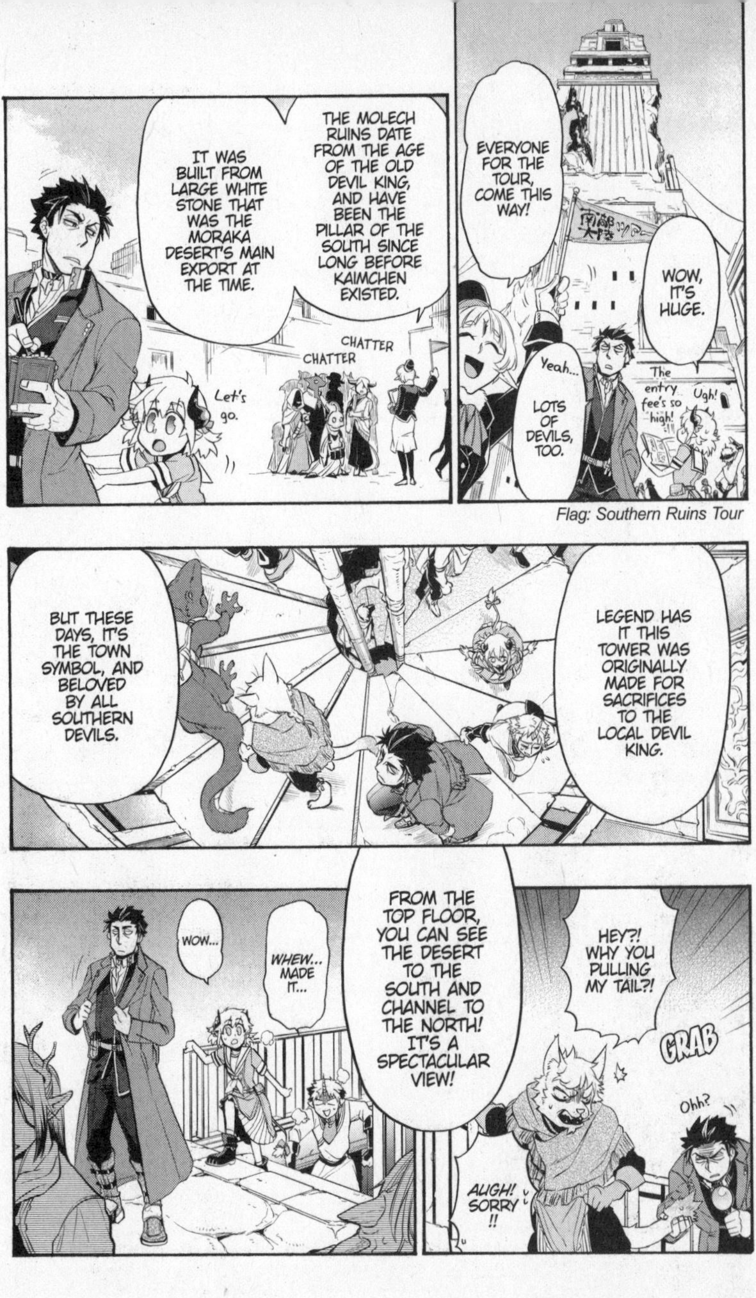
EVERYONE FOR THE TOUR, COME THIS WAY!
WOW, IT'S HUGE.
Yeah...
LOTS OF DEVILS, TOO.
Ugh!
The entry fee's so high!
THE MOLECH RUINS DATE FROM THE AGE OF THE OLD DEVIL KING, AND HAVE BEEN THE PILLAR OF THE SOUTH SINCE LONG BEFORE KAIMCHEN EXISTED.
IT WAS BUILT FROM LARGE WHITE STONE THAT WAS THE MORAKA DESERT'S MAIN EXPORT AT THE TIME.
CHATTER
CHATTER
Let's go.
LEGEND HAS IT THIS TOWER WAS ORIGINALLY MADE FOR SACRIFICES TO THE LOCAL DEVIL KING.
BUT THESE DAYS, IT'S THE TOWN SYMBOL, AND BELOVED BY ALL SOUTHERN DEVILS.
HEY?! WHY YOU PULLING MY TAIL?!
GRAB
Ohh?
AUGH! SORRY!!
FROM THE TOP FLOOR, YOU CAN SEE THE DESERT TO THE SOUTH AND CHANNEL TO THE NORTH! IT'S A SPECTACULAR VIEW!
WOW...
WHEW... MADE IT...

Flag: Southern Ruins Tour

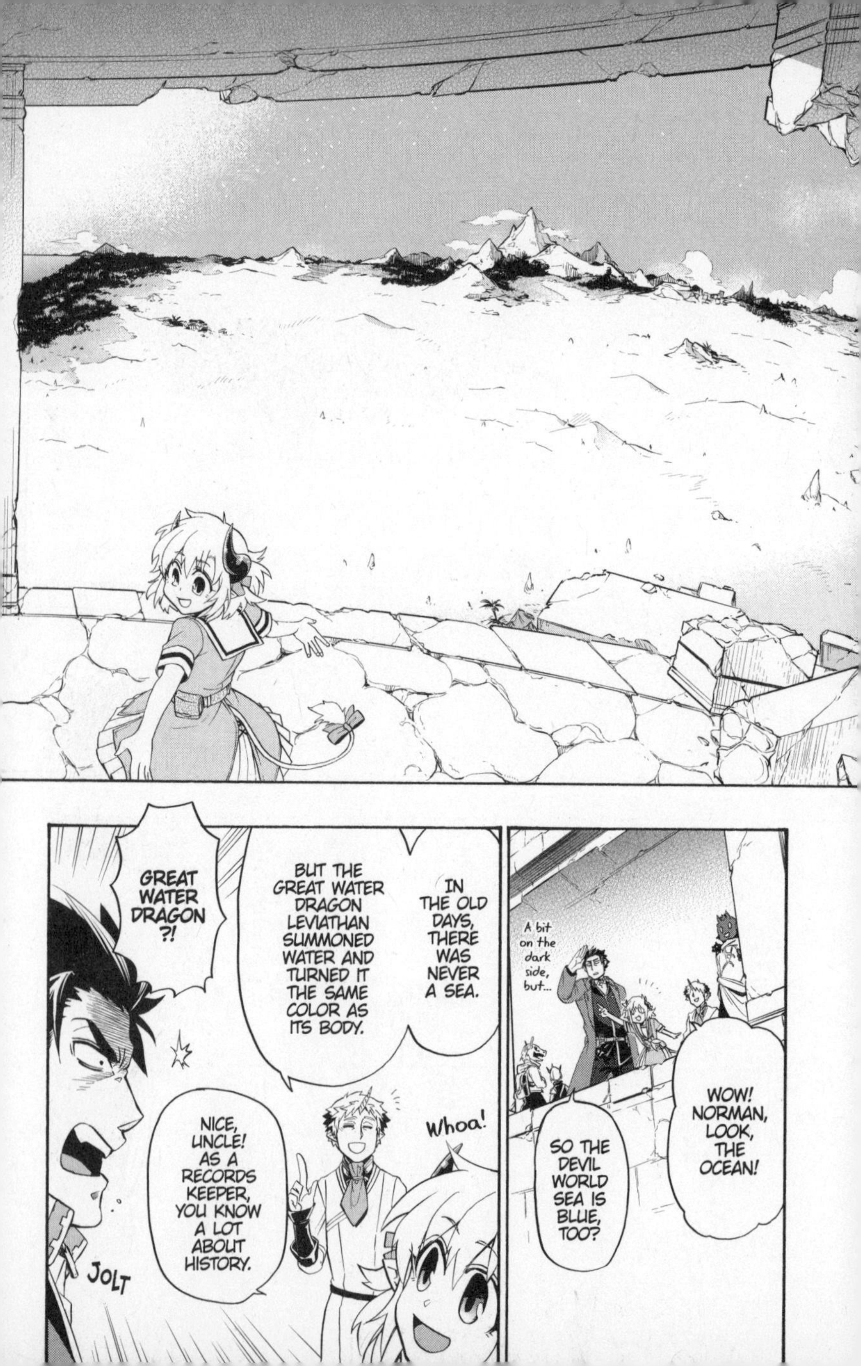
WOW! NORMAN, LOOK, THE OCEAN!
SO THE DEVIL WORLD SEA IS BLUE, TOO?
A bit on the dark side, but...
IN THE OLD DAYS, THERE WAS NEVER A SEA.
BUT THE GREAT WATER DRAGON LEVIATHAN SUMMONED WATER AND TURNED IT THE SAME COLOR AS ITS BODY.
GREAT WATER DRAGON?!
Whoa!
NICE, UNCLE! AS A RECORDS KEEPER, YOU KNOW A LOT ABOUT HISTORY.
JOLT

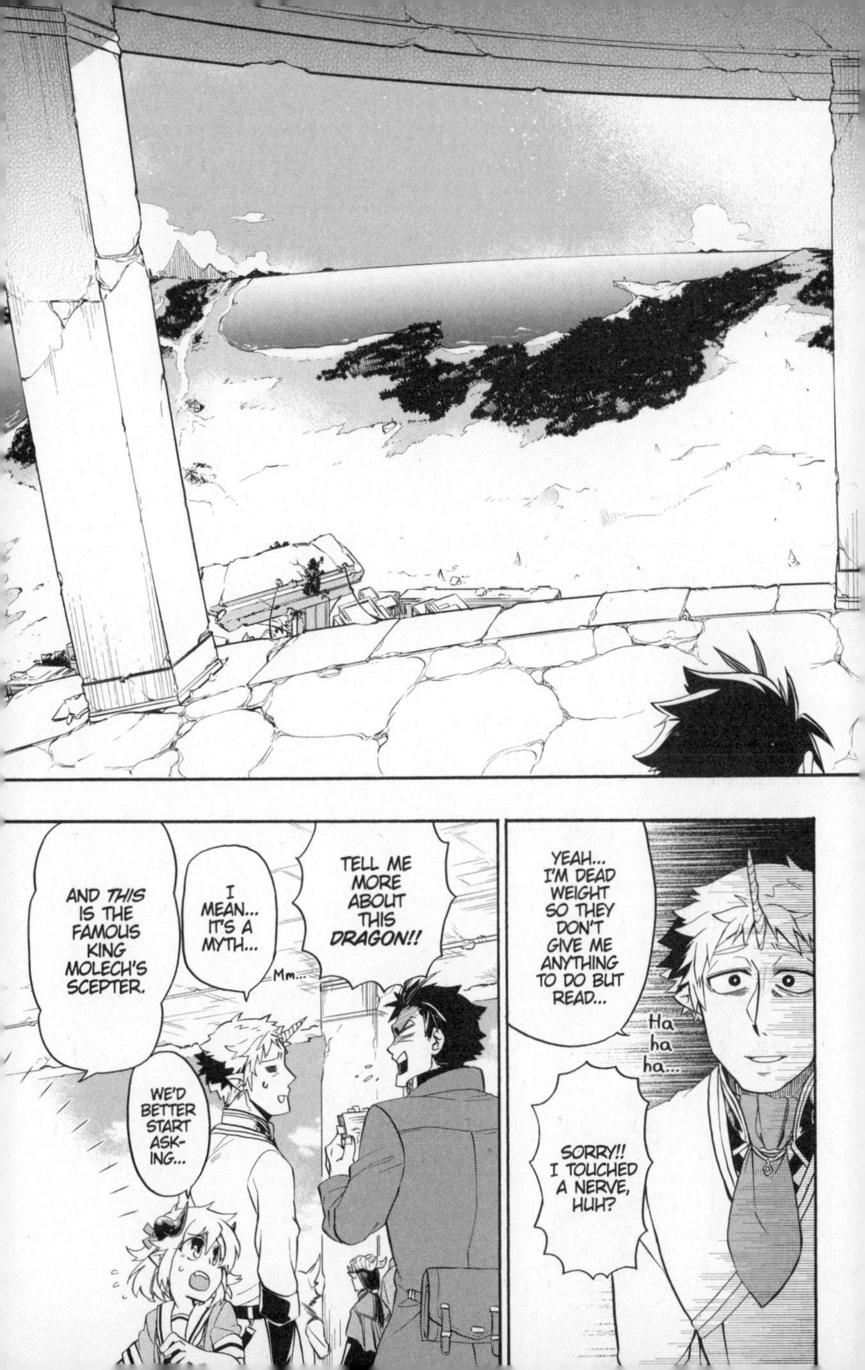
YEAH... I'M DEAD WEIGHT SO THEY DON'T GIVE ME ANYTHING TO DO BUT READ...
Ha ha ha...
SORRY!! I TOUCHED A NERVE, HUH?
TELL ME MORE ABOUT THIS *DRAGON!!*
I MEAN... IT'S A MYTH...
Mm...
AND *THIS* IS THE FAMOUS KING MOLECH'S SCEPTER.
WE'D BETTER START ASK-ING...

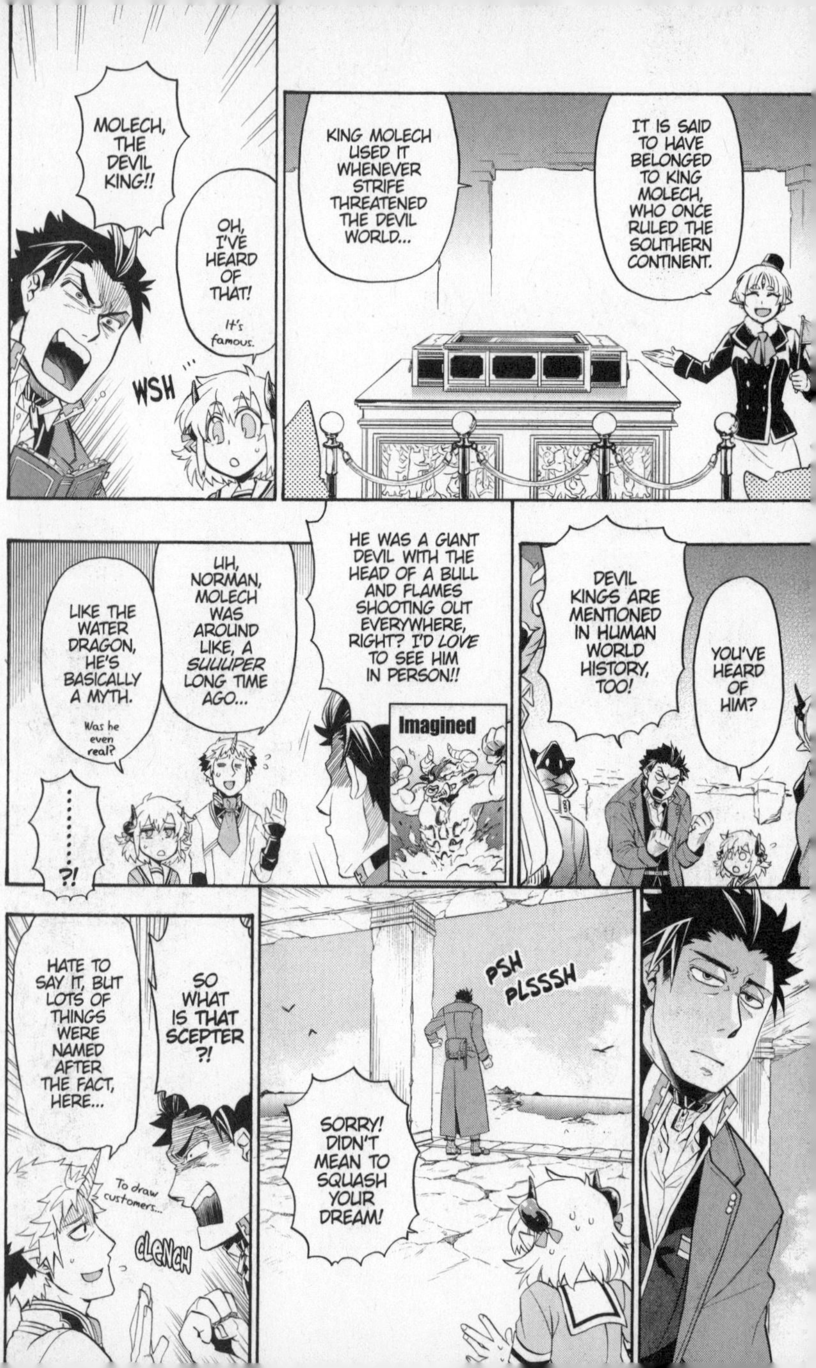
IT IS SAID TO HAVE BELONGED TO KING MOLECH, WHO ONCE RULED THE SOUTHERN CONTINENT.
KING MOLECH USED IT WHENEVER STRIFE THREATENED THE DEVIL WORLD...
MOLECH, THE DEVIL KING!!
OH, I'VE HEARD OF THAT!
It's famous.
WSH
YOU'VE HEARD OF HIM?
DEVIL KINGS ARE MENTIONED IN HUMAN WORLD HISTORY, TOO!
HE WAS A GIANT DEVIL WITH THE HEAD OF A BULL AND FLAMES SHOOTING OUT EVERYWHERE, RIGHT? I'D *LOVE* TO SEE HIM IN PERSON!!
Imagined
UH, NORMAN, MOLECH WAS AROUND LIKE, A *SUUUPER* LONG TIME AGO...
LIKE THE WATER DRAGON, HE'S BASICALLY A MYTH.
Was he even real?
........?!
PSH PLSSSH
SORRY! DIDN'T MEAN TO SQUASH YOUR DREAM!
SO WHAT IS THAT SCEPTER?!
HATE TO SAY IT, BUT LOTS OF THINGS WERE NAMED AFTER THE FACT, HERE...
To draw customers...
CLENCH

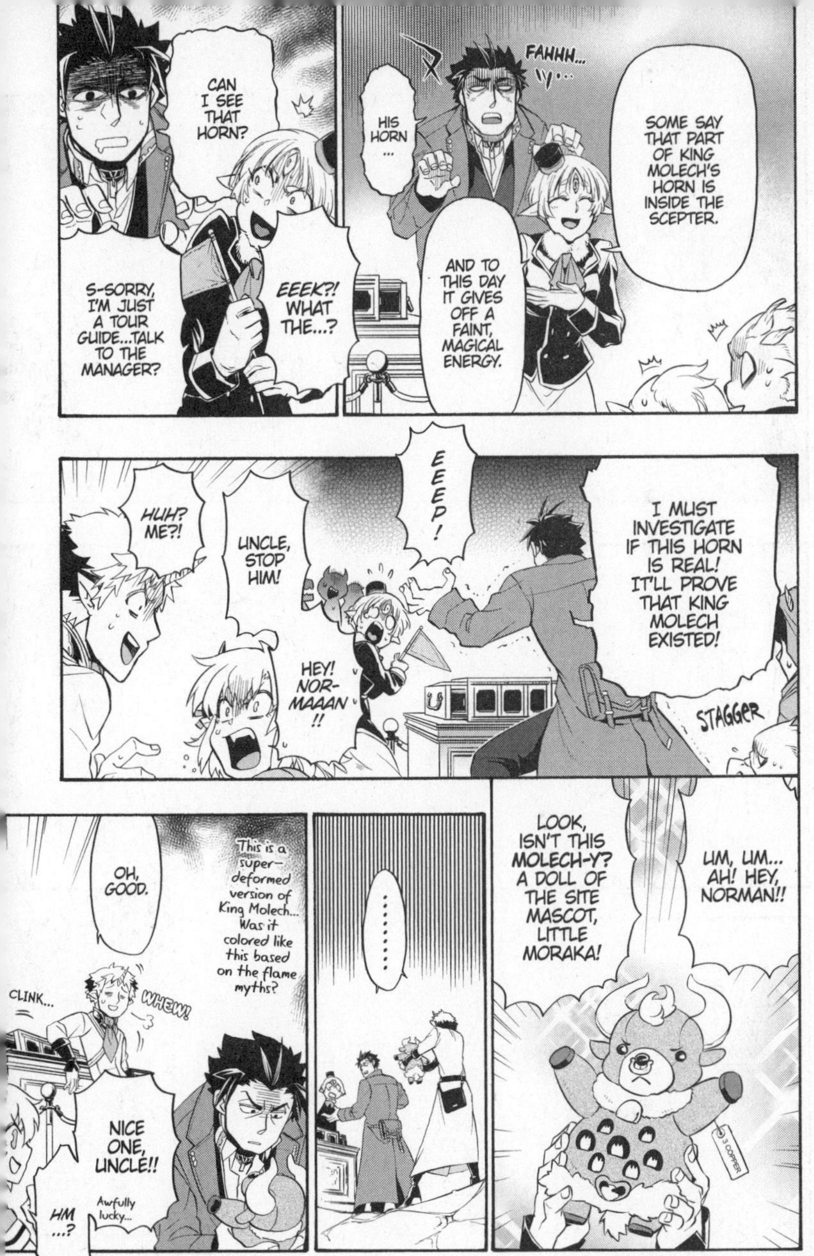

FAHHH...
SOME SAY THAT PART OF KING MOLECH'S HORN IS INSIDE THE SCEPTER.
HIS HORN ...
AND TO THIS DAY IT GIVES OFF A FAINT, MAGICAL ENERGY.
CAN I SEE THAT HORN?
EEEK?! WHAT THE...?
S-SORRY, I'M JUST A TOUR GUIDE...TALK TO THE MANAGER?
I MUST INVESTIGATE IF THIS HORN IS REAL! IT'LL PROVE THAT KING MOLECH EXISTED!
EEEP!
UNCLE, STOP HIM!
HUH? ME?!
HEY! NOR-MAAAN!!
STAGGER
UM, UM... AH! HEY, NORMAN!!
LOOK, ISN'T THIS MOLECH-Y? A DOLL OF THE SITE MASCOT, LITTLE MORAKA!
3 COPPER
....
This is a super-deformed version of King Molech... Was it colored like this based on the flame myths?
OH, GOOD.
CLINK...
WHEW!
NICE ONE, UNCLE!!
HM ...?
Awfully lucky...

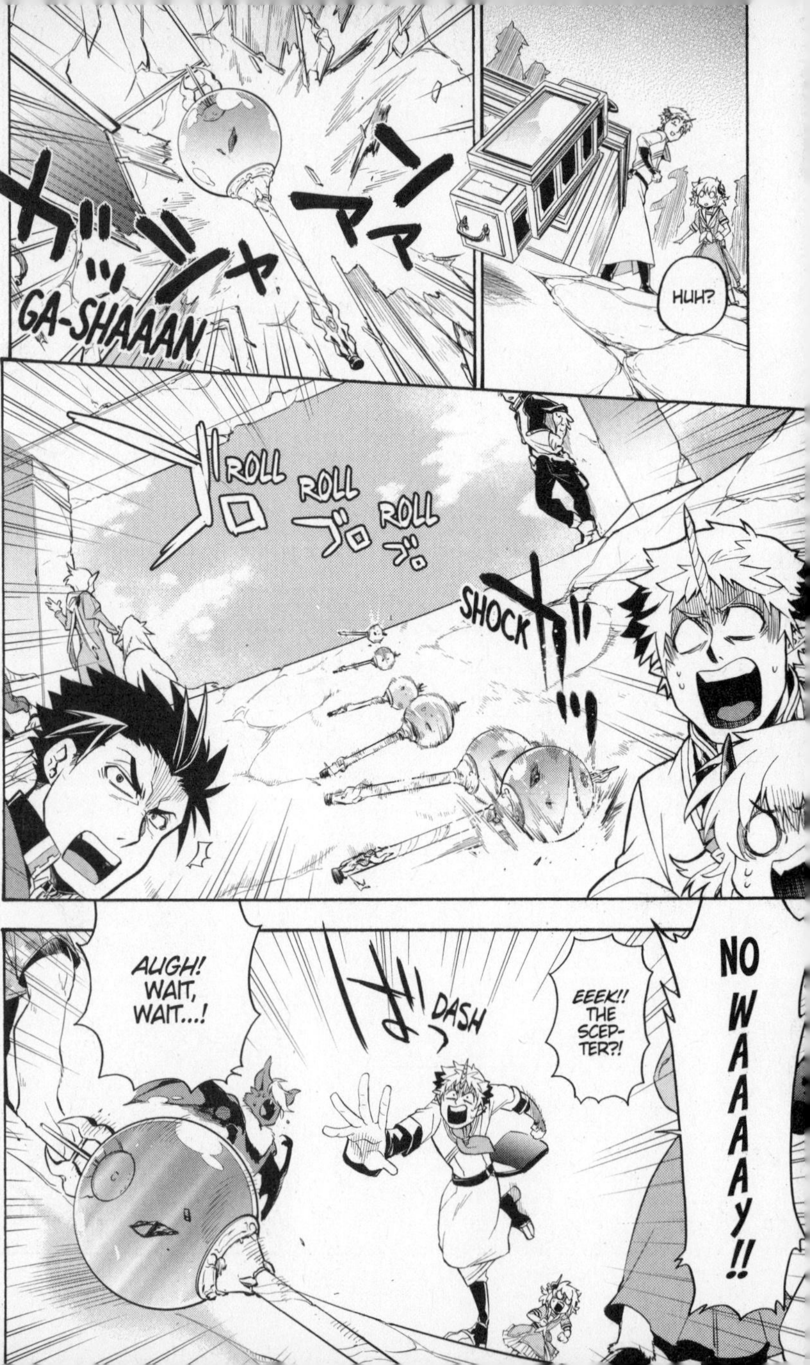
HUH?
GA-SHAAAN
SHOCK
ROLL
ROLL
ROLL
NO WAAAAAY!!
EEEK!! THE SCEP-TER?!
DASH
AUGH! WAIT, WAIT...!

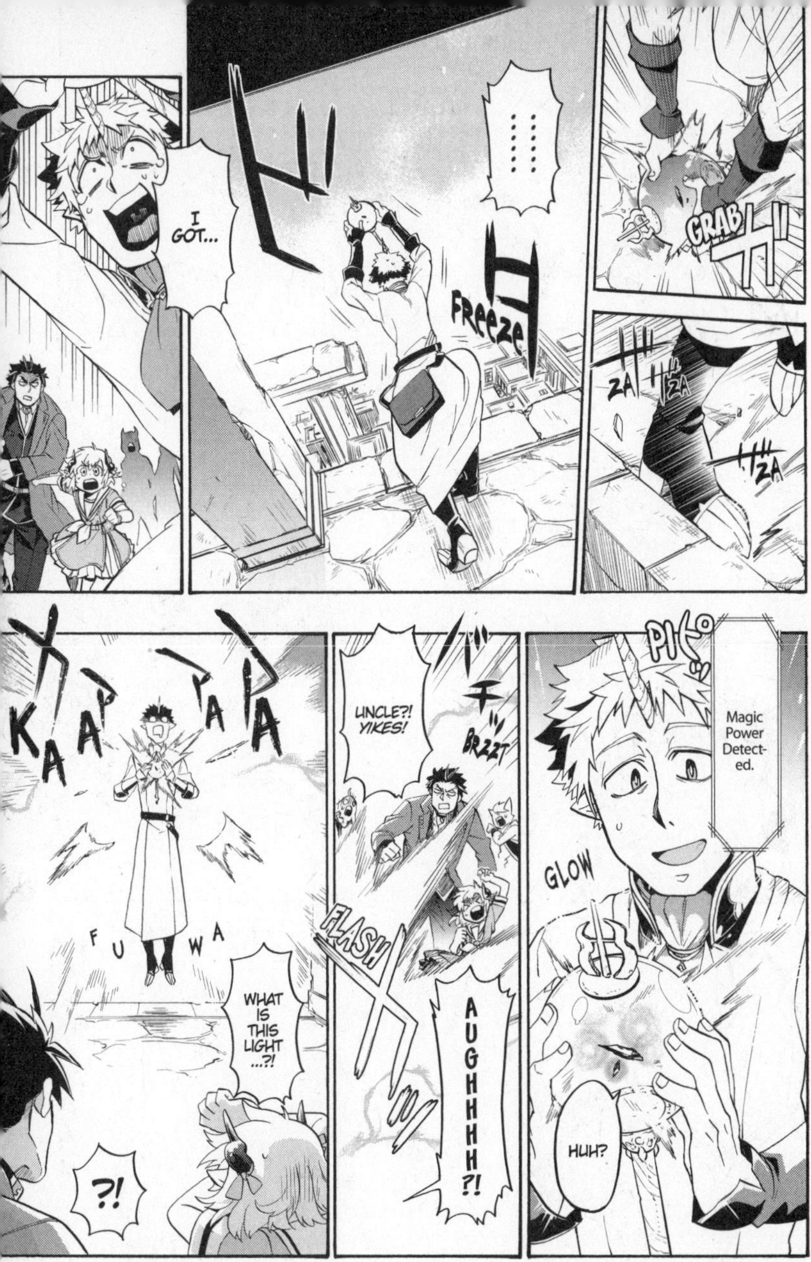
GRAB
ZA
ZA
ZA
......
FREEZE
I GOT...
PI
Magic Power Detected.
GLOW
HUH?
UNCLE?! YIKES!
BRZZT
FLASH
AUGHHHHH?!
KA PA PA
FUWA
WHAT IS THIS LIGHT ...?!
?!

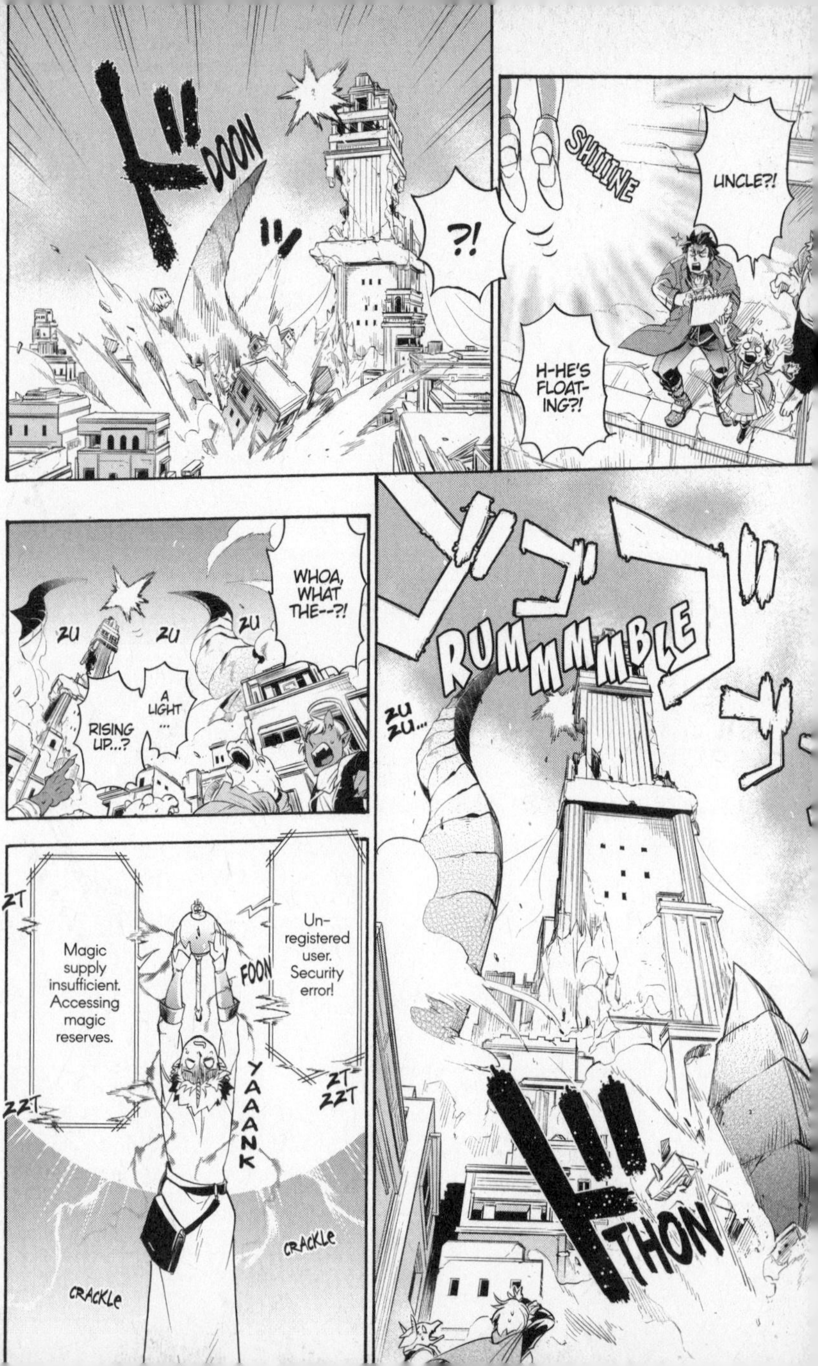
UNCLE?!
SHIIINE
H-HE'S FLOATING?!
?!
DOON
RUMMMMBLE
ZU ZU...
THON
WHOA, WHAT THE--?!
ZU
ZU
ZU
A LIGHT ...
RISING UP...?
Un-registered user. Security error!
ZT
FOON
Magic supply insufficient. Accessing magic reserves.
ZT ZZT
YAAAANK
ZZT
CRACKLe
CRACKLe

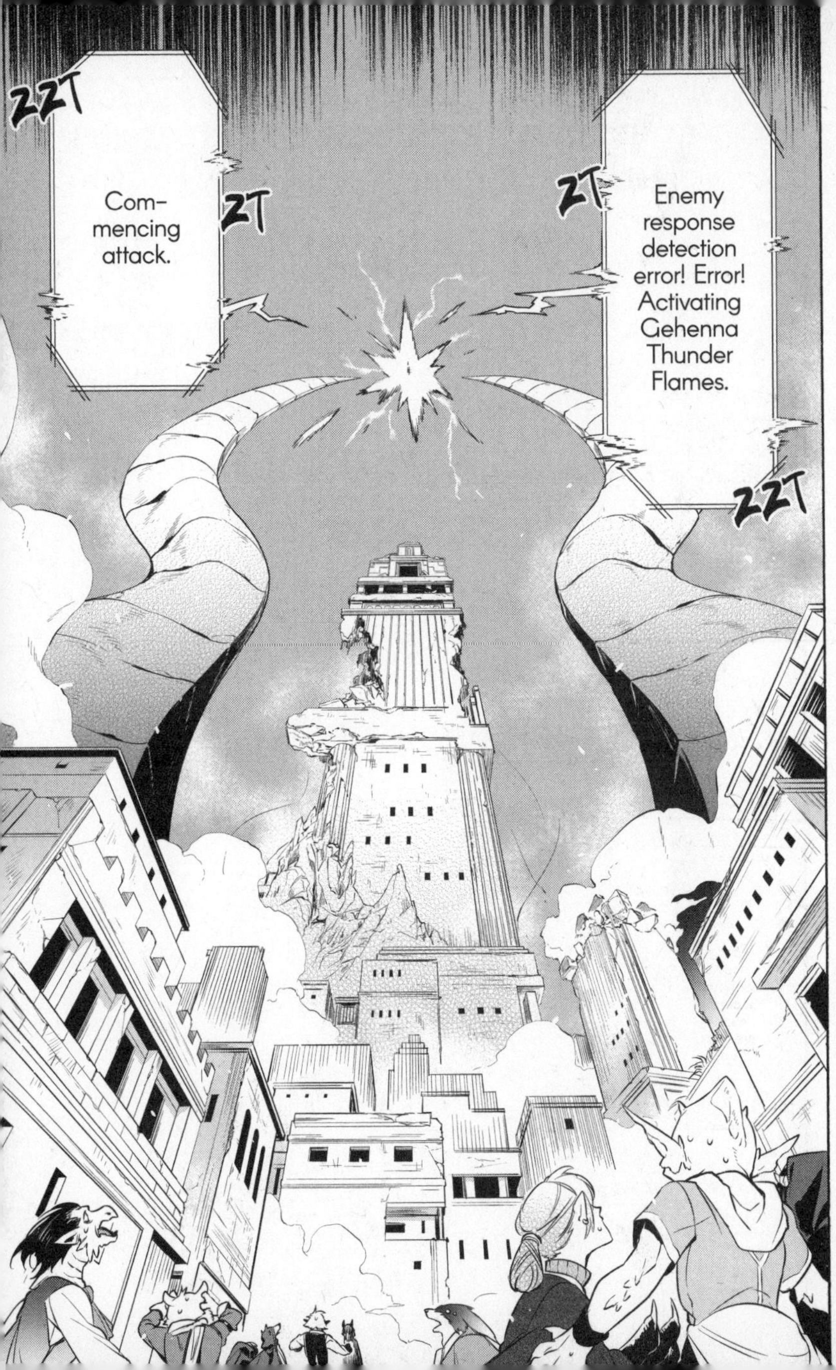
ZT
Enemy response detection error! Error! Activating Gehenna Thunder Flames.
ZZT
ZZT
Com-mencing attack.
ZT

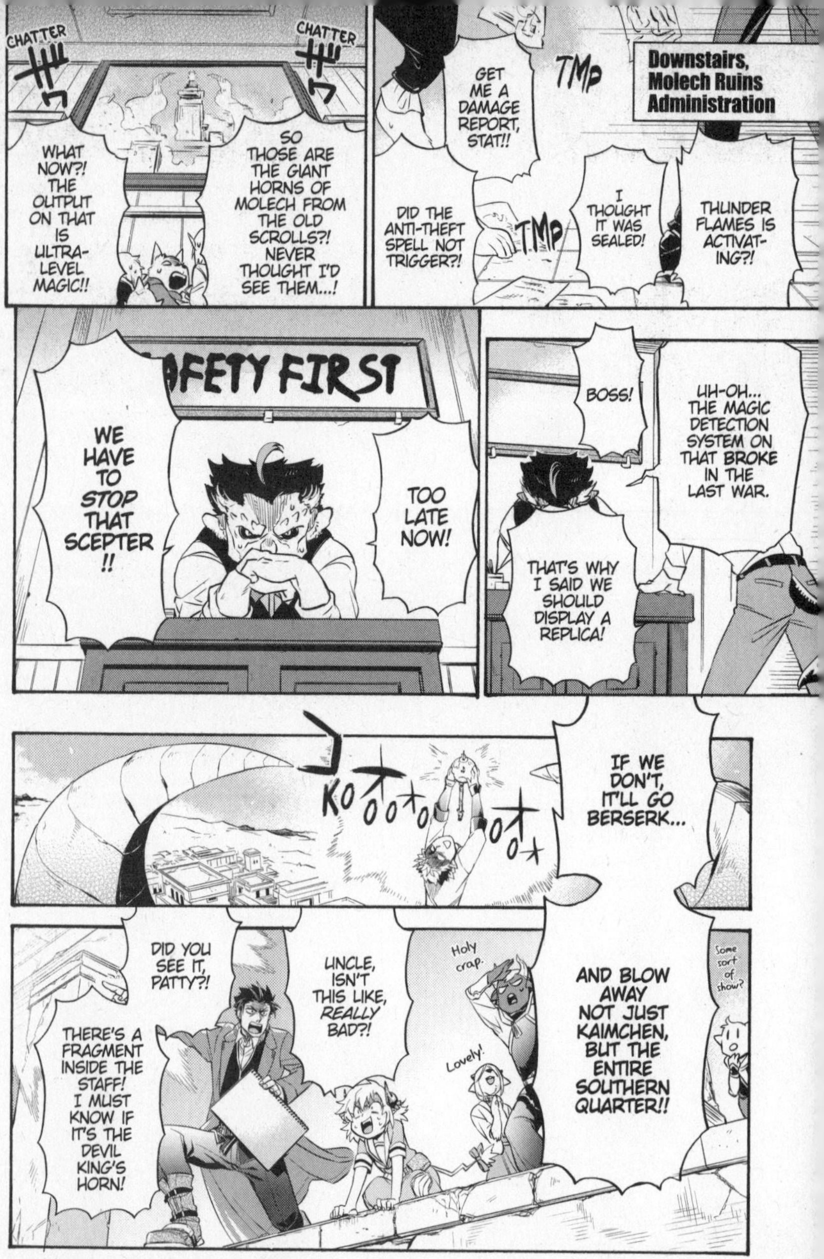
Downstairs, Molech Ruins Administration
TMP
GET ME A DAMAGE REPORT, STAT!!
THUNDER FLAMES IS ACTIVATING?!
I THOUGHT IT WAS SEALED!
TMP
DID THE ANTI-THEFT SPELL NOT TRIGGER?!
CHATTER
CHATTER
SO THOSE ARE THE GIANT HORNS OF MOLECH FROM THE OLD SCROLLS?! NEVER THOUGHT I'D SEE THEM...!
WHAT NOW?! THE OUTPUT ON THAT IS ULTRA-LEVEL MAGIC!!
UH-OH... THE MAGIC DETECTION SYSTEM ON THAT BROKE IN THE LAST WAR.
BOSS!
THAT'S WHY I SAID WE SHOULD DISPLAY A REPLICA!
AFETY FIRST
TOO LATE NOW!
WE HAVE TO *STOP* THAT SCEPTER!!
IF WE DON'T, IT'LL GO BERSERK...
KOOOOOOO
AND BLOW AWAY NOT JUST KAIMCHEN, BUT THE ENTIRE SOUTHERN QUARTER!!
Some sort of show?
Holy crap.
Lovely!
UNCLE, ISN'T THIS LIKE, *REALLY* BAD?!
DID YOU SEE IT, PATTY?!
THERE'S A FRAGMENT INSIDE THE STAFF! I MUST KNOW IF IT'S THE DEVIL KING'S HORN!

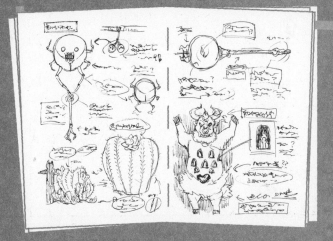

Sorry For My Familiar

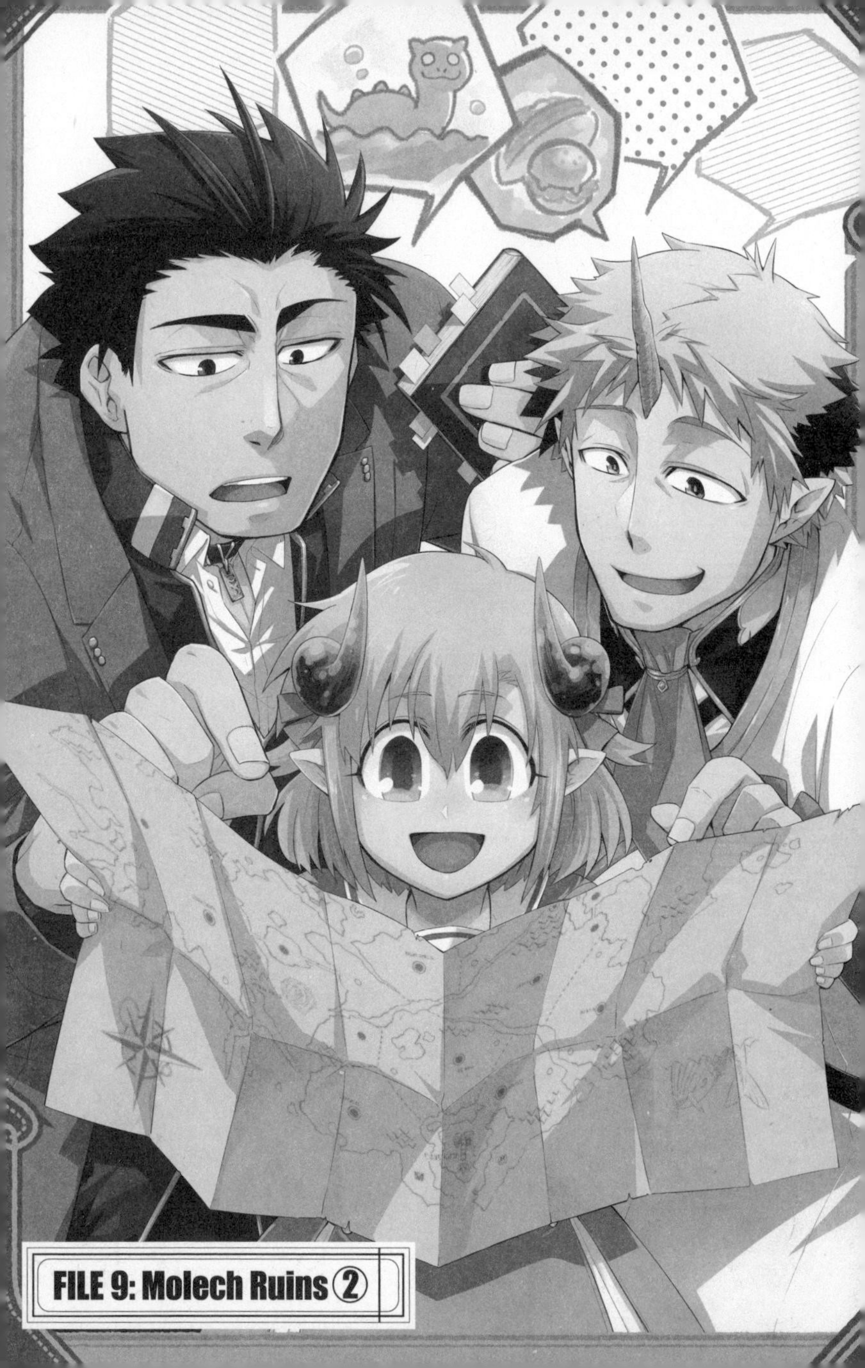
FILE 9: Molech Ruins ②

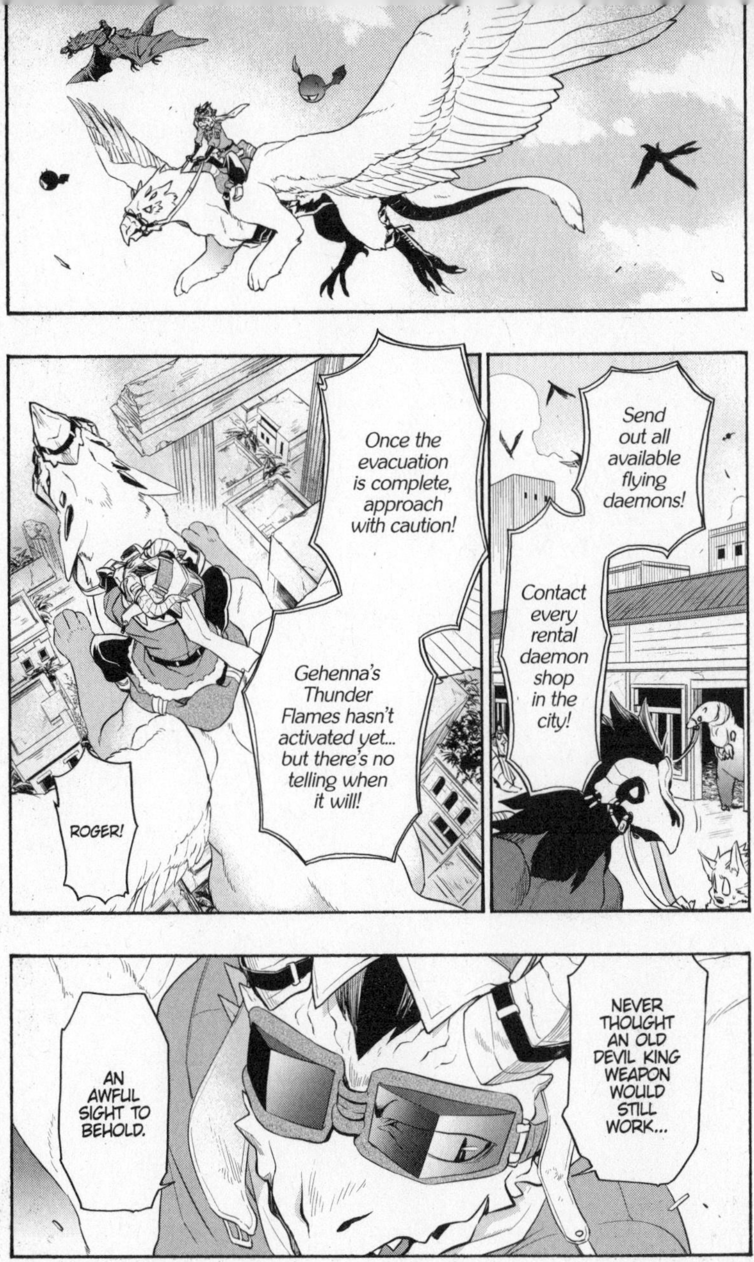
Send out all available flying daemons!
Contact every rental daemon shop in the city!
Once the evacuation is complete, approach with caution!
Gehenna's Thunder Flames hasn't activated yet... but there's no telling when it will!
ROGER!
NEVER THOUGHT AN OLD DEVIL KING WEAPON WOULD STILL WORK...
AN AWFUL SIGHT TO BEHOLD.

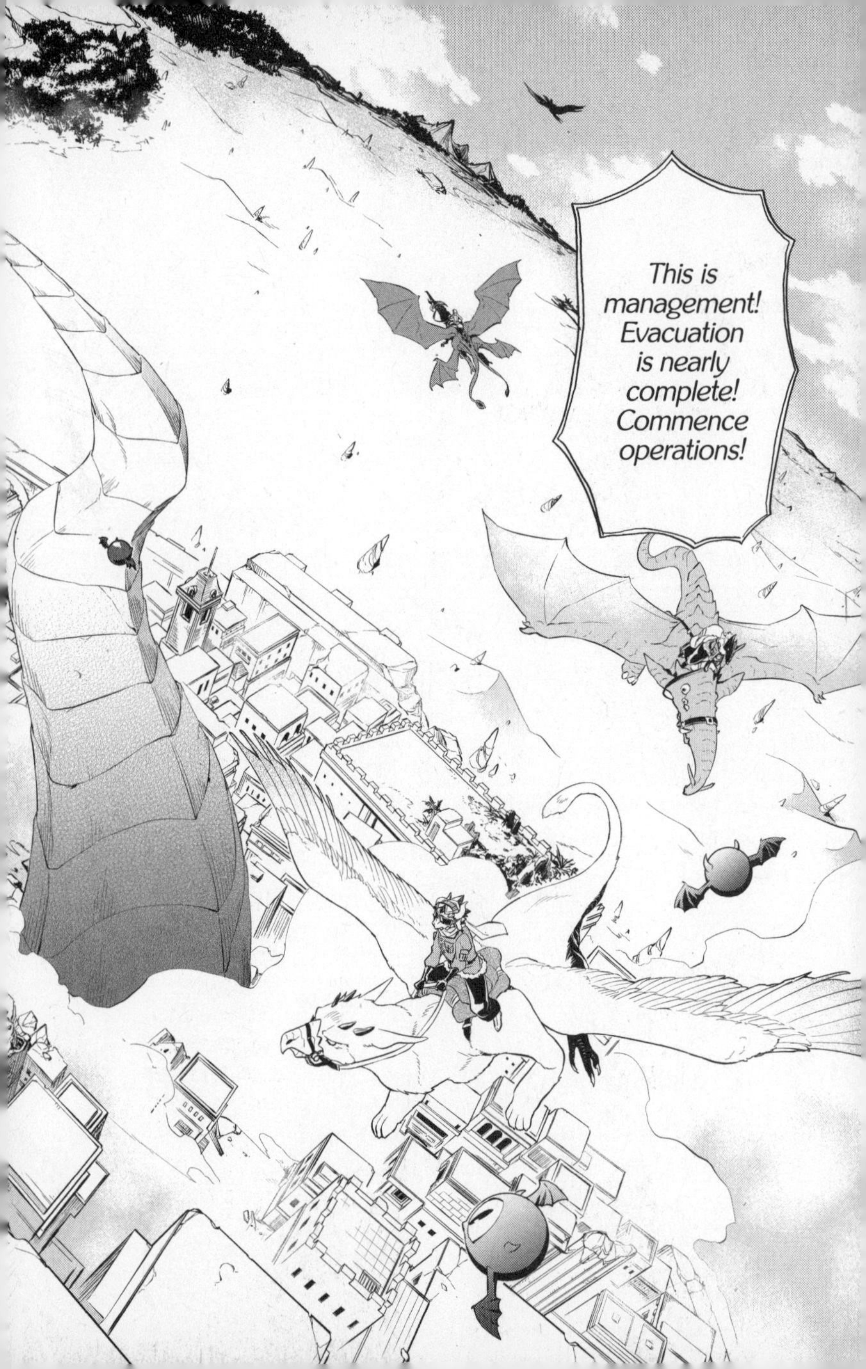
This is management! Evacuation is nearly complete! Commence operations!

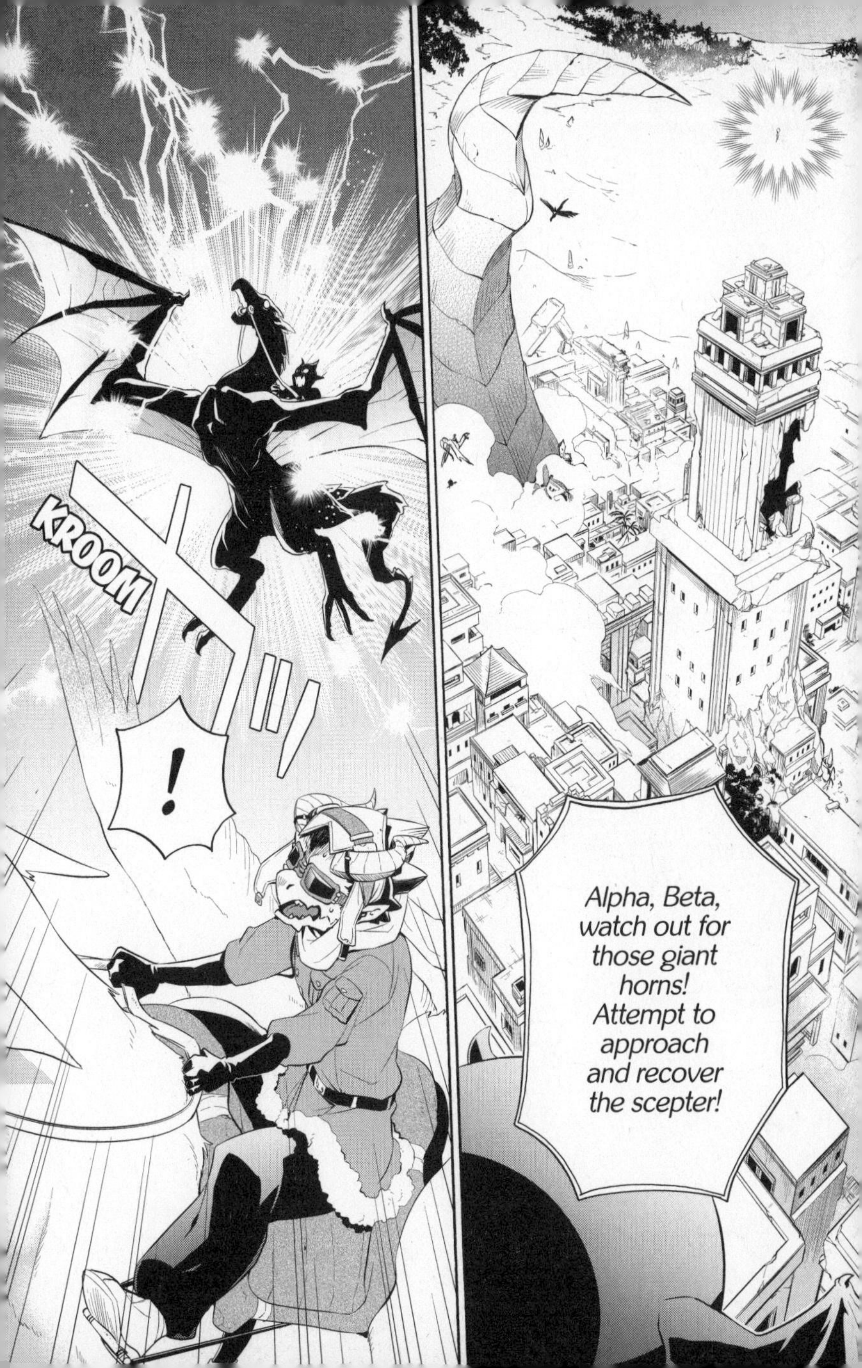
Alpha, Beta, watch out for those giant horns! Attempt to approach and recover the scepter!
KROOM
!

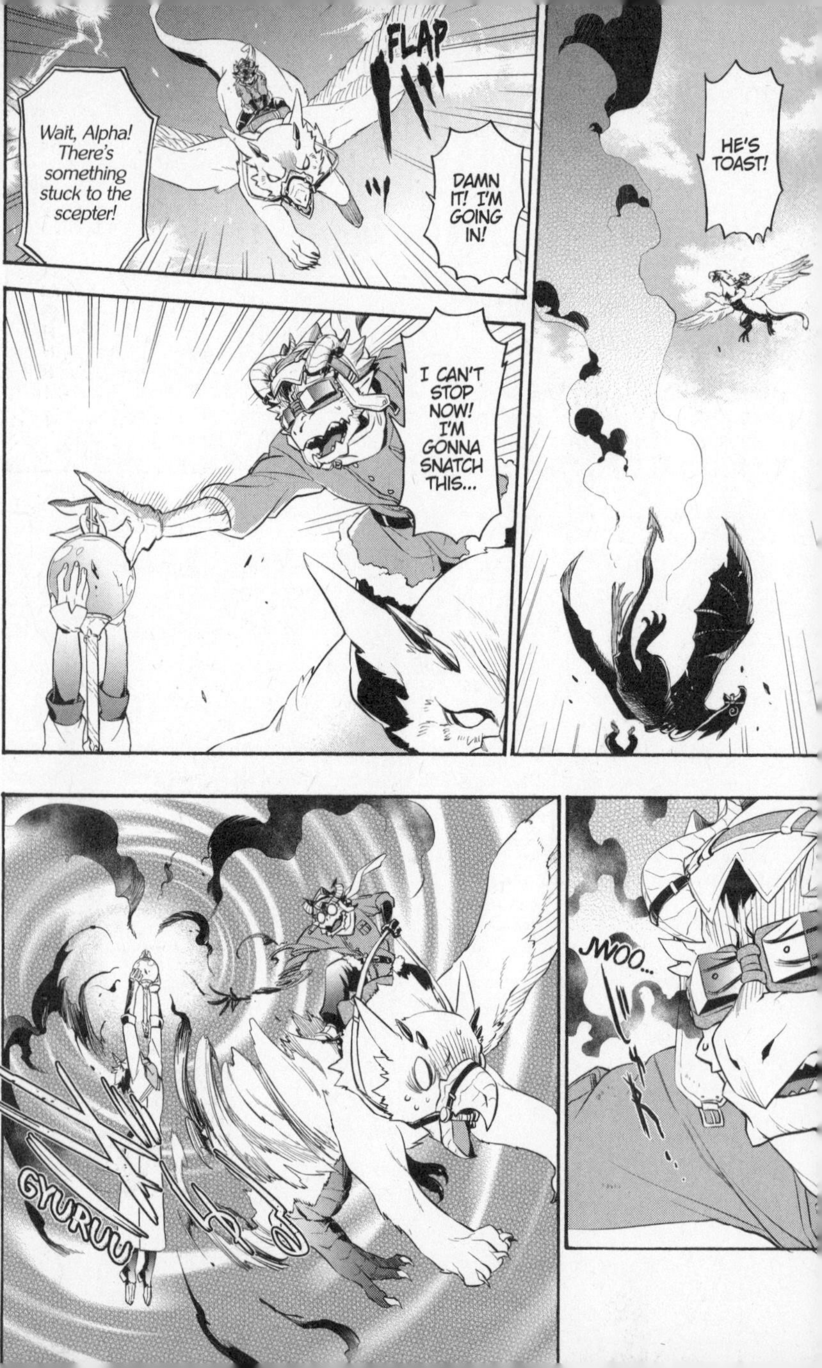
HE'S TOAST!
FLAP
DAMN IT! I'M GOING IN!
Wait, Alpha! There's something stuck to the scepter!
I CAN'T STOP NOW! I'M GONNA SNATCH THIS...
JWOO...
GYURUU

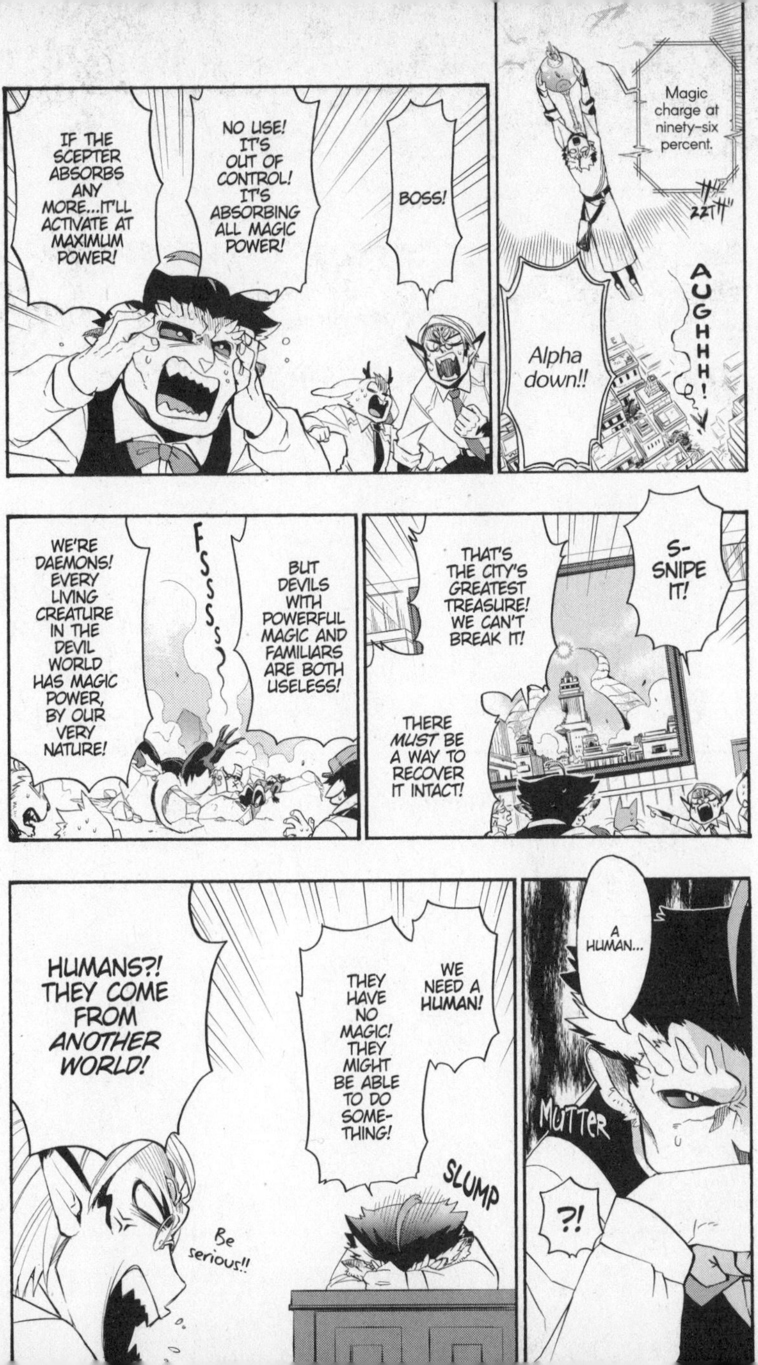

Magic charge at ninety-six percent.
ZZT
AUGHHH!
Alpha down!!
BOSS!
NO USE! IT'S OUT OF CONTROL! IT'S ABSORBING ALL MAGIC POWER!
IF THE SCEPTER ABSORBS ANY MORE...IT'LL ACTIVATE AT MAXIMUM POWER!
S-SNIPE IT!
THAT'S THE CITY'S GREATEST TREASURE! WE CAN'T BREAK IT!
THERE *MUST* BE A WAY TO RECOVER IT INTACT!
FSSSS
BUT DEVILS WITH POWERFUL MAGIC AND FAMILIARS ARE BOTH USELESS!
WE'RE DAEMONS! EVERY LIVING CREATURE IN THE DEVIL WORLD HAS MAGIC POWER, BY OUR VERY NATURE!
A HUMAN...
MUTTER
?!
WE NEED A HUMAN!
THEY HAVE NO MAGIC! THEY MIGHT BE ABLE TO DO SOME-THING!
HUMANS?! THEY COME FROM *ANOTHER WORLD!*
SLUMP
Be serious!!

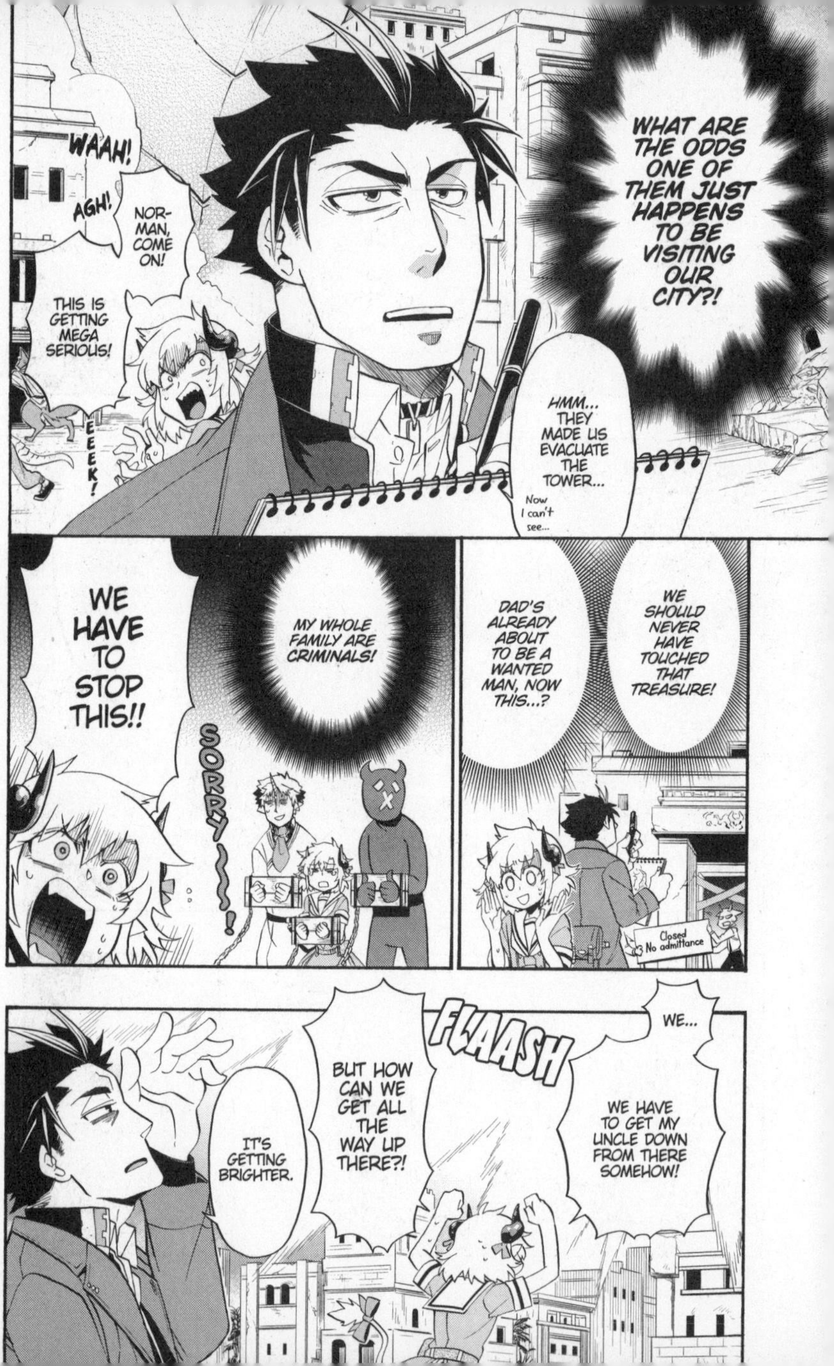
WHAT ARE THE ODDS ONE OF THEM JUST HAPPENS TO BE VISITING OUR CITY?!
HMM... THEY MADE US EVACUATE THE TOWER...
Now I can't see...
WAAH!
AGH!
NOR-MAN, COME ON!
THIS IS GETTING MEGA SERIOUS!
EEEK!
WE SHOULD NEVER HAVE TOUCHED THAT TREASURE!
DAD'S ALREADY ABOUT TO BE A WANTED MAN, NOW THIS...?
Closed
No admittance
MY WHOLE FAMILY ARE CRIMINALS!
WE HAVE TO STOP THIS!!
SORRY~~!
WE...
FLAASH
WE HAVE TO GET MY UNCLE DOWN FROM THERE SOMEHOW!
BUT HOW CAN WE GET ALL THE WAY UP THERE?!
IT'S GETTING BRIGHTER.

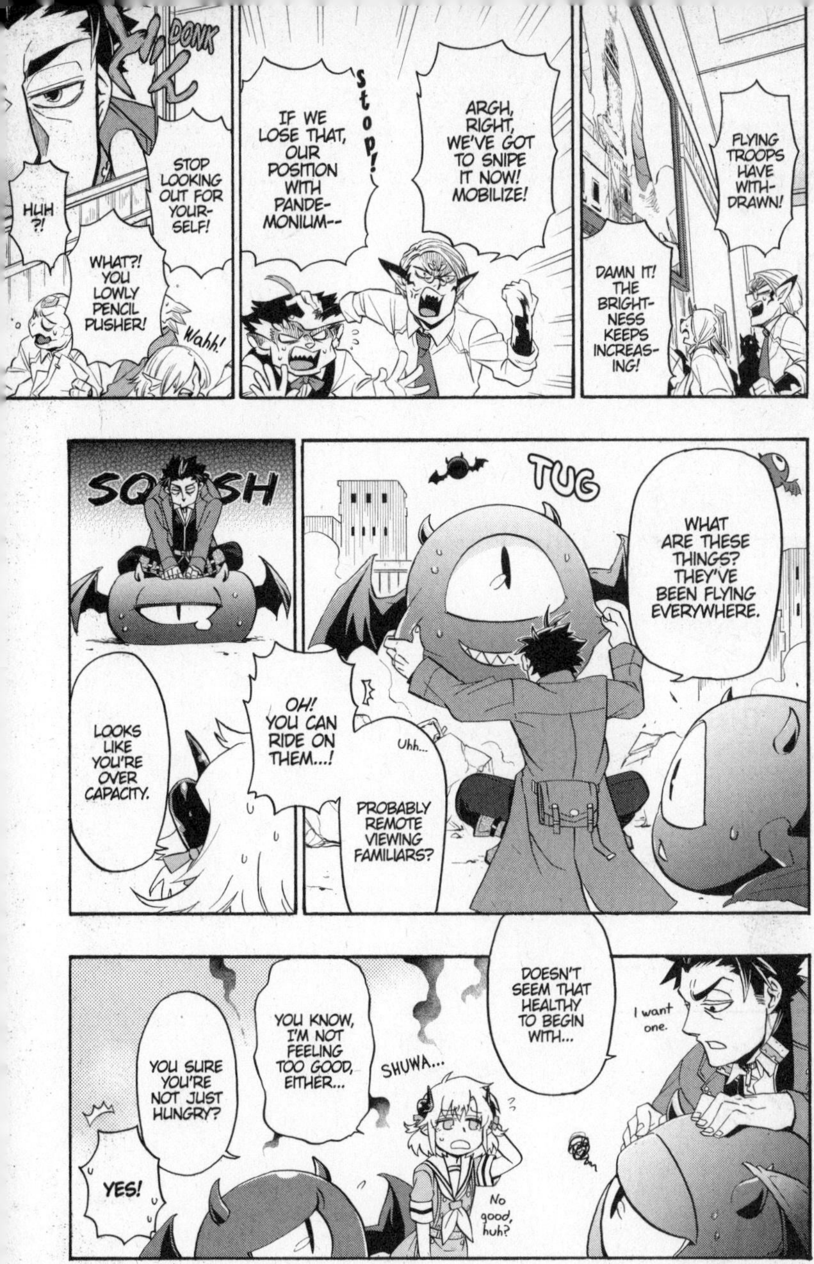

FLYING TROOPS HAVE WITH-DRAWN!
DAMN IT! THE BRIGHT-NESS KEEPS INCREAS-ING!
ARGH, RIGHT, WE'VE GOT TO SNIPE IT NOW! MOBILIZE!
stop!
IF WE LOSE THAT, OUR POSITION WITH PANDE-MONIUM--
DONK
STOP LOOKING OUT FOR YOUR-SELF!
HUH?!
WHAT?! YOU LOWLY PENCIL PUSHER!
Wahh!
TUG
WHAT ARE THESE THINGS? THEY'VE BEEN FLYING EVERYWHERE.
OH! YOU CAN RIDE ON THEM...!
Uhh...
PROBABLY REMOTE VIEWING FAMILIARS?
SQ SH
LOOKS LIKE YOU'RE OVER CAPACITY.
I want one.
DOESN'T SEEM THAT HEALTHY TO BEGIN WITH...
No good, huh?
SHUWA...
YOU KNOW, I'M NOT FEELING TOO GOOD, EITHER...
YOU SURE YOU'RE NOT JUST HUNGRY?
YES!

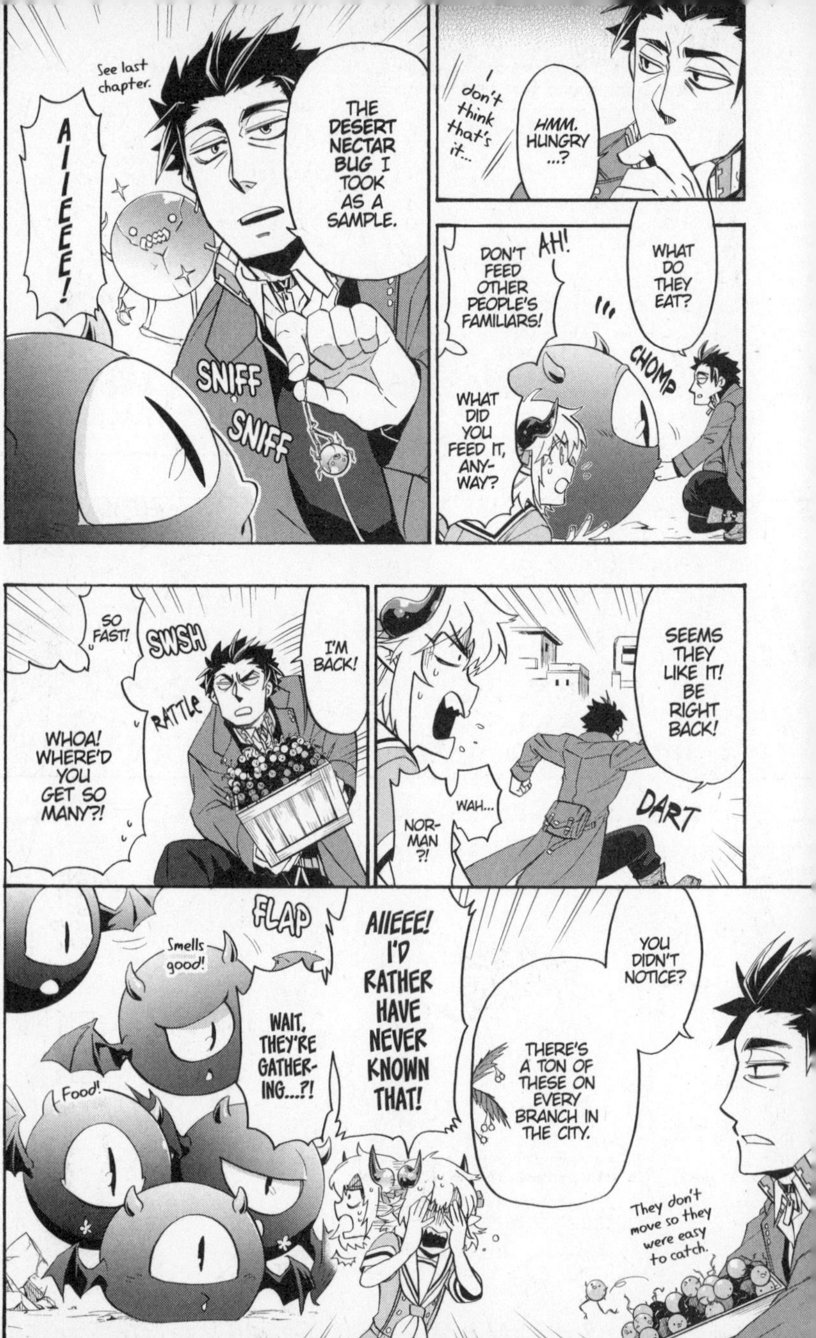
HMM. HUNGRY ...?
I don't think that's it...
WHAT DO THEY EAT?
AH!
DON'T FEED OTHER PEOPLE'S FAMILIARS!
CHOMP
WHAT DID YOU FEED IT, ANYWAY?
THE DESERT NECTAR BUG I TOOK AS A SAMPLE.
See last chapter.
AIIEEE!
SNIFF
SNIFF
SEEMS THEY LIKE IT! BE RIGHT BACK!
DART
WAH...
NOR-MAN?!
I'M BACK!
SWSH
SO FAST!
RATTLE
WHOA! WHERE'D YOU GET SO MANY?!
YOU DIDN'T NOTICE?
THERE'S A TON OF THESE ON EVERY BRANCH IN THE CITY.
They don't move so they were easy to catch.
AIIEEE! I'D RATHER HAVE NEVER KNOWN THAT!
FLAP
WAIT, THEY'RE GATHERING...?!
Smells good!
Food!

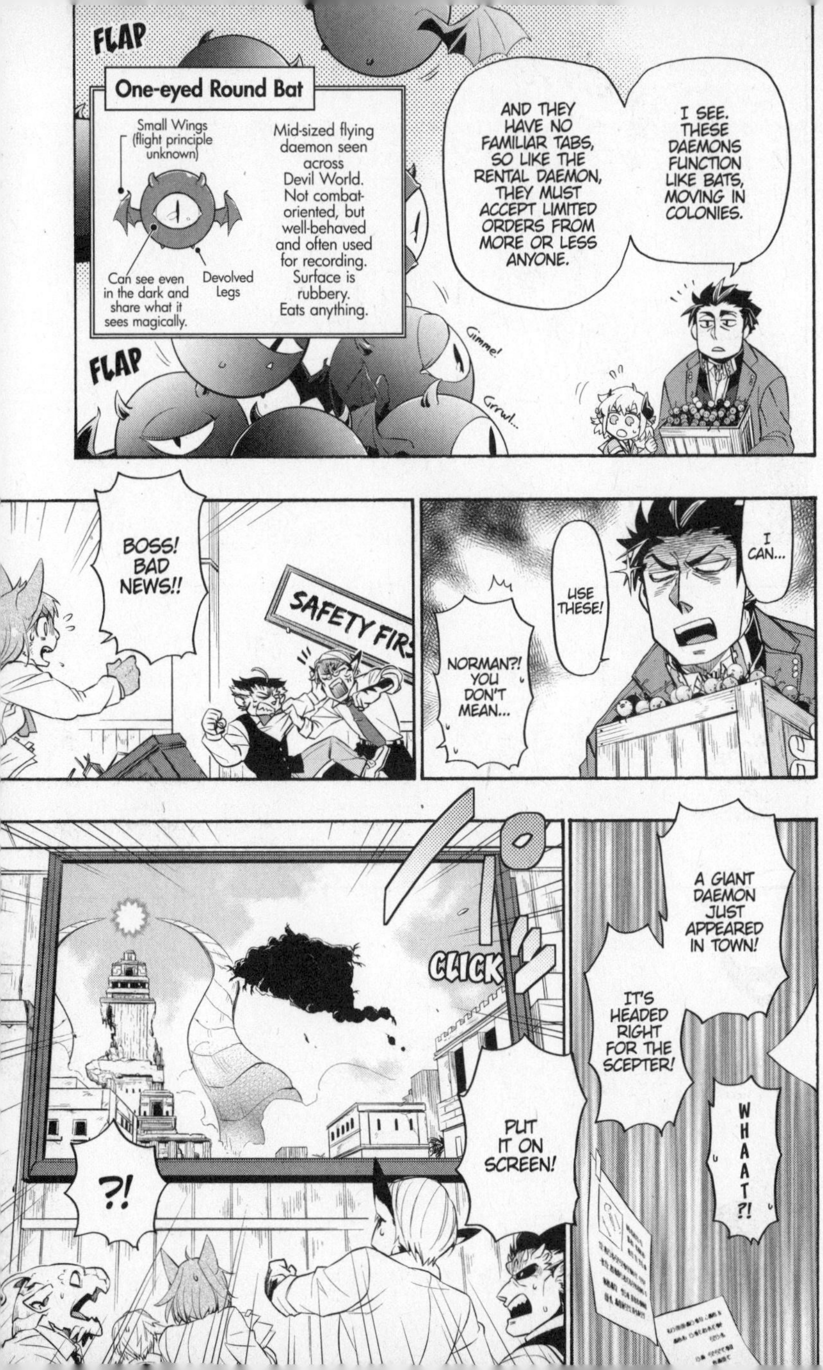

I SEE. THESE DAEMONS FUNCTION LIKE BATS, MOVING IN COLONIES.
AND THEY HAVE NO FAMILIAR TABS, SO LIKE THE RENTAL DAEMON, THEY MUST ACCEPT LIMITED ORDERS FROM MORE OR LESS ANYONE.
FLAP
One-eyed Round Bat
Small Wings (flight principle unknown)
Can see even in the dark and share what it sees magically.
Devolved Legs
Mid-sized flying daemon seen across Devil World. Not combat-oriented, but well-behaved and often used for recording. Surface is rubbery. Eats anything.
Gimme!
Grrwl...
FLAP
I CAN...
USE THESE!
NORMAN?! YOU DON'T MEAN...
SAFETY FIRS
BOSS! BAD NEWS!!
A GIANT DAEMON JUST APPEARED IN TOWN!
IT'S HEADED RIGHT FOR THE SCEPTER!
WHAAAT?!
CLICK
PUT IT ON SCREEN!
?!

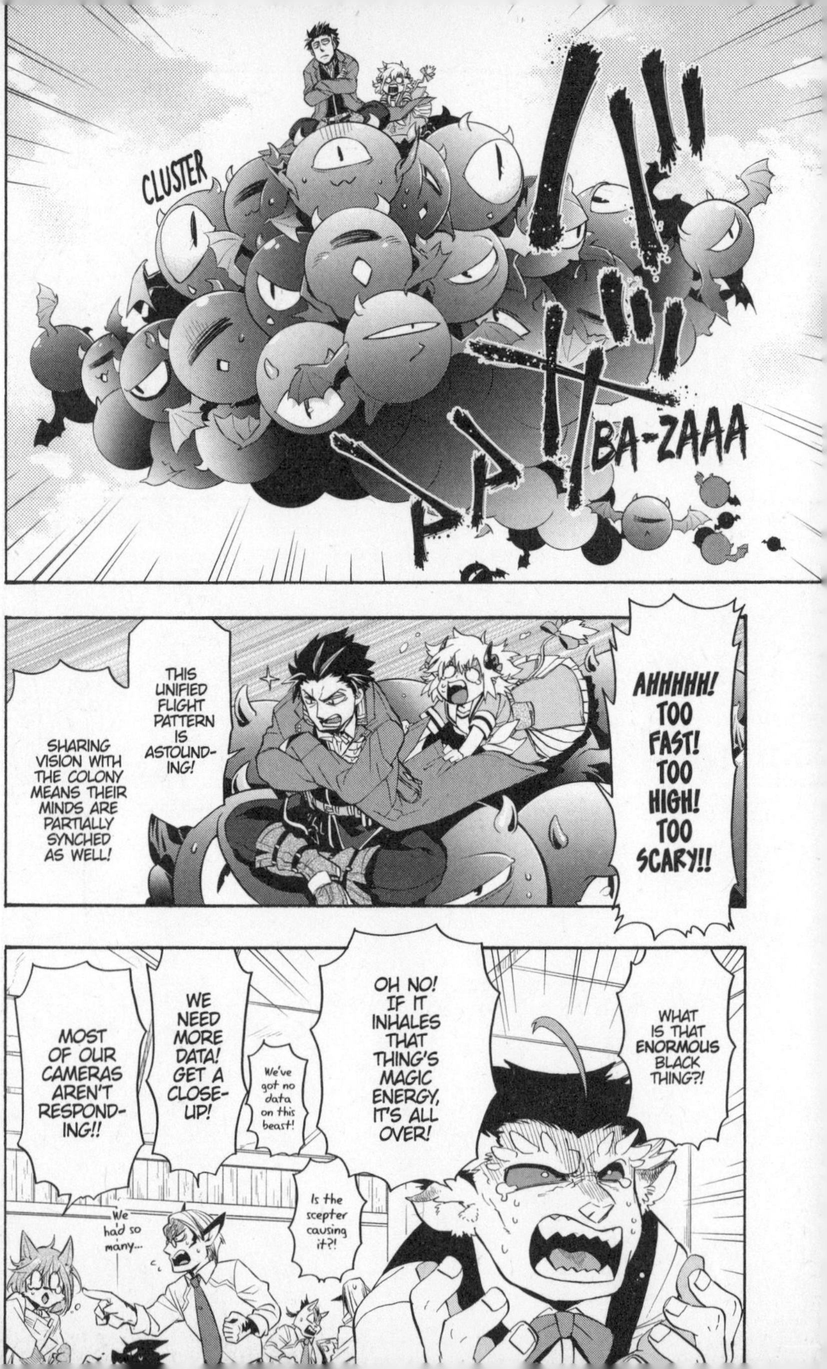
BA-ZAAA
CLUSTER
AHHHHH! TOO FAST! TOO HIGH! TOO SCARY!!
THIS UNIFIED FLIGHT PATTERN IS ASTOUND-ING!
SHARING VISION WITH THE COLONY MEANS THEIR MINDS ARE PARTIALLY SYNCHED AS WELL!
WHAT IS THAT ENORMOUS BLACK THING?!
OH NO! IF IT INHALES THAT THING'S MAGIC ENERGY, IT'S ALL OVER!
We've got no data on this beast!
WE NEED MORE DATA! GET A CLOSE-UP!
MOST OF OUR CAMERAS AREN'T RESPOND-ING!!
Is the scepter causing it?!
We had so many...

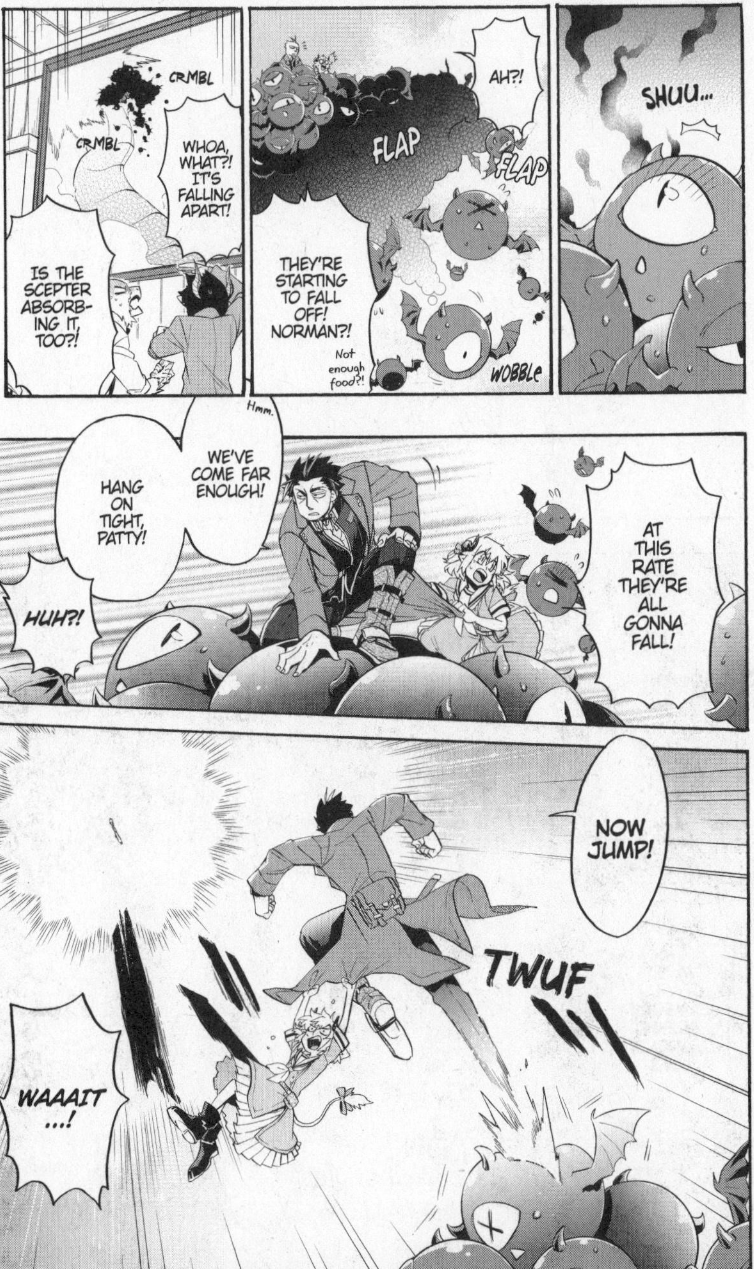
SHUU...
AH?!
FLAP
FLAP
THEY'RE STARTING TO FALL OFF! NORMAN?!
Not enough food?!
WOBBLE
CRMBL
CRMBL
WHOA, WHAT?! IT'S FALLING APART!
IS THE SCEPTER ABSORBING IT, TOO?!
AT THIS RATE THEY'RE ALL GONNA FALL!
Hmm.
WE'VE COME FAR ENOUGH!
HANG ON TIGHT, PATTY!
HUH?!
NOW JUMP!
TWUF
WAAAIT ...!

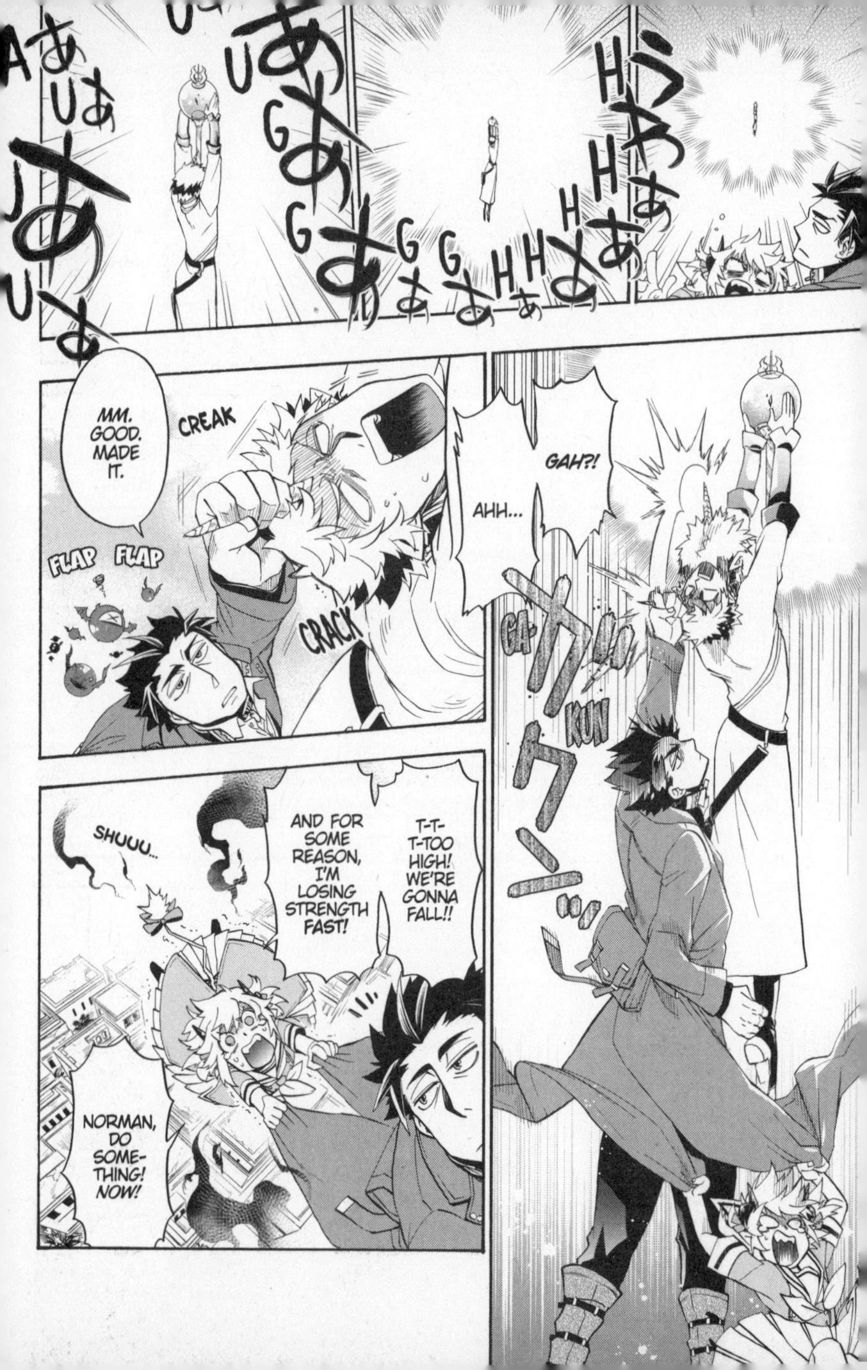
GAH?!
AHH...
GA-
KUN
MM. GOOD. MADE IT.
CREAK
FLAP FLAP
CRACK
T-T-T-TOO HIGH! WE'RE GONNA FALL!!
AND FOR SOME REASON, I'M LOSING STRENGTH FAST!
SHUUU...
NORMAN, DO SOME-THING! NOW!

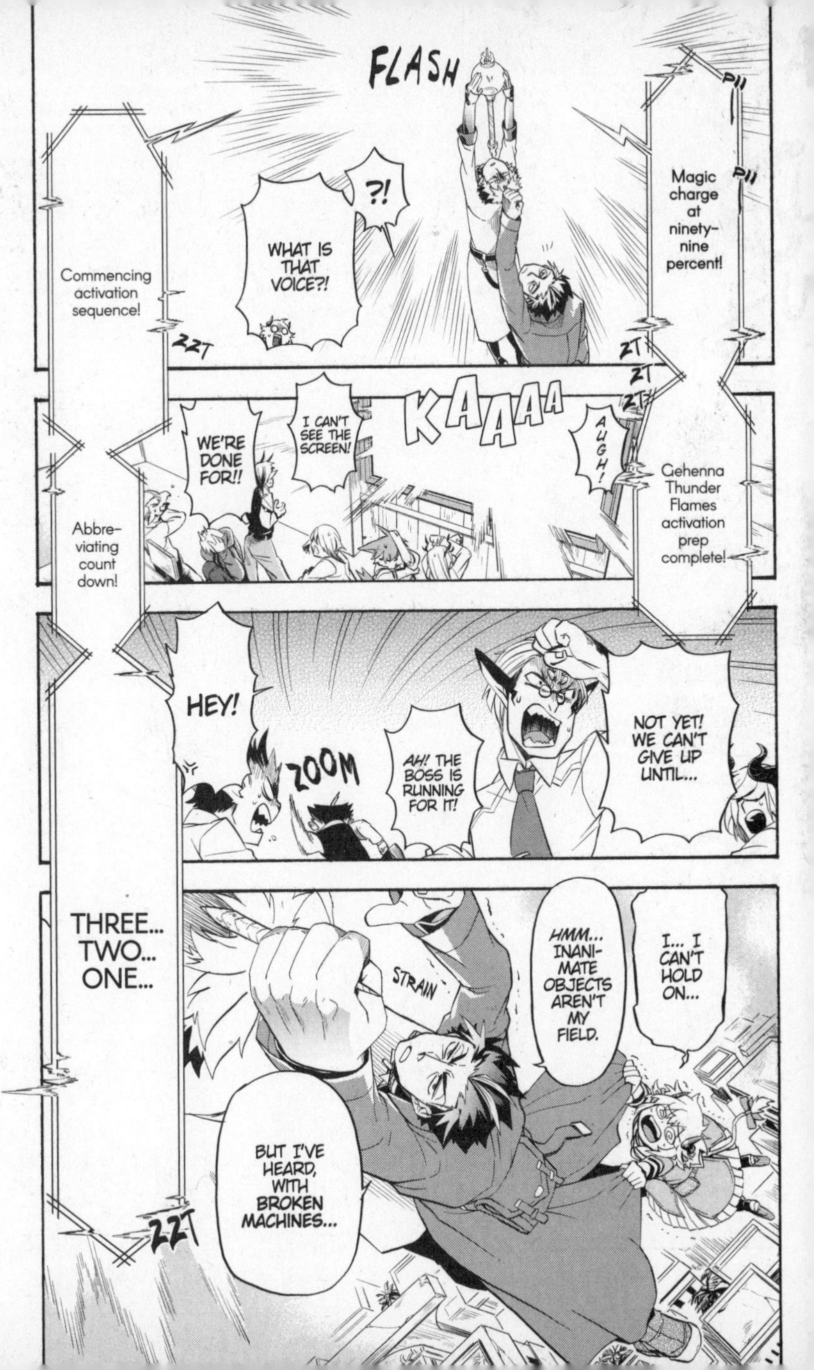
FLASH
PII
PII
Magic charge at ninety-nine percent!
?!
WHAT IS THAT VOICE?!
Commencing activation sequence!
ZZT
ZT
ZT
ZT
AUGH!
KAAAAA
Gehenna Thunder Flames activation prep complete!
I CAN'T SEE THE SCREEN!
WE'RE DONE FOR!!
Abbre-viating count down!
NOT YET! WE CAN'T GIVE UP UNTIL...
AH! THE BOSS IS RUNNING FOR IT!
ZOOM
HEY!
I... I CAN'T HOLD ON...
HMM... INANI-MATE OBJECTS AREN'T MY FIELD.
STRAIN
BUT I'VE HEARD, WITH BROKEN MACHINES...
THREE... TWO... ONE...
ZZT

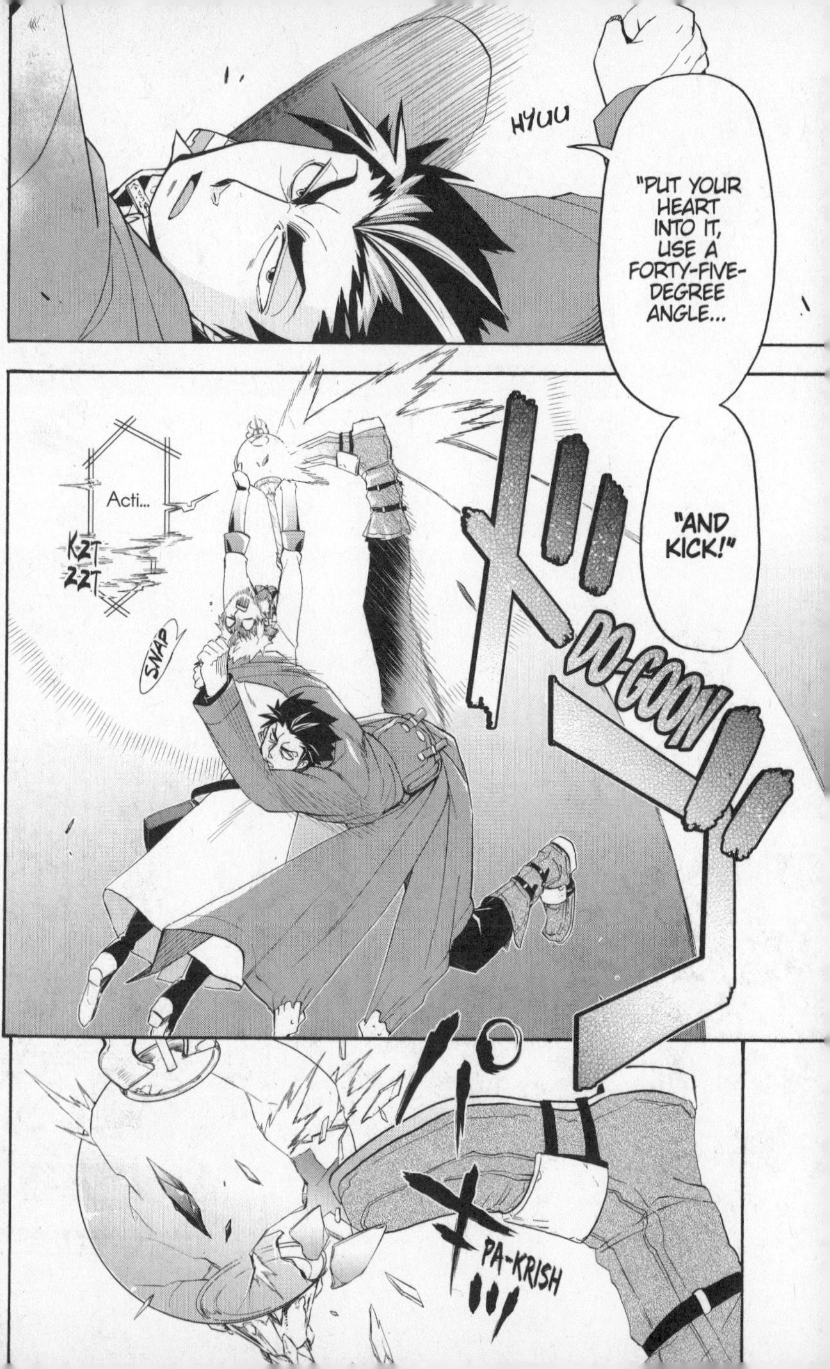
"PUT YOUR HEART INTO IT, USE A FORTY-FIVE-DEGREE ANGLE...
HYUU
"AND KICK!"
DO-GOON
Acti...
K-ZT Z-ZT
SNAP
PA-KRISH

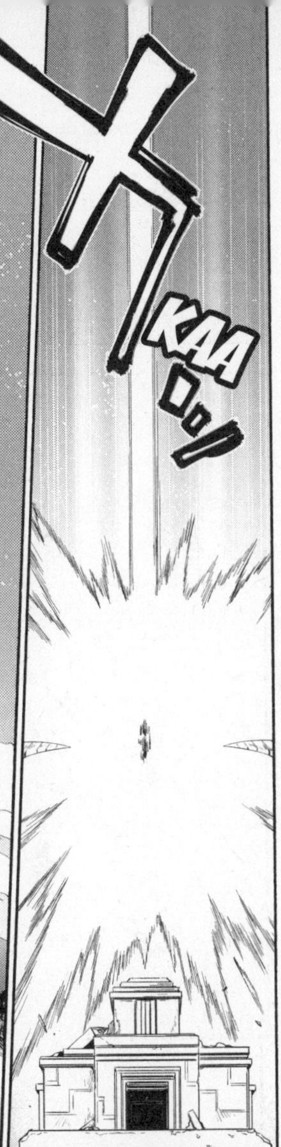
KAA
Do!
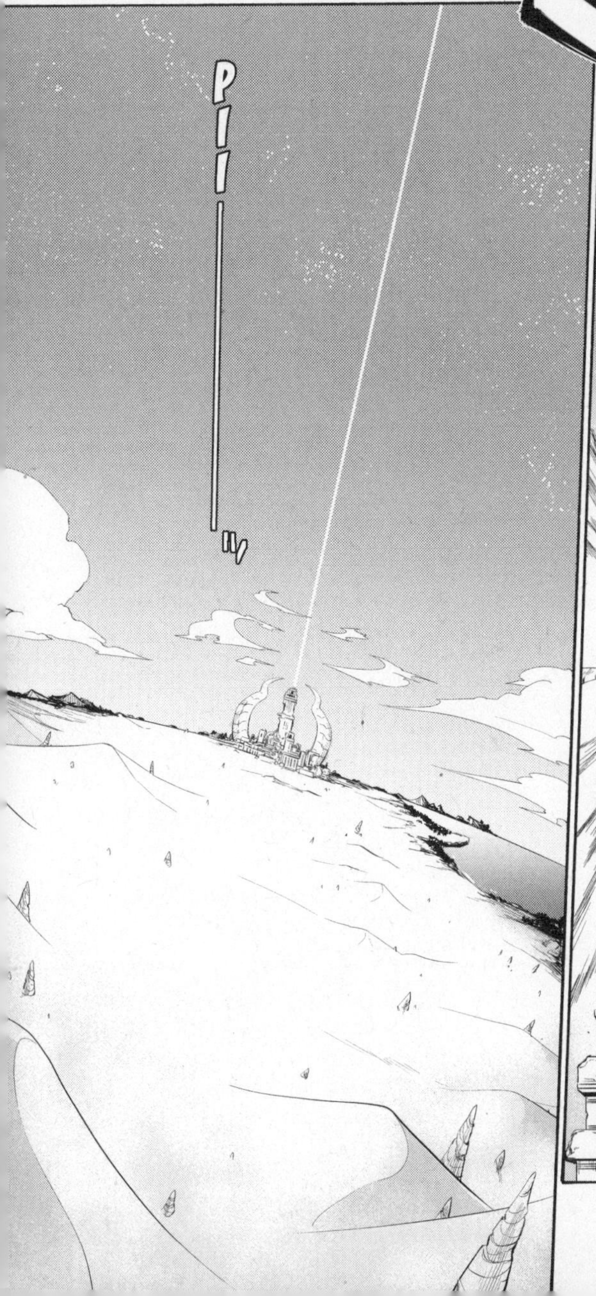
PIII—!!

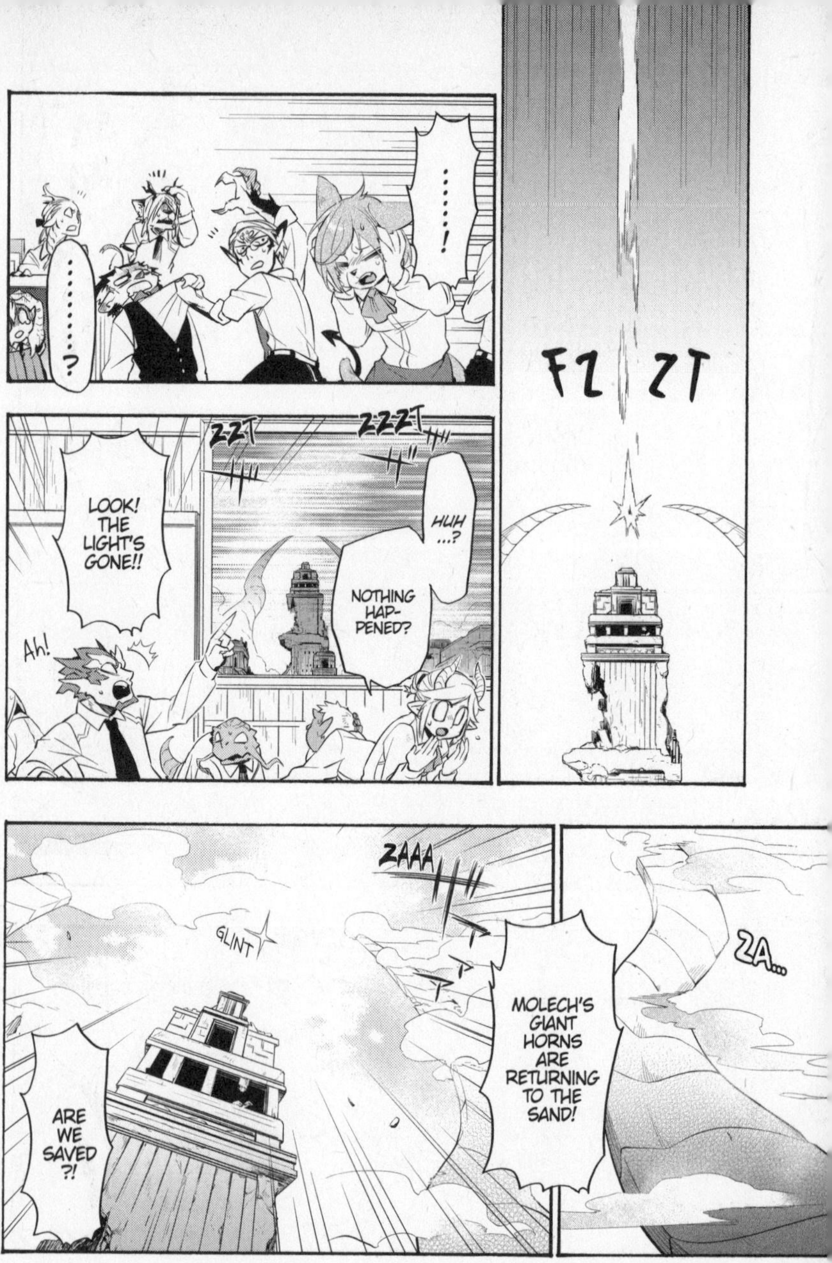
FZ ZT
......!
......?
ZZZT
ZZT
HUH ...?
NOTHING HAP-PENED?
LOOK! THE LIGHT'S GONE!!
Ah!
ZA...
ZAAA
MOLECH'S GIANT HORNS ARE RETURNING TO THE SAND!
GLINT
ARE WE SAVED?!

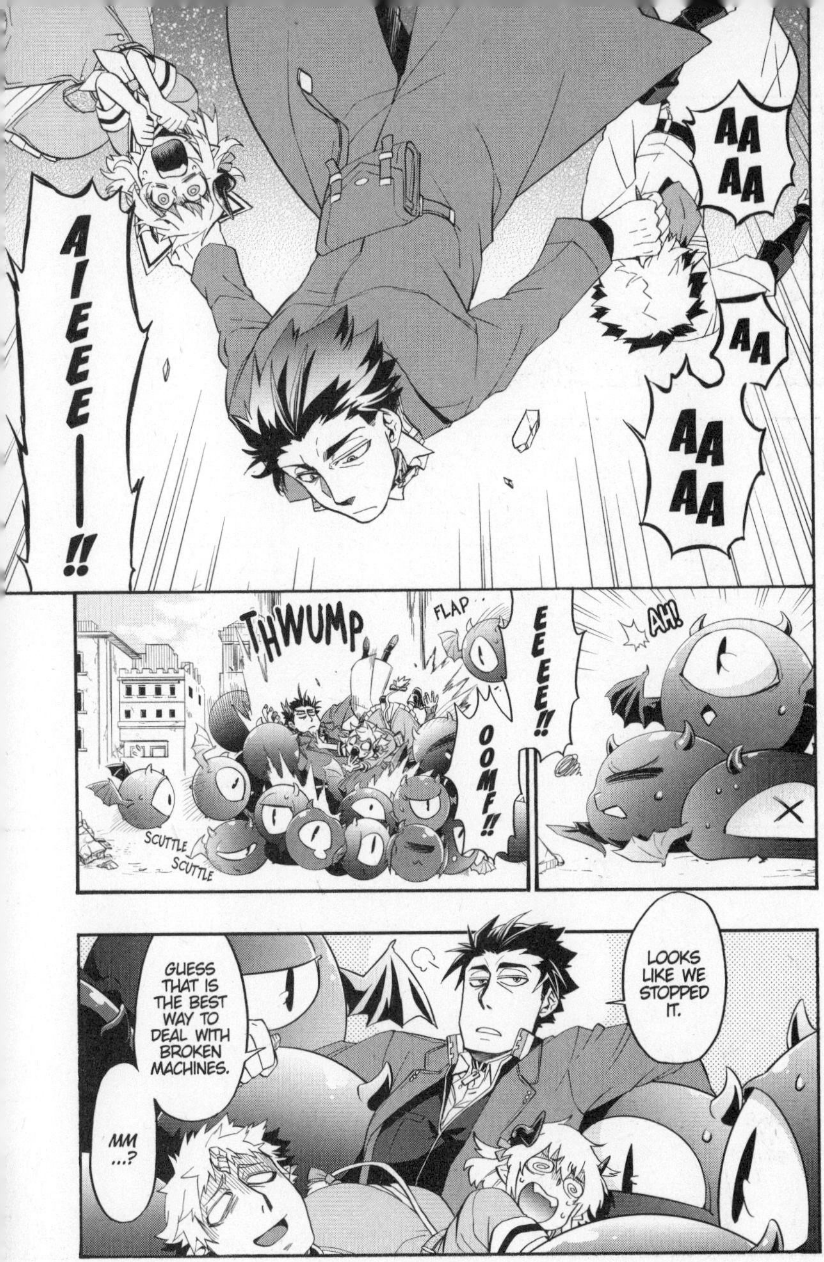
AAAA
AA
AAAA
AIEEEE!!
AH!
EEEE!!
FLAP
THWUMP
OOMF!!
SCUTTLE SCUTTLE
LOOKS LIKE WE STOPPED IT.
GUESS THAT IS THE BEST WAY TO DEAL WITH BROKEN MACHINES.
MM ...?

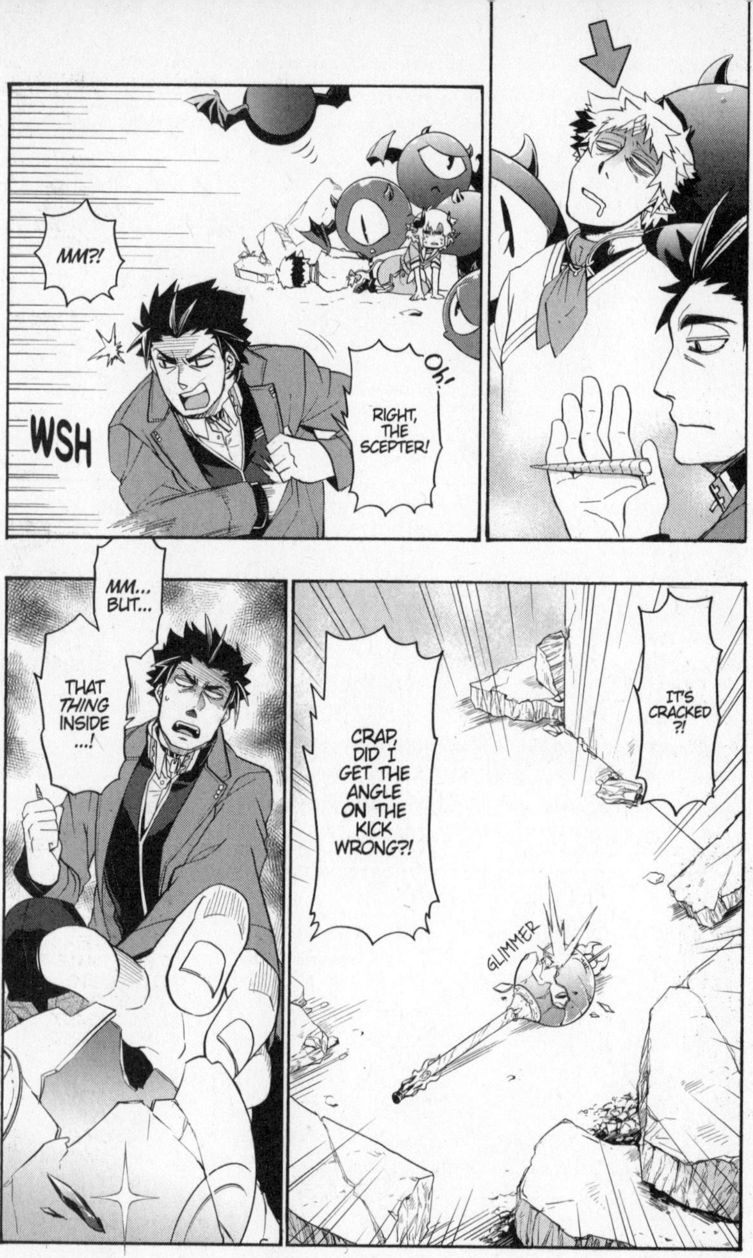
MM?!
Oh!
RIGHT, THE SCEPTER!
WSH
IT'S CRACKED?!
CRAP, DID I GET THE ANGLE ON THE KICK WRONG?!
GLIMMER
MM... BUT...
THAT *THING* INSIDE ...!

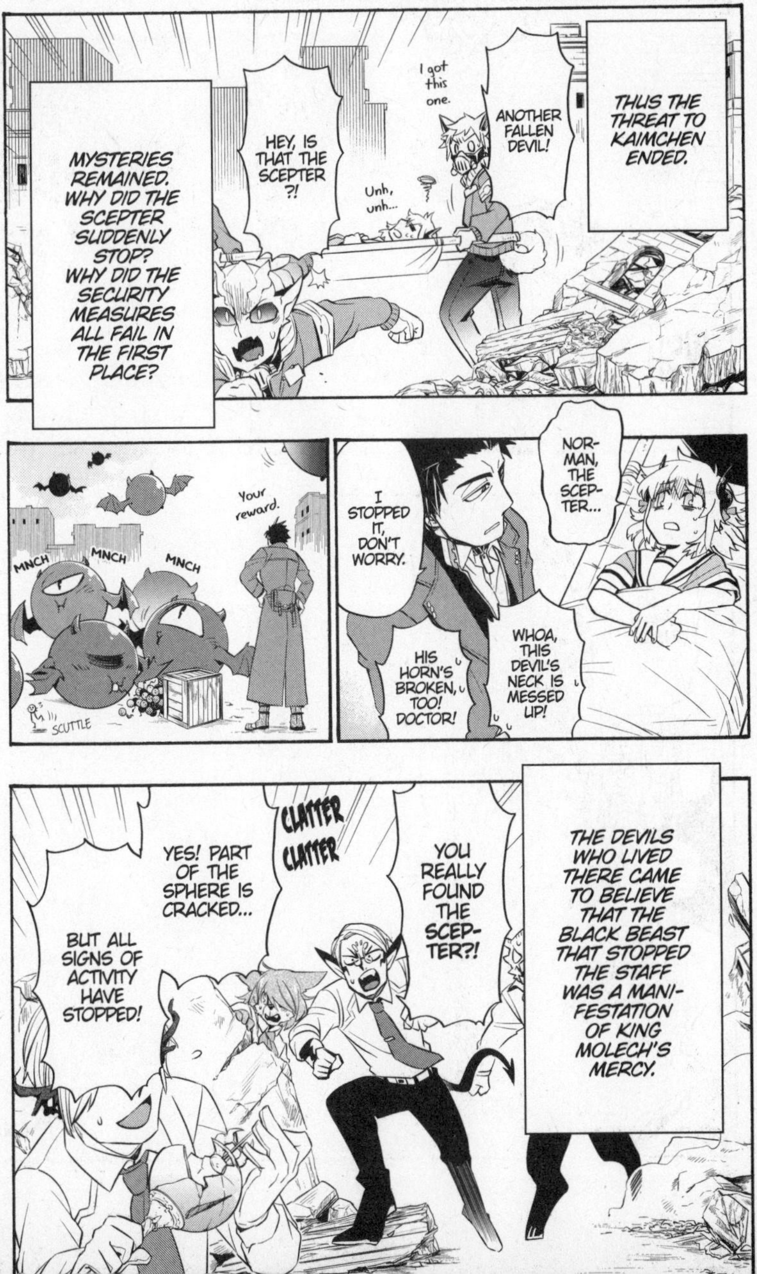
THUS THE THREAT TO KAIMCHEN ENDED.
ANOTHER FALLEN DEVIL!
I got this one.
Unh, unh...
HEY, IS THAT THE SCEPTER?!
MYSTERIES REMAINED. WHY DID THE SCEPTER SUDDENLY STOP? WHY DID THE SECURITY MEASURES ALL FAIL IN THE FIRST PLACE?
NOR-MAN, THE SCEP-TER...
I STOPPED IT, DON'T WORRY.
WHOA, THIS DEVIL'S NECK IS MESSED UP!
HIS HORN'S BROKEN, TOO! DOCTOR!
Your reward.
MNCH
MNCH
MNCH
SCUTTLE
THE DEVILS WHO LIVED THERE CAME TO BELIEVE THAT THE BLACK BEAST THAT STOPPED THE STAFF WAS A MANI-FESTATION OF KING MOLECH'S MERCY.
YOU REALLY FOUND THE SCEP-TER?!
CLATTER CLATTER
YES! PART OF THE SPHERE IS CRACKED...
BUT ALL SIGNS OF ACTIVITY HAVE STOPPED!

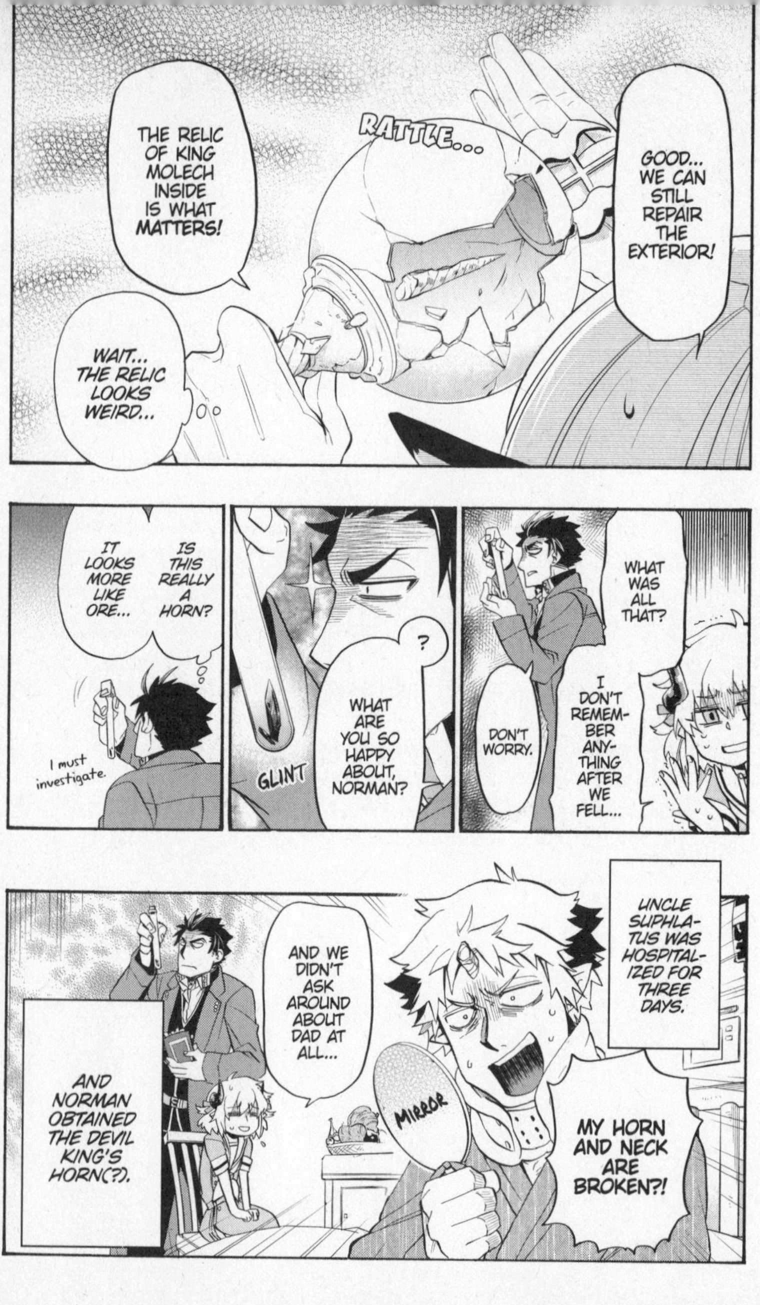
GOOD... WE CAN STILL REPAIR THE EXTERIOR!
RATTLE...
THE RELIC OF KING MOLECH INSIDE IS WHAT MATTERS!
WAIT... THE RELIC LOOKS WEIRD...
WHAT WAS ALL THAT?
I DON'T REMEMBER ANYTHING AFTER WE FELL...
DON'T WORRY.
?
WHAT ARE YOU SO HAPPY ABOUT, NORMAN?
GLINT
IS THIS REALLY A HORN?
IT LOOKS MORE LIKE ORE...
I must investigate.
UNCLE SUPHLATUS WAS HOSPITALIZED FOR THREE DAYS.
MY HORN AND NECK ARE BROKEN?!
MIRROR
AND WE DIDN'T ASK AROUND ABOUT DAD AT ALL...
AND NORMAN OBTAINED THE DEVIL KING'S HORN(?).

Sorry For My Familiar

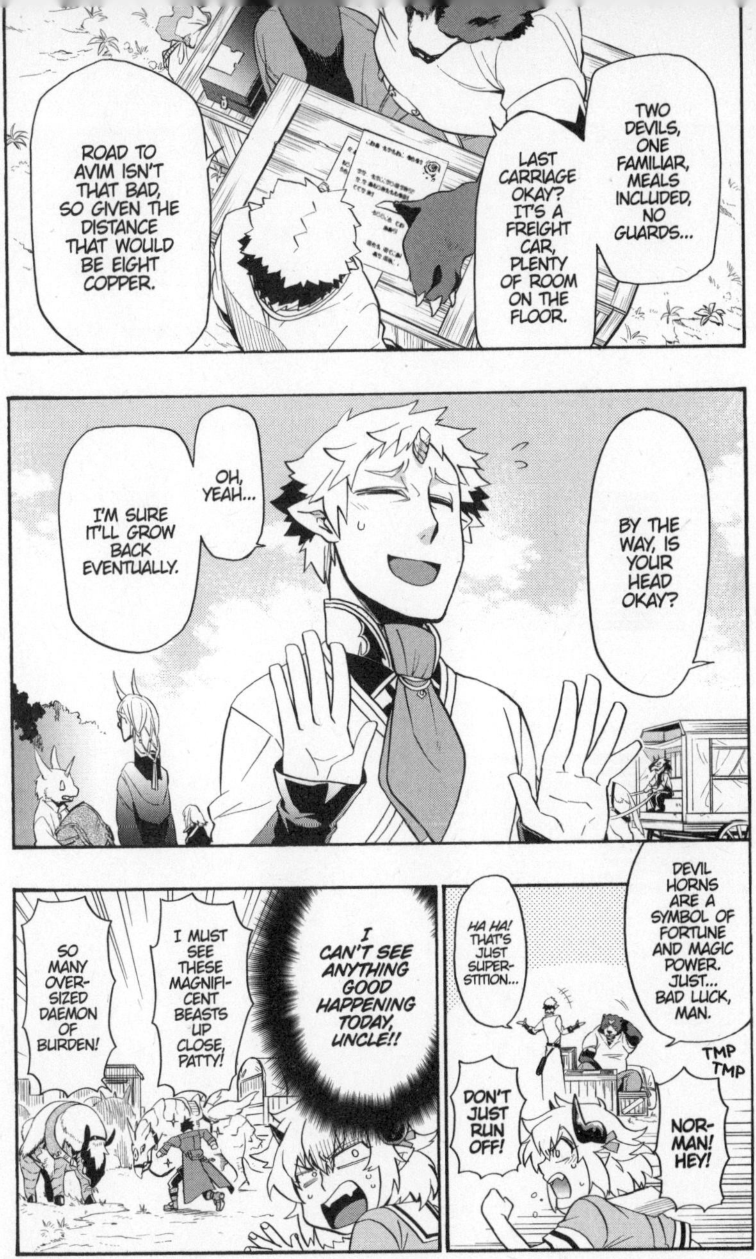
TWO DEVILS, ONE FAMILIAR, MEALS INCLUDED, NO GUARDS...
LAST CARRIAGE OKAY? IT'S A FREIGHT CAR, PLENTY OF ROOM ON THE FLOOR.
ROAD TO AVIM ISN'T THAT BAD, SO GIVEN THE DISTANCE THAT WOULD BE EIGHT COPPER.
BY THE WAY, IS YOUR HEAD OKAY?
OH, YEAH...
I'M SURE IT'LL GROW BACK EVENTUALLY.
DEVIL HORNS ARE A SYMBOL OF FORTUNE AND MAGIC POWER. JUST... BAD LUCK, MAN.
HA HA! THAT'S JUST SUPER-STITION...
TMP TMP
NOR-MAN! HEY!
DON'T JUST RUN OFF!
I CAN'T SEE ANYTHING GOOD HAPPENING TODAY, UNCLE!!
I MUST SEE THESE MAGNIFI-CENT BEASTS UP CLOSE, PATTY!
SO MANY OVER-SIZED DAEMON OF BURDEN!

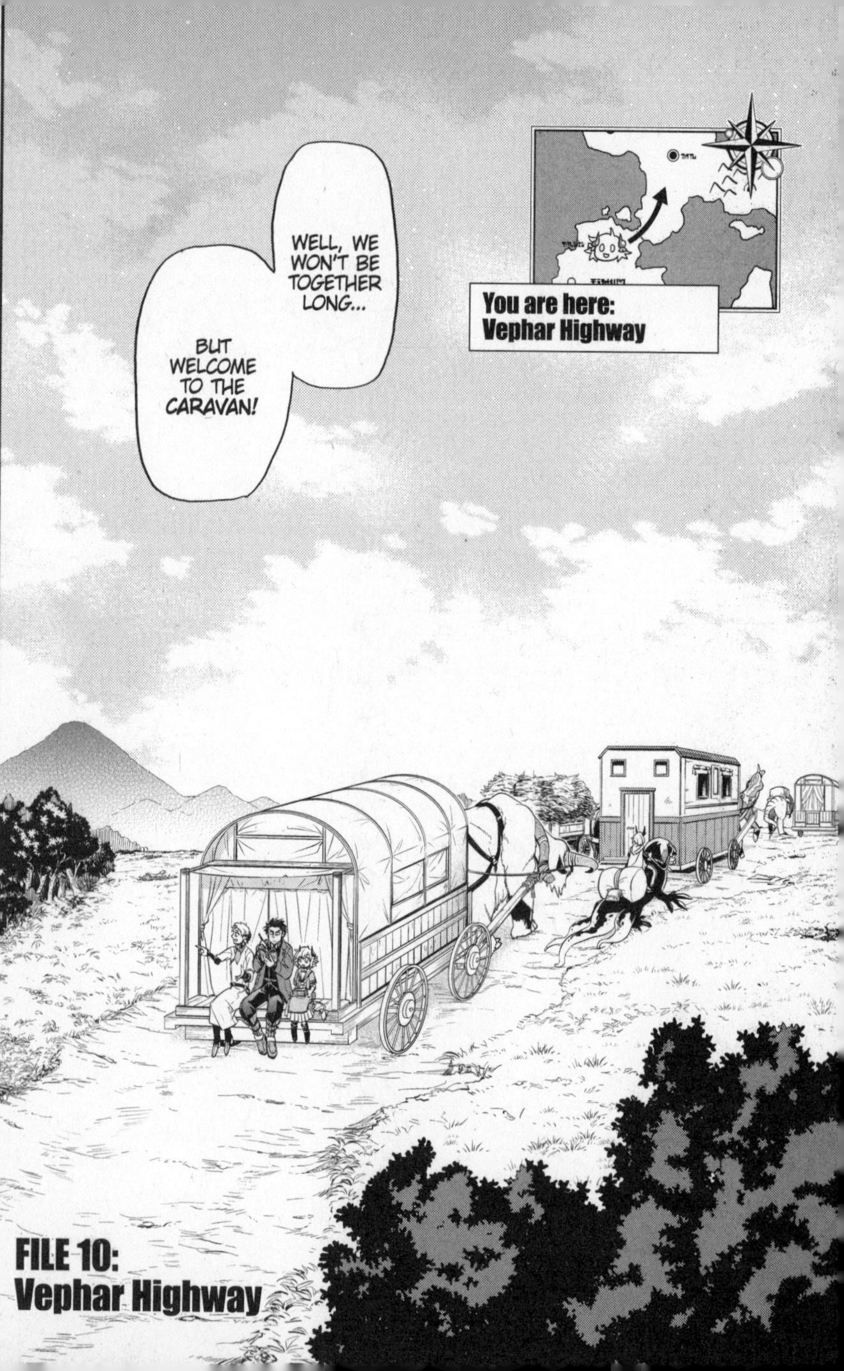
You are here: Vephar Highway
WELL, WE WON'T BE TOGETHER LONG...
BUT WELCOME TO THE CARAVAN!
FILE 10: Vephar Highway

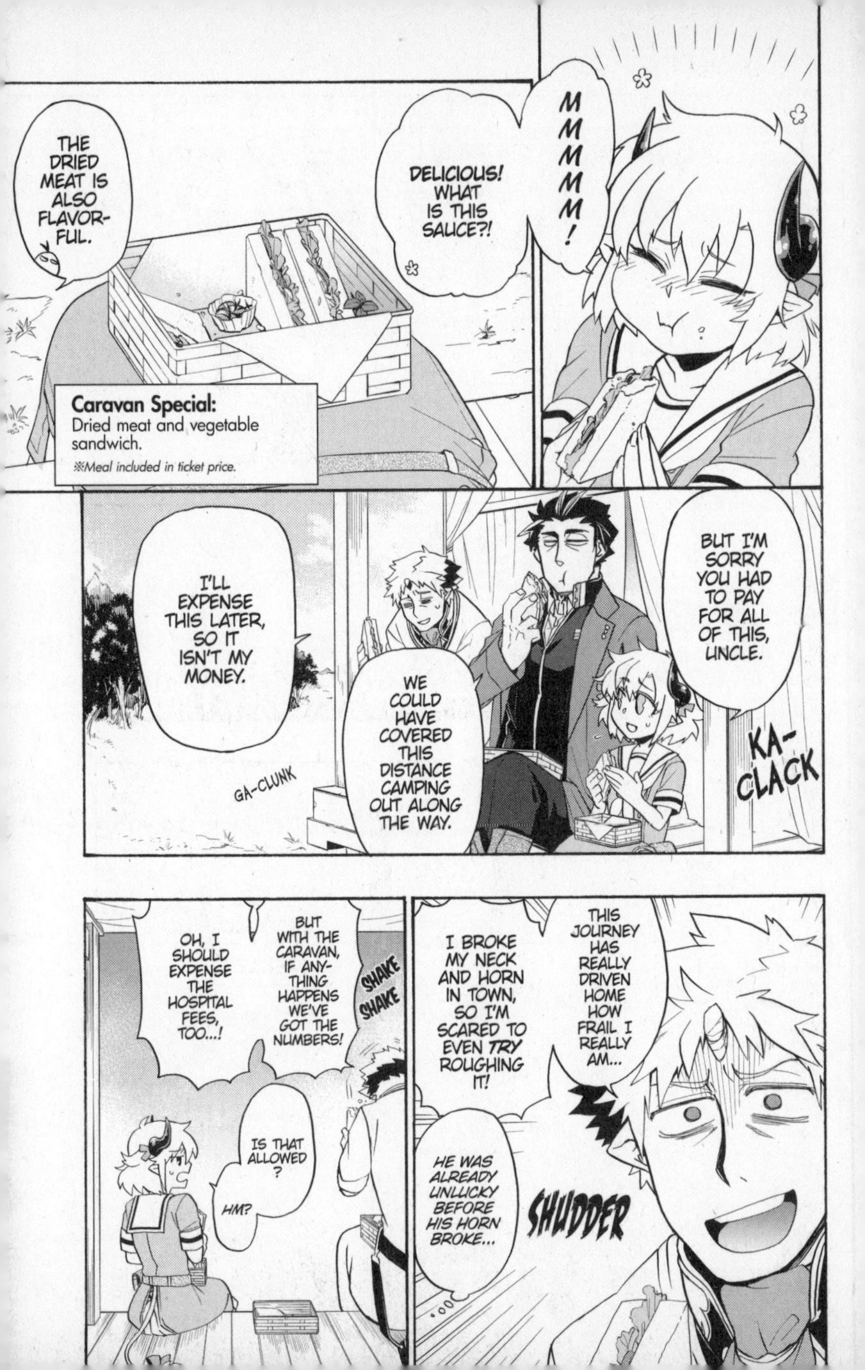
MMMMMM!
DELICIOUS! WHAT IS THIS SAUCE?!
THE DRIED MEAT IS ALSO FLAVOR-FUL.
Caravan Special:
Dried meat and vegetable sandwich.
※Meal included in ticket price.
BUT I'M SORRY YOU HAD TO PAY FOR ALL OF THIS, UNCLE.
KA-CLACK
I'LL EXPENSE THIS LATER, SO IT ISN'T MY MONEY.
WE COULD HAVE COVERED THIS DISTANCE CAMPING OUT ALONG THE WAY.
GA-CLUNK
THIS JOURNEY HAS REALLY DRIVEN HOME HOW FRAIL I REALLY AM...
I BROKE MY NECK AND HORN IN TOWN, SO I'M SCARED TO EVEN *TRY* ROUGHING IT!
SHUDDER
HE WAS ALREADY UNLUCKY BEFORE HIS HORN BROKE...
BUT WITH THE CARAVAN, IF ANY-THING HAPPENS WE'VE GOT THE NUMBERS!
SHAKE SHAKE
OH, I SHOULD EXPENSE THE HOSPITAL FEES, TOO...!
IS THAT ALLOWED?
HM?

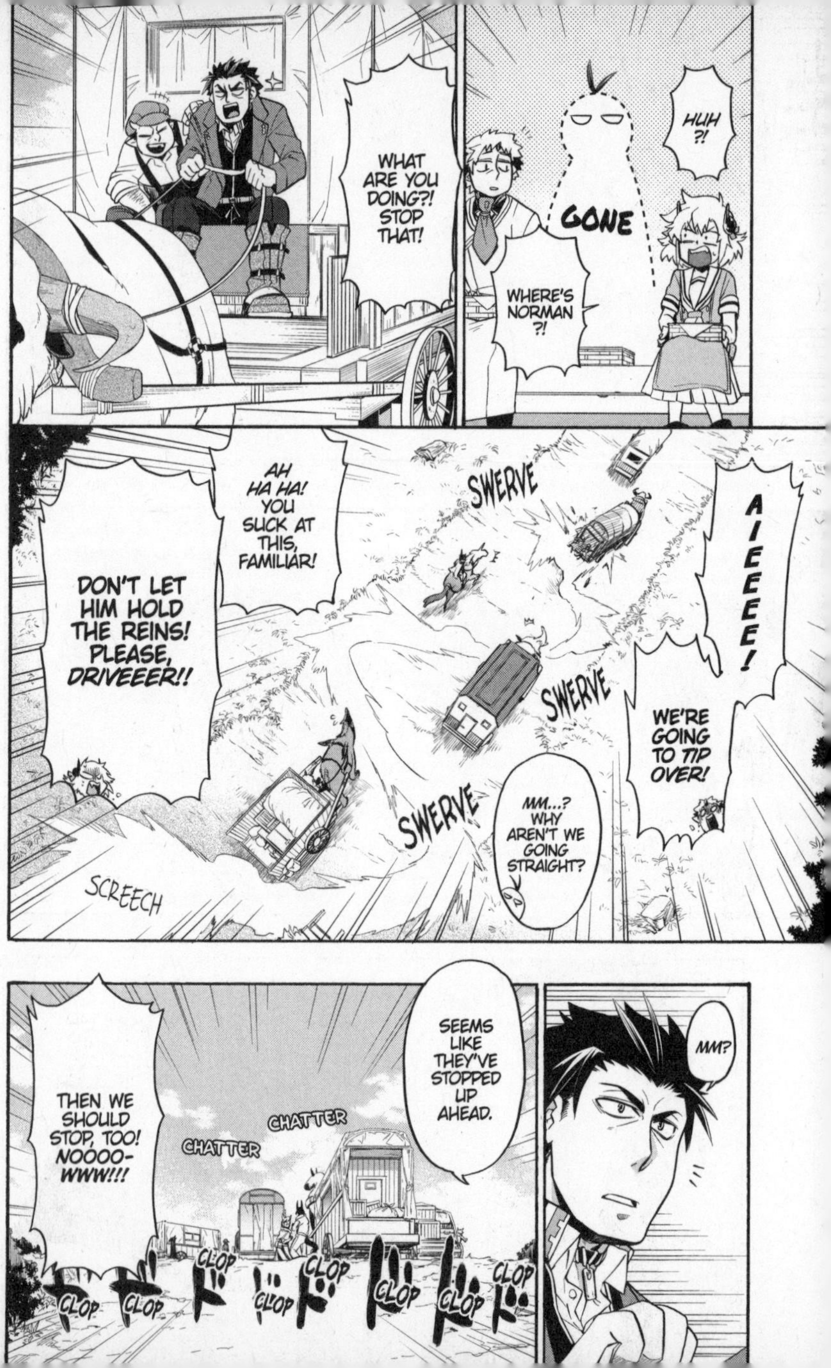
HUH?!
GONE
WHERE'S NORMAN?!
WHAT ARE YOU DOING?! STOP THAT!
AIEEEE!
WE'RE GOING TO TIP OVER!
SWERVE
AH HA HA! YOU SUCK AT THIS, FAMILIAR!
SWERVE
MM...? WHY AREN'T WE GOING STRAIGHT?
SWERVE
DON'T LET HIM HOLD THE REINS! PLEASE, DRIVEEER!!
SCREECH
MM?
SEEMS LIKE THEY'VE STOPPED UP AHEAD.
CHATTER
CHATTER
THEN WE SHOULD STOP, TOO! NOOOO-WWW!!!
CLOP
CLOP
CLOP
CLOP
CLOP
CLOP
CLOP
CLOP

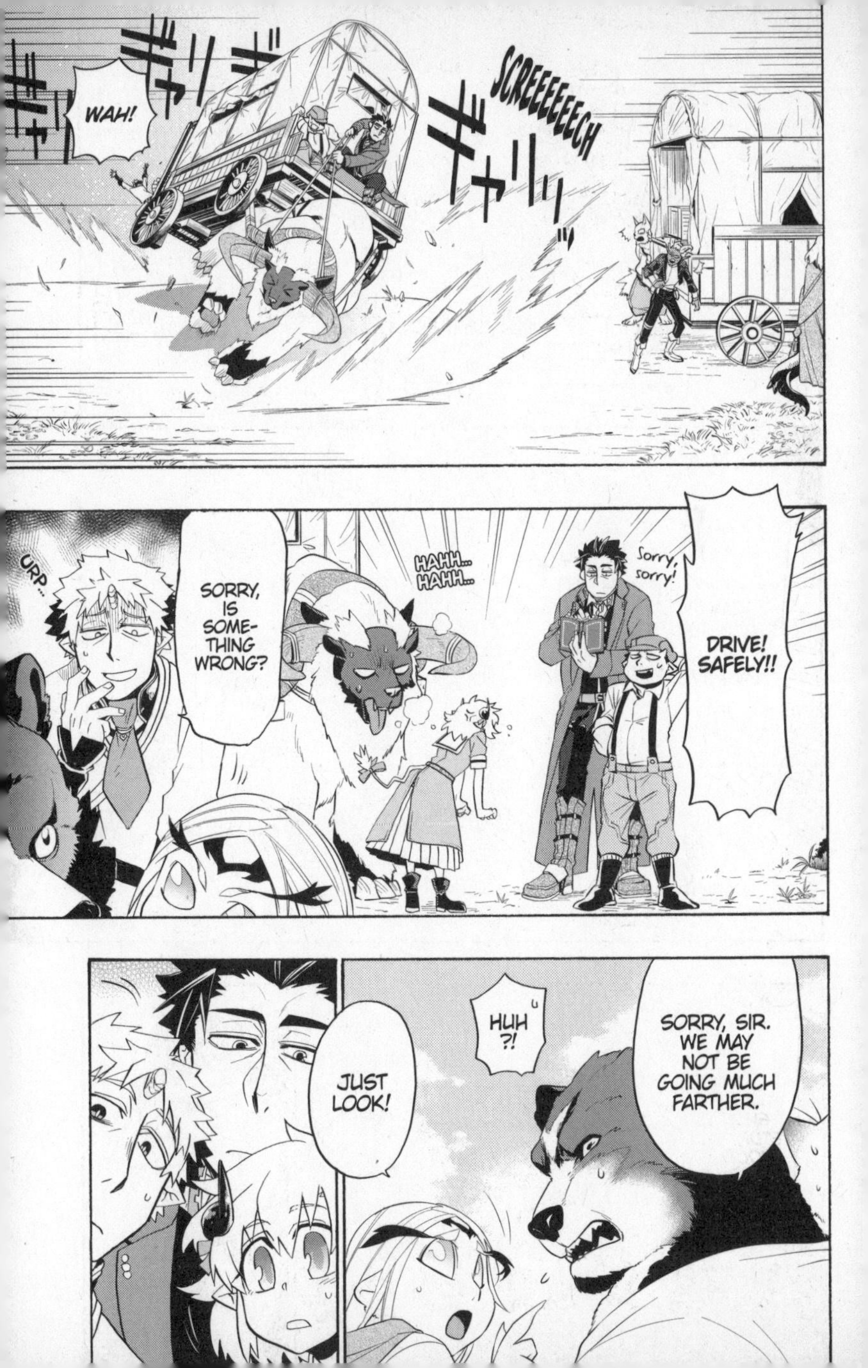
SCREEEEEEECH
WAH!
DRIVE! SAFELY!!
Sorry, sorry!
HAHH... HAHH...
SORRY, IS SOME-THING WRONG?
URP...
SORRY, SIR. WE MAY NOT BE GOING MUCH FARTHER.
HUH ?!
JUST LOOK!

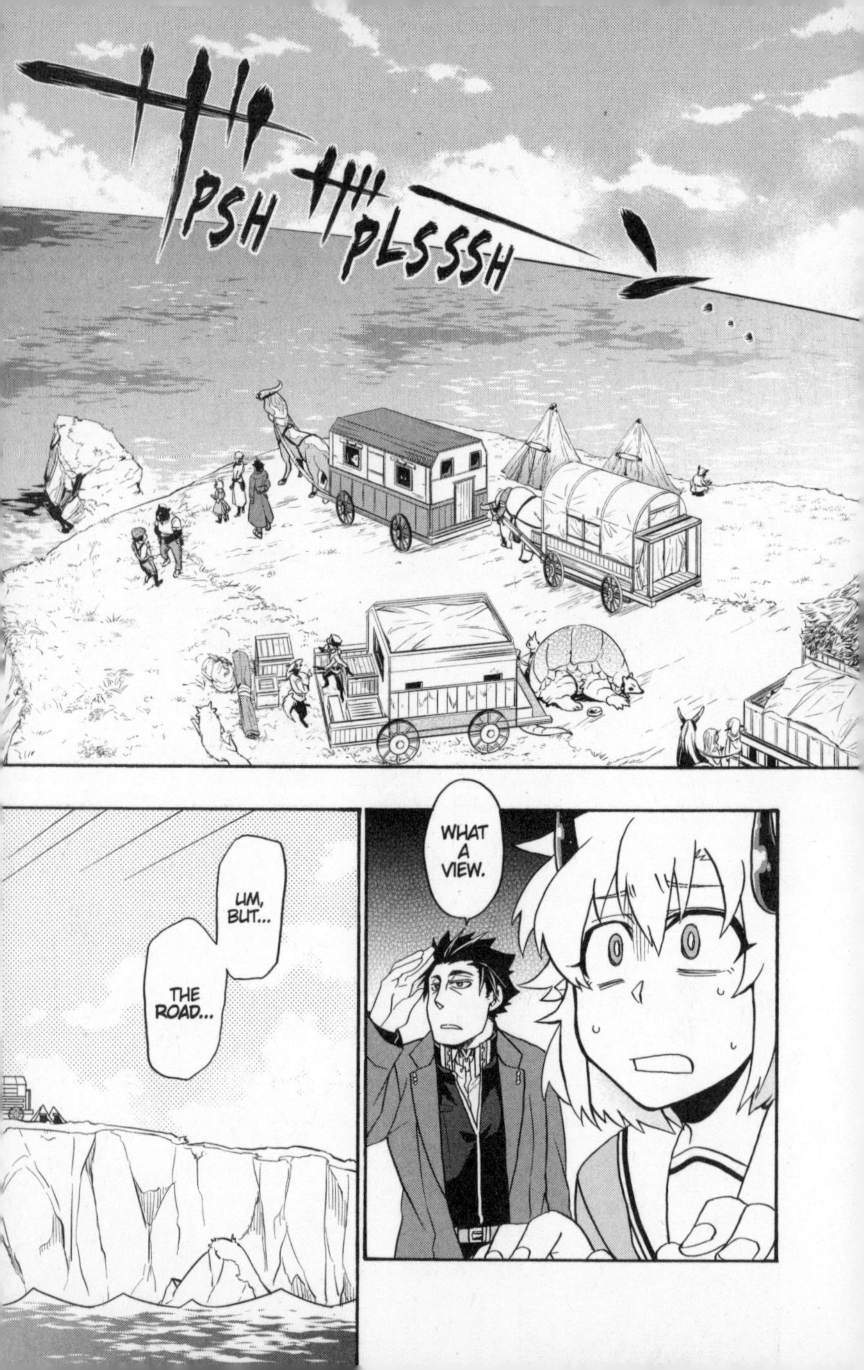
PSH
PLSSSH
WHAT A VIEW.
UM, BUT...
THE ROAD...

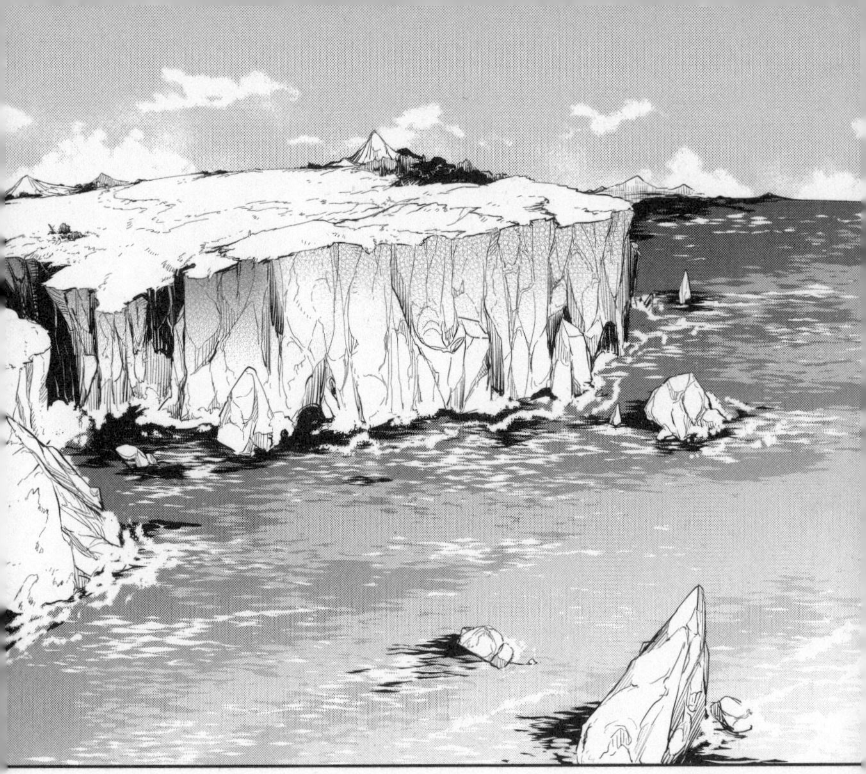

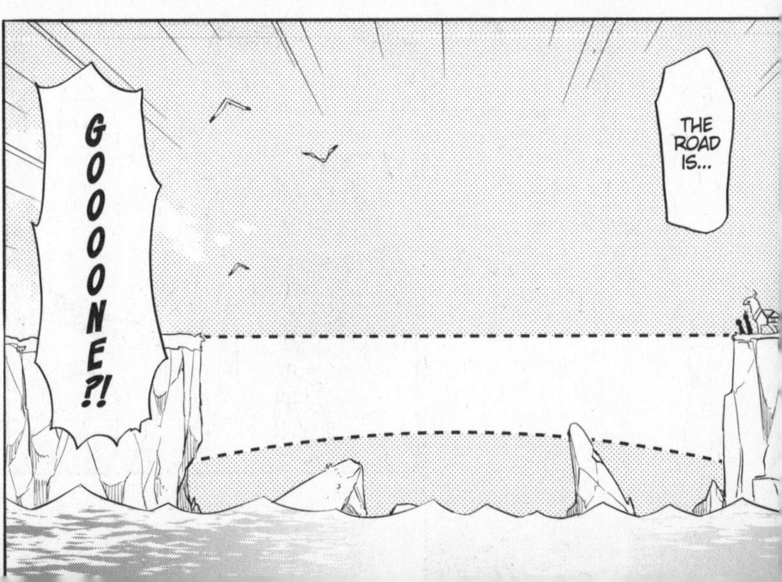
THE ROAD IS...
GOOOOONE?!

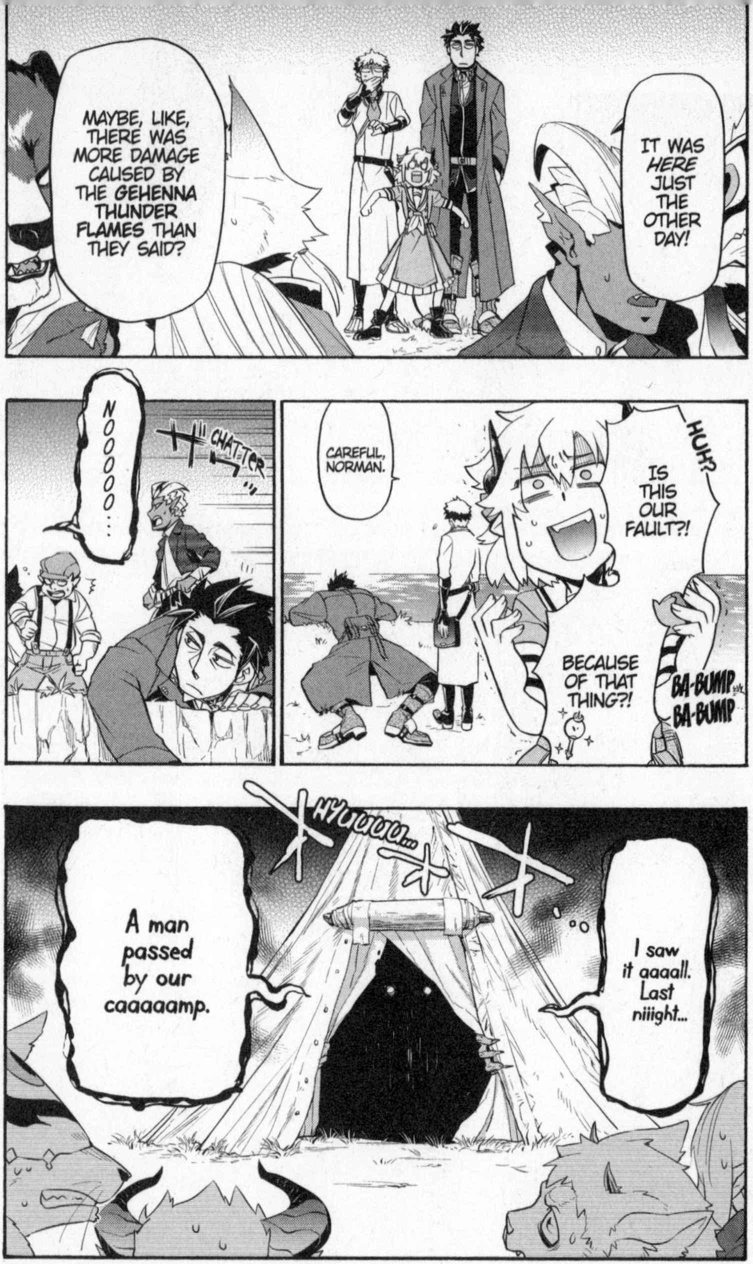
IT WAS HERE JUST THE OTHER DAY!
MAYBE, LIKE, THERE WAS MORE DAMAGE CAUSED BY THE GEHENNA THUNDER FLAMES THAN THEY SAID?
HUH?
IS THIS OUR FAULT?!
BECAUSE OF THAT THING?!
BA-BUMP BA-BUMP
CAREFUL, NORMAN.
NOOOOOO...
CHATTER
HYUUUUU...
I saw it aaaall. Last niiight...
A man passed by our caaaaamp.

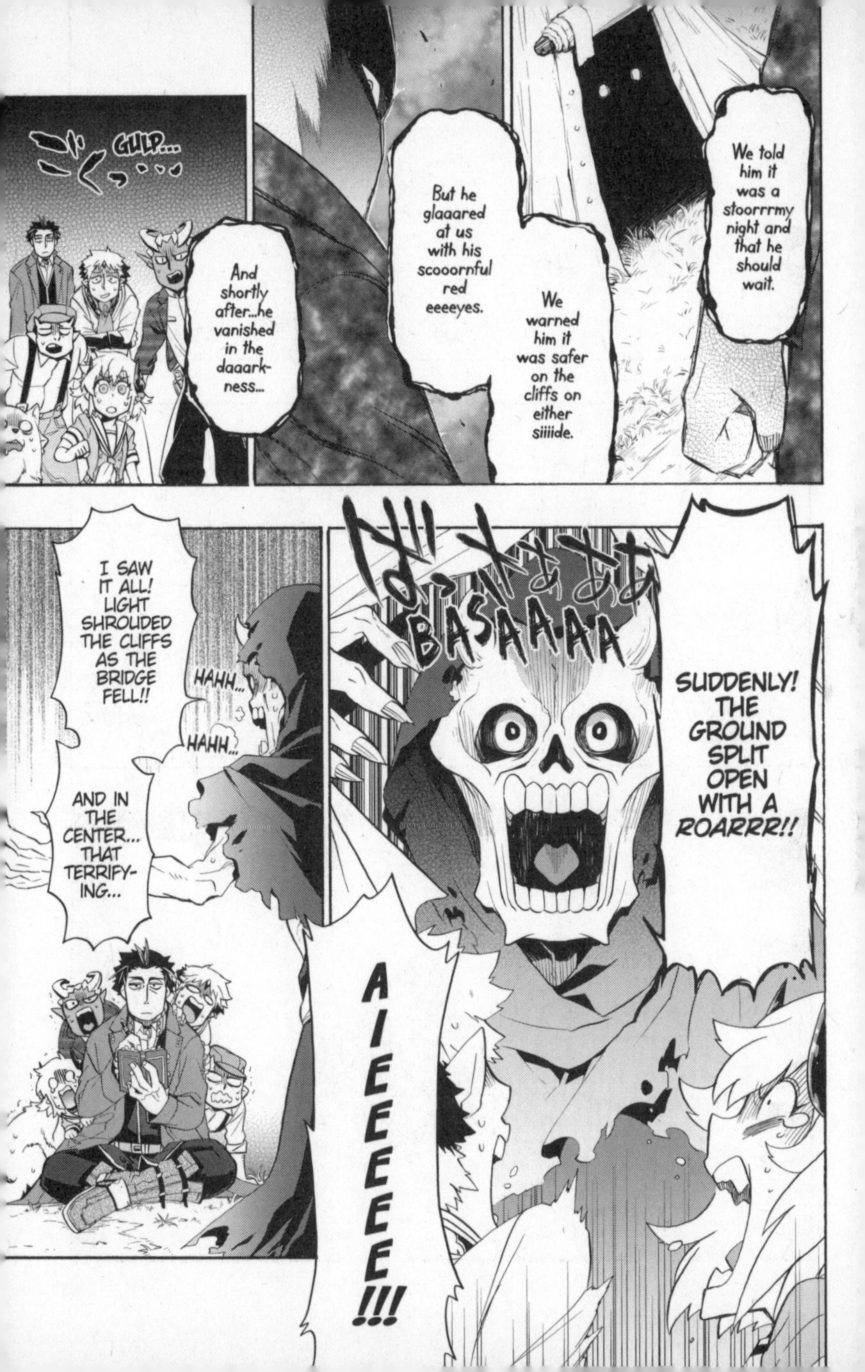
We told him it was a stoorrrmy night and that he should wait.
We warned him it was safer on the cliffs on either siiiide.
But he glaaared at us with his scooornful red eeeeyes.
And shortly after...he vanished in the daaark-ness...
ごくっ…
GULP...
ばさあああ
BASAAAA
SUDDENLY! THE GROUND SPLIT OPEN WITH A ROARRR!!
I SAW IT ALL! LIGHT SHROUDED THE CLIFFS AS THE BRIDGE FELL!!
HAHH...
HAHH...
AND IN THE CENTER... THAT TERRIFY-ING...
AIEEEEEE!!!

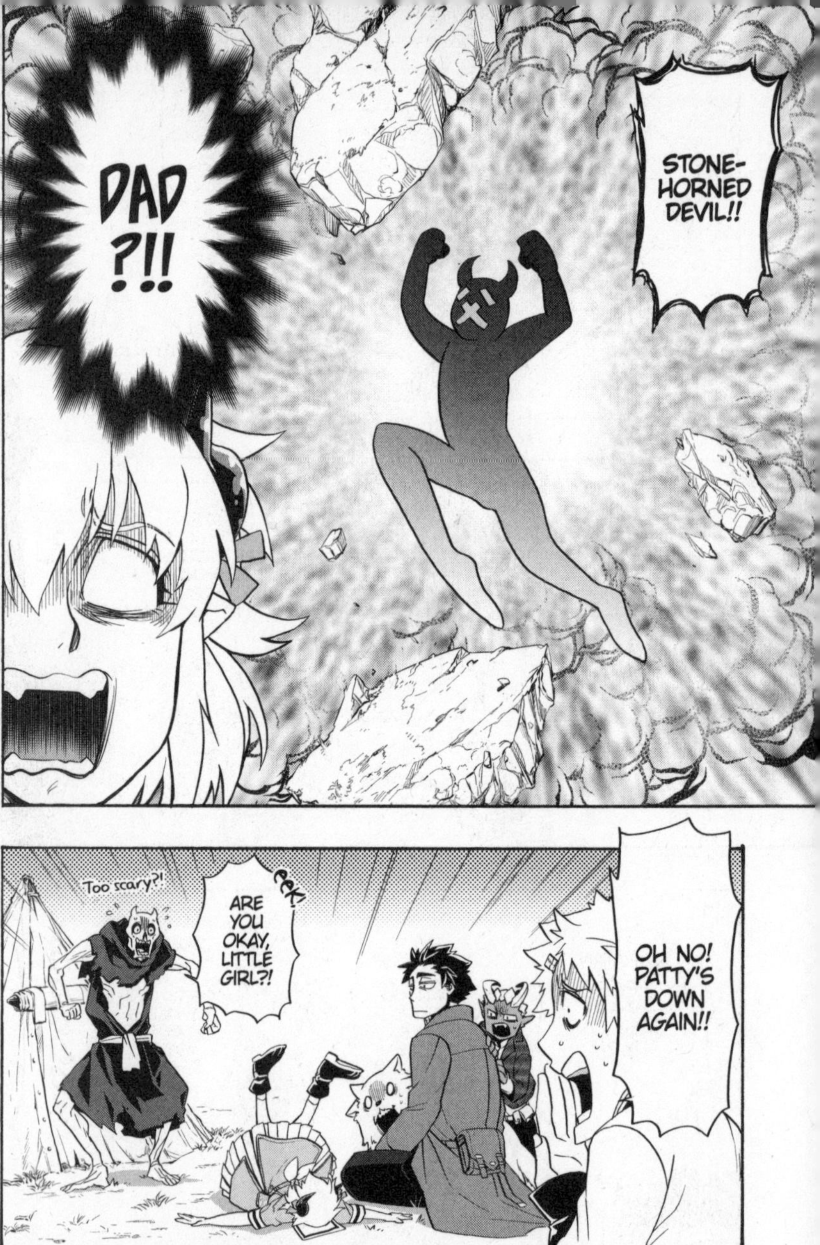
STONE-HORNED DEVIL!!
DAD ?!!
OH NO! PATTY'S DOWN AGAIN!!
eek!
ARE YOU OKAY, LITTLE GIRL?!
Too scary?!

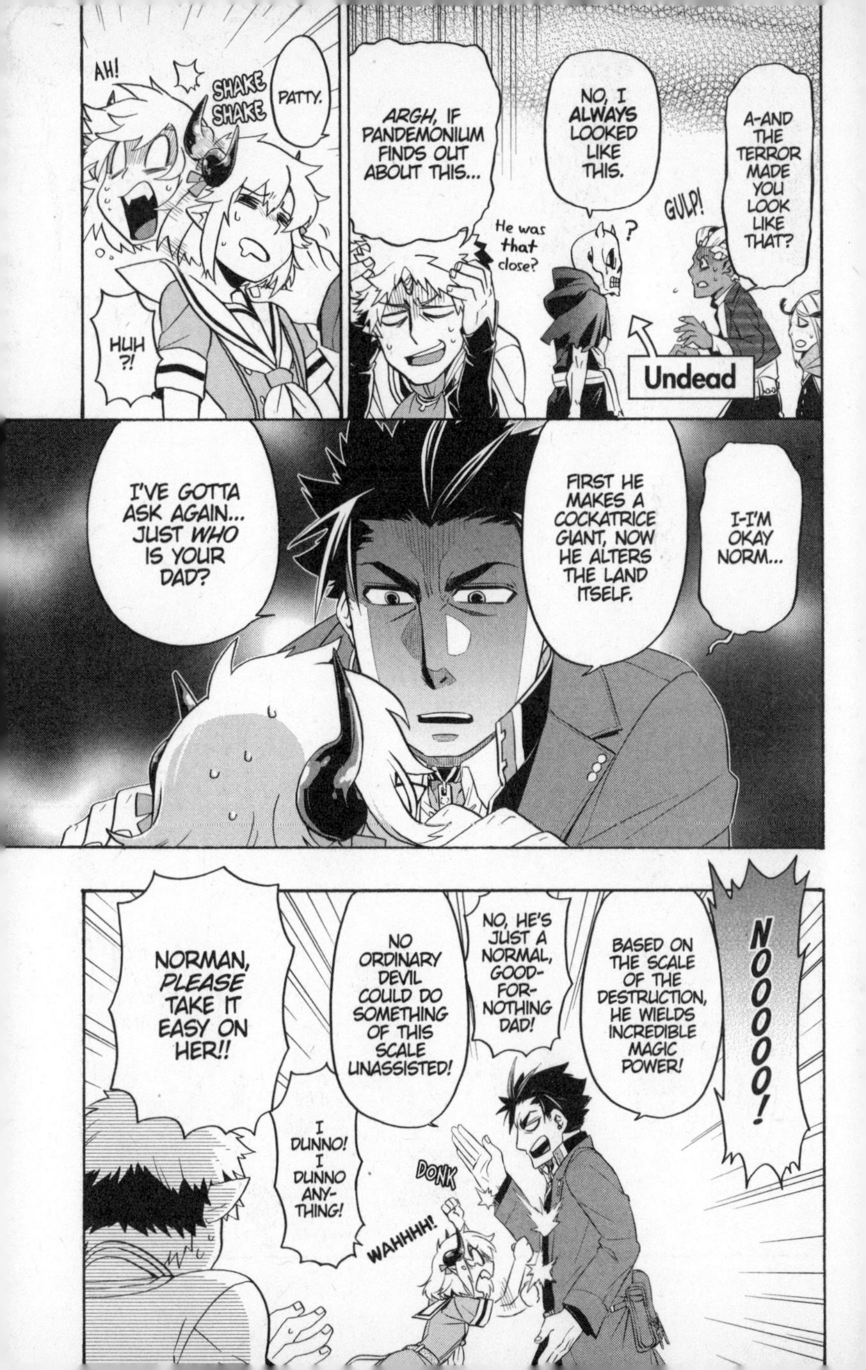

A-AND THE TERROR MADE YOU LOOK LIKE THAT?
GULP!
NO, I ALWAYS LOOKED LIKE THIS.
?
Undead
ARGH, IF PANDEMONIUM FINDS OUT ABOUT THIS...
He was that close?
PATTY.
SHAKE SHAKE
AH!
HUH ?!
I-I'M OKAY NORM...
FIRST HE MAKES A COCKATRICE GIANT, NOW HE ALTERS THE LAND ITSELF.
I'VE GOTTA ASK AGAIN... JUST WHO IS YOUR DAD?
NOOOOOO!
BASED ON THE SCALE OF THE DESTRUCTION, HE WIELDS INCREDIBLE MAGIC POWER!
NO, HE'S JUST A NORMAL, GOOD-FOR-NOTHING DAD!
NO ORDINARY DEVIL COULD DO SOMETHING OF THIS SCALE UNASSISTED!
NORMAN, PLEASE TAKE IT EASY ON HER!!
I DUNNO! I DUNNO ANYTHING!
DONK
WAHHHH!

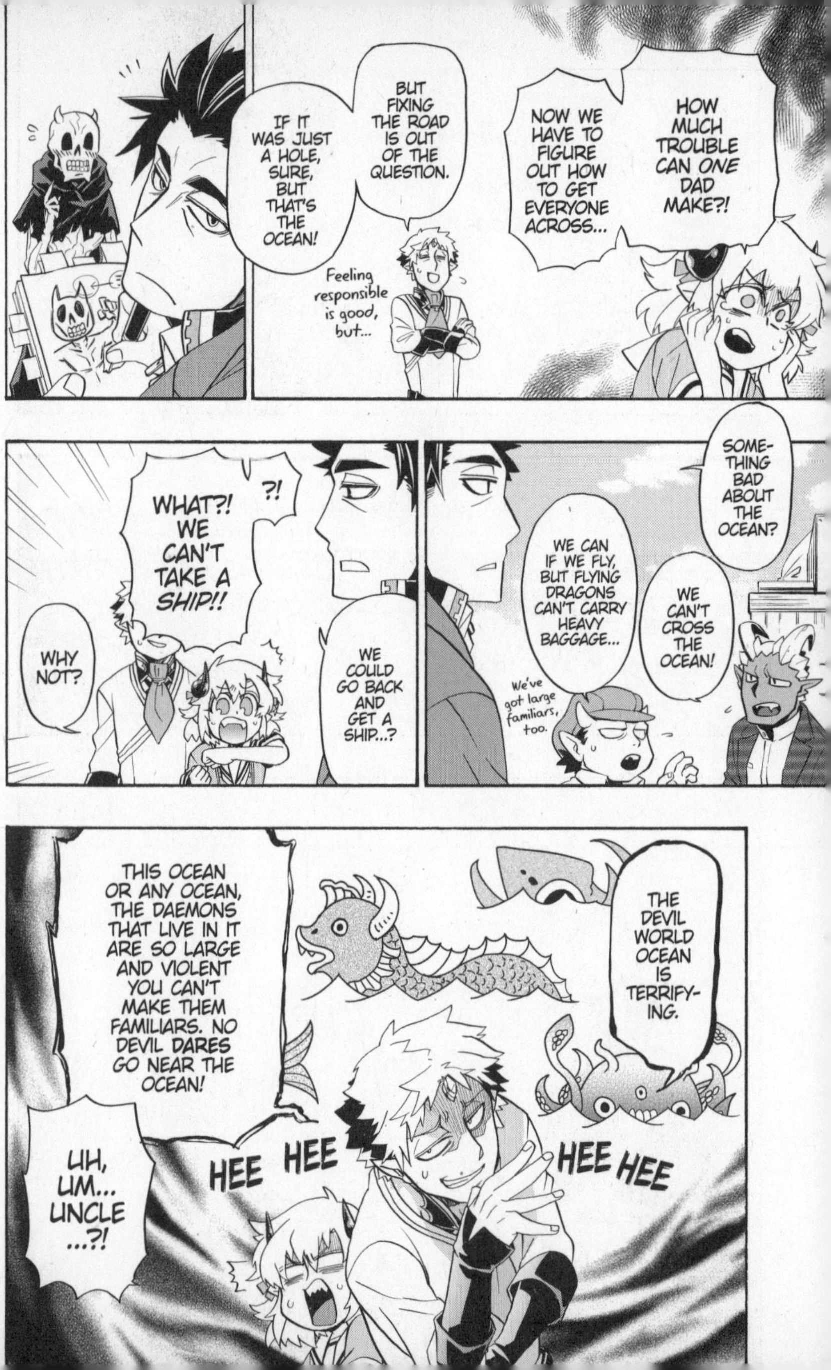
HOW MUCH TROUBLE CAN *ONE* DAD MAKE?!
NOW WE HAVE TO FIGURE OUT HOW TO GET EVERYONE ACROSS...
BUT FIXING THE ROAD IS OUT OF THE QUESTION.
IF IT WAS JUST A HOLE, SURE, BUT THAT'S THE OCEAN!
Feeling responsible is good, but...
SOME-THING BAD ABOUT THE OCEAN?
WE CAN'T CROSS THE OCEAN!
WE CAN IF WE FLY, BUT FLYING DRAGONS CAN'T CARRY HEAVY BAGGAGE...
We've got large familiars, too.
WE COULD GO BACK AND GET A SHIP...?
?!
WHAT?! WE CAN'T TAKE A *SHIP!!*
WHY NOT?
THE DEVIL WORLD OCEAN IS TERRIFY-ING.
THIS OCEAN OR ANY OCEAN, THE DAEMONS THAT LIVE IN IT ARE SO LARGE AND VIOLENT YOU CAN'T MAKE THEM FAMILIARS. NO DEVIL DARES GO NEAR THE OCEAN!
HEE HEE
HEE HEE
UH, UM... UNCLE ...?!

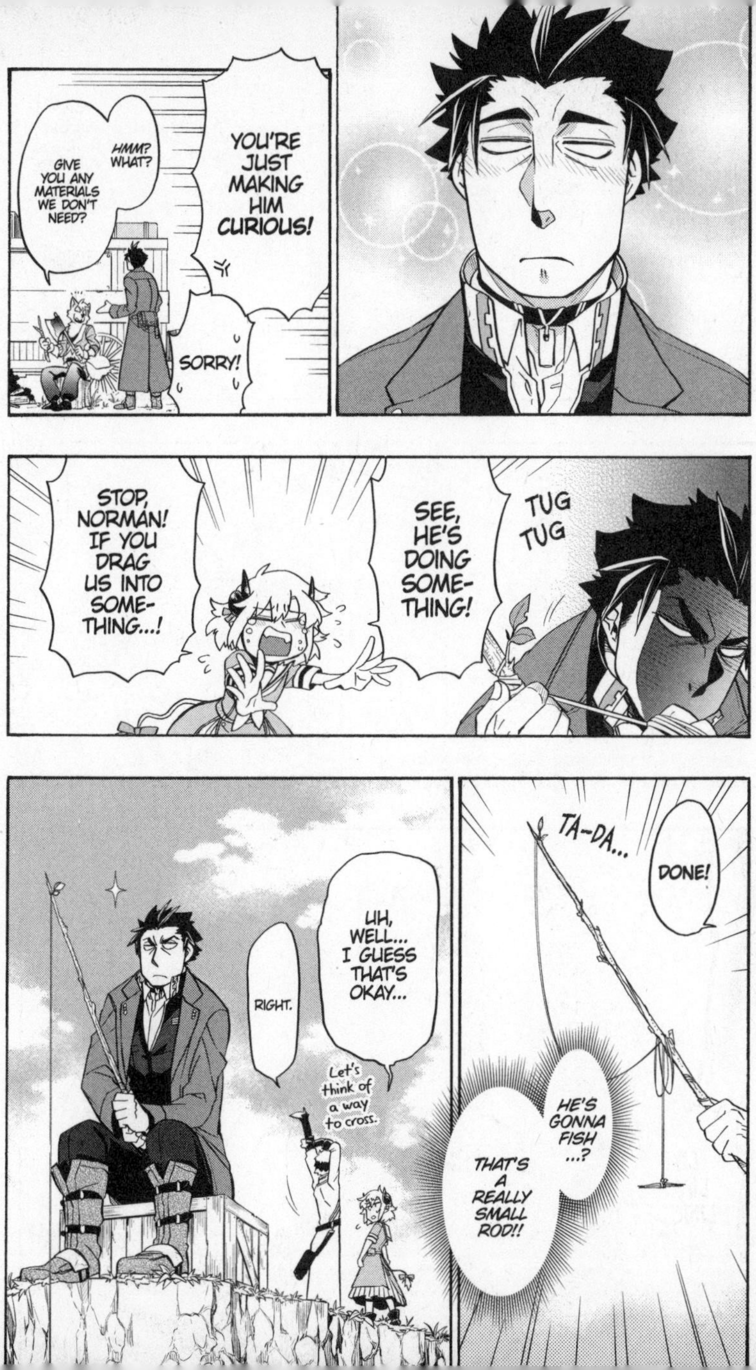

YOU'RE JUST MAKING HIM CURIOUS!
HMM? WHAT?
GIVE YOU ANY MATERIALS WE DON'T NEED?
SORRY!
TUG TUG
SEE, HE'S DOING SOMETHING!
STOP, NORMAN! IF YOU DRAG US INTO SOMETHING...!
TA-DA...
DONE!
HE'S GONNA FISH ...?
THAT'S A REALLY SMALL ROD!!
UH, WELL... I GUESS THAT'S OKAY...
RIGHT.
Let's think of a way to cross.

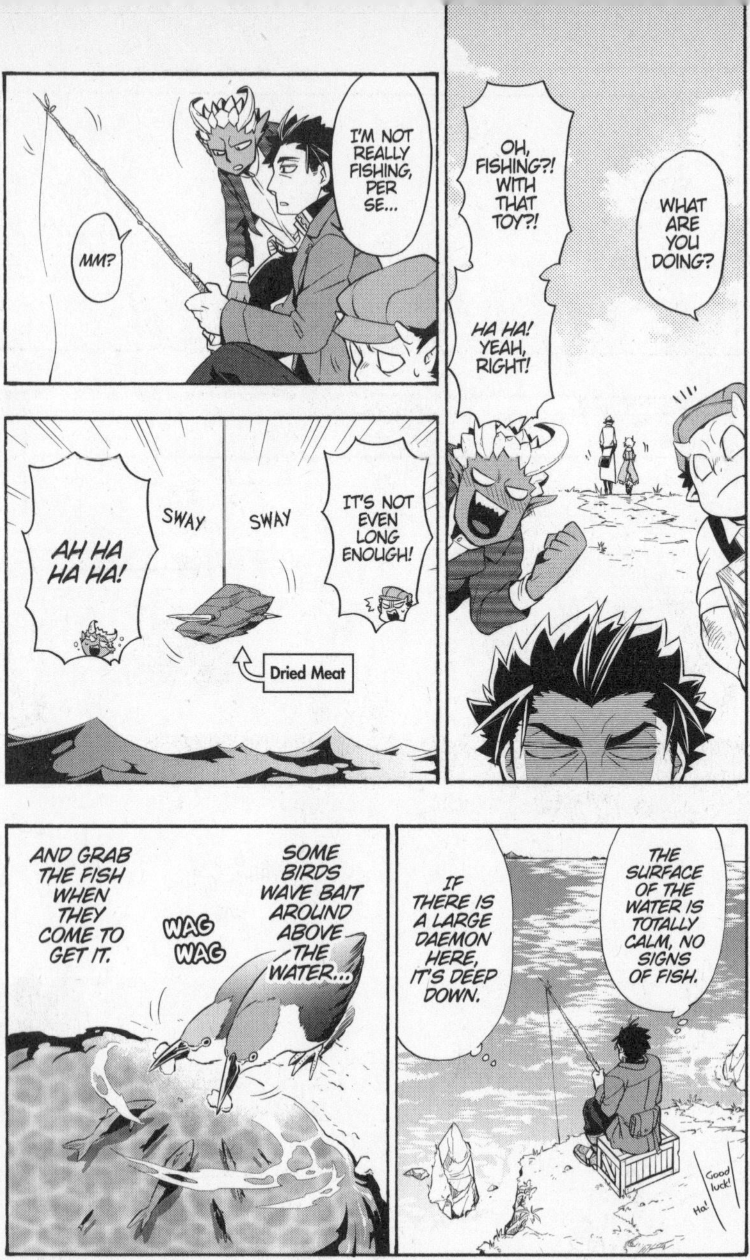
WHAT ARE YOU DOING?
OH, FISHING?! WITH THAT TOY?!
HA HA! YEAH, RIGHT!
I'M NOT REALLY FISHING, PER SE...
MM?
IT'S NOT EVEN LONG ENOUGH!
SWAY
SWAY
Dried Meat
AH HA HA HA!
THE SURFACE OF THE WATER IS TOTALLY CALM, NO SIGNS OF FISH.
IF THERE IS A LARGE DAEMON HERE, IT'S DEEP DOWN.
Good luck!
Ha!
SOME BIRDS WAVE BAIT AROUND ABOVE THE WATER...
WAG WAG
AND GRAB THE FISH WHEN THEY COME TO GET IT.

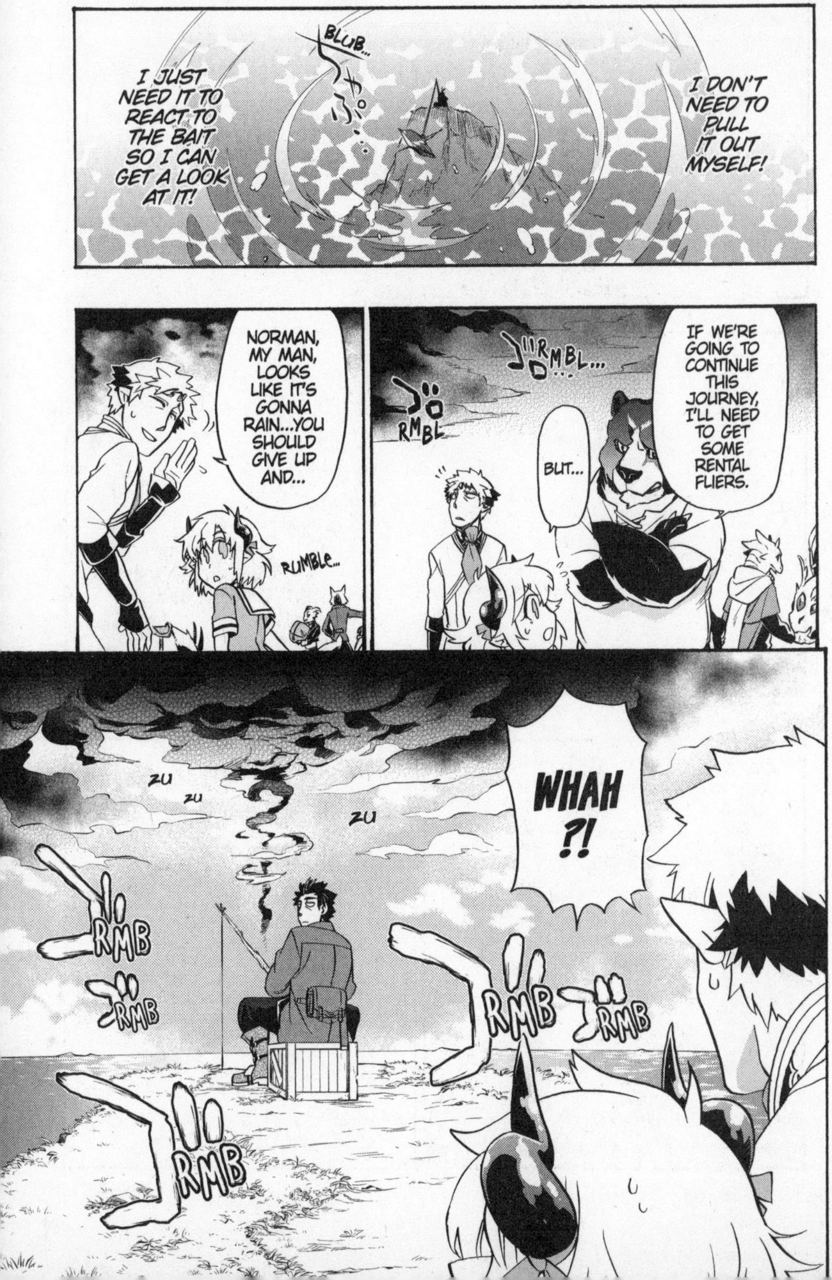
I DON'T NEED TO PULL IT OUT MYSELF!
BLUB...
I JUST NEED IT TO REACT TO THE BAIT SO I CAN GET A LOOK AT IT!
IF WE'RE GOING TO CONTINUE THIS JOURNEY, I'LL NEED TO GET SOME RENTAL FLIERS.
RMBL...
BUT...
RMBL
NORMAN, MY MAN, LOOKS LIKE IT'S GONNA RAIN...YOU SHOULD GIVE UP AND...
RUMBLE...
WHAH ?!
ZU
ZU
ZU
RMB
RMB
RMB
RMB
RMB

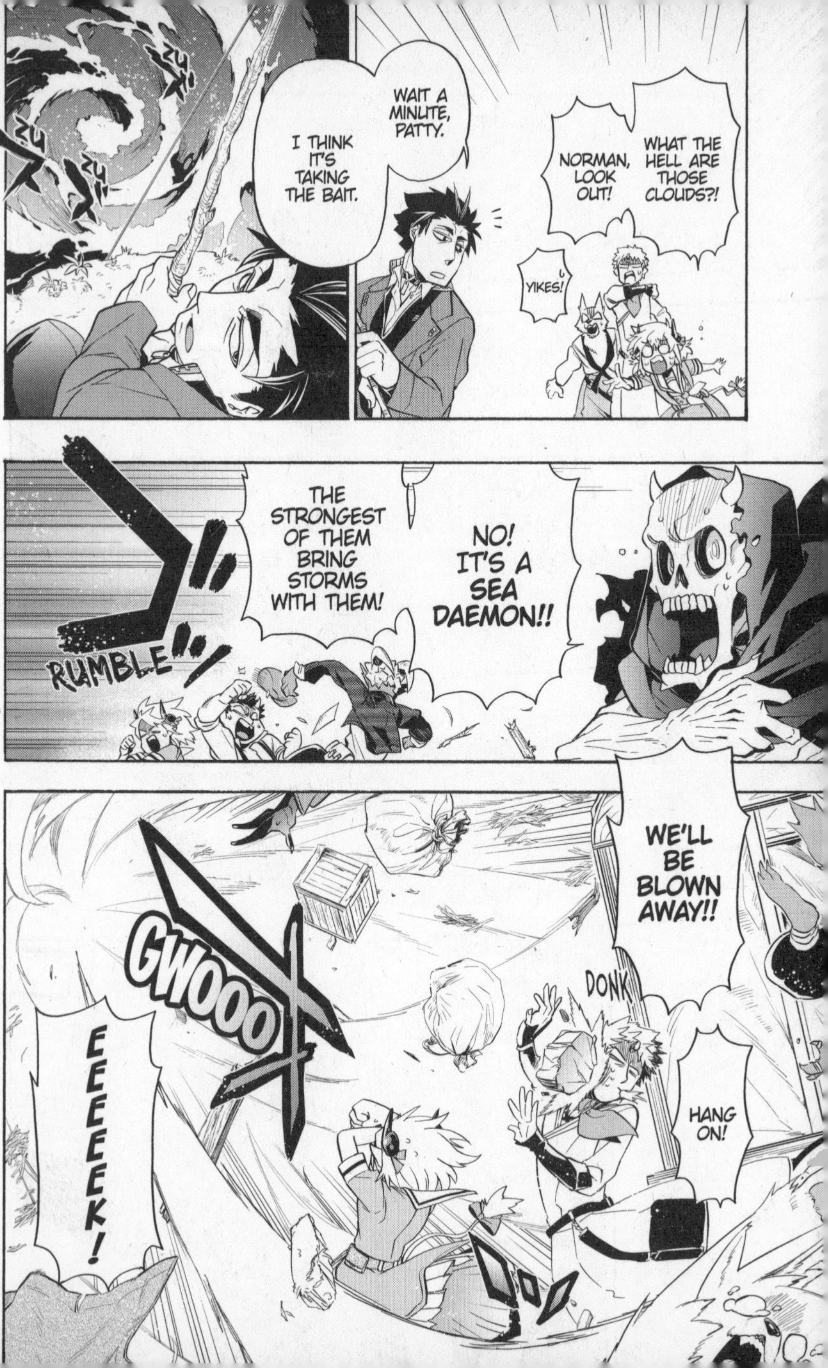
WHAT THE HELL ARE THOSE CLOUDS?!
NORMAN, LOOK OUT!
YIKES!
WAIT A MINUTE, PATTY.
I THINK IT'S TAKING THE BAIT.
NO! IT'S A SEA DAEMON!!
THE STRONGEST OF THEM BRING STORMS WITH THEM!
RUMBLE
WE'LL BE BLOWN AWAY!!
HANG ON!
DONK
GWOOO
EEEEEEK!

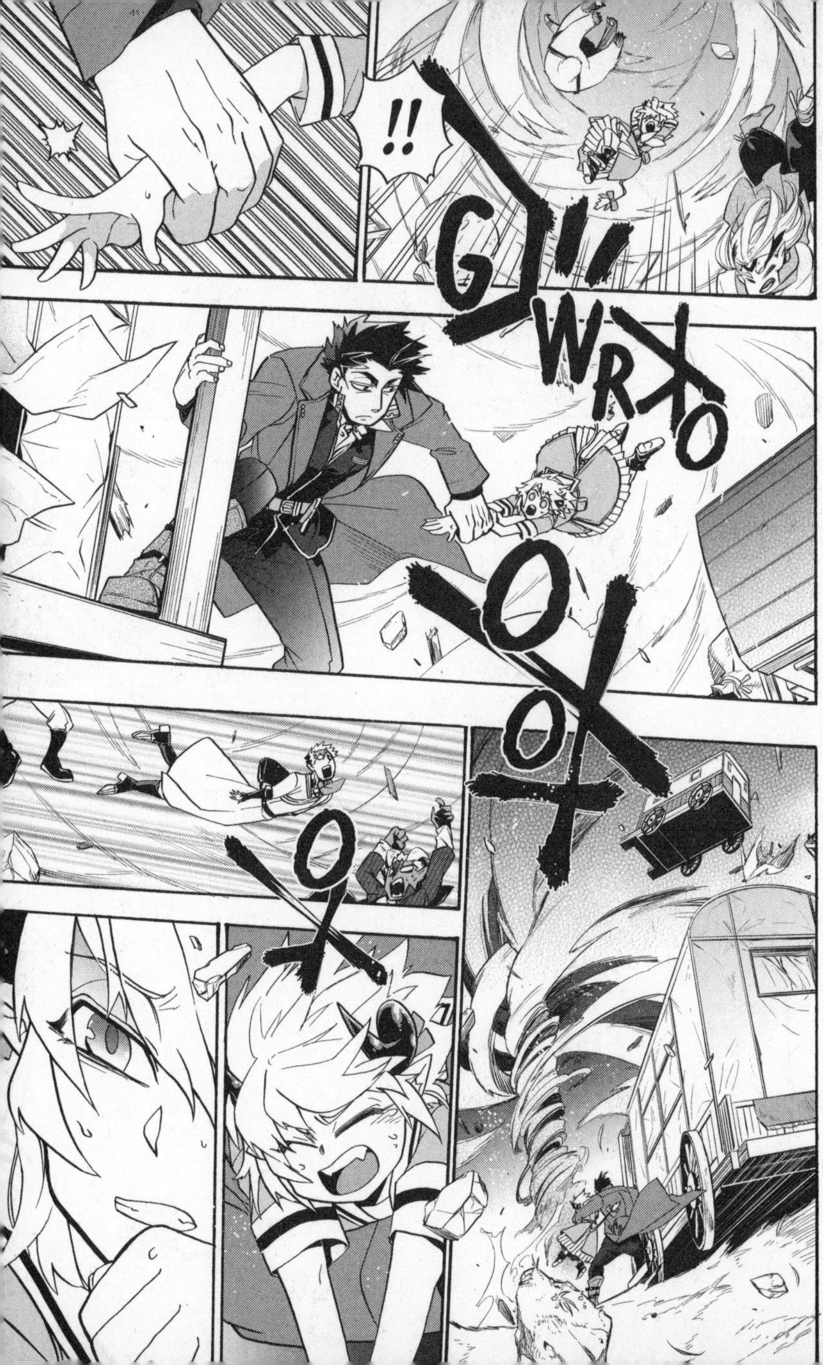
GWROOOO
!!

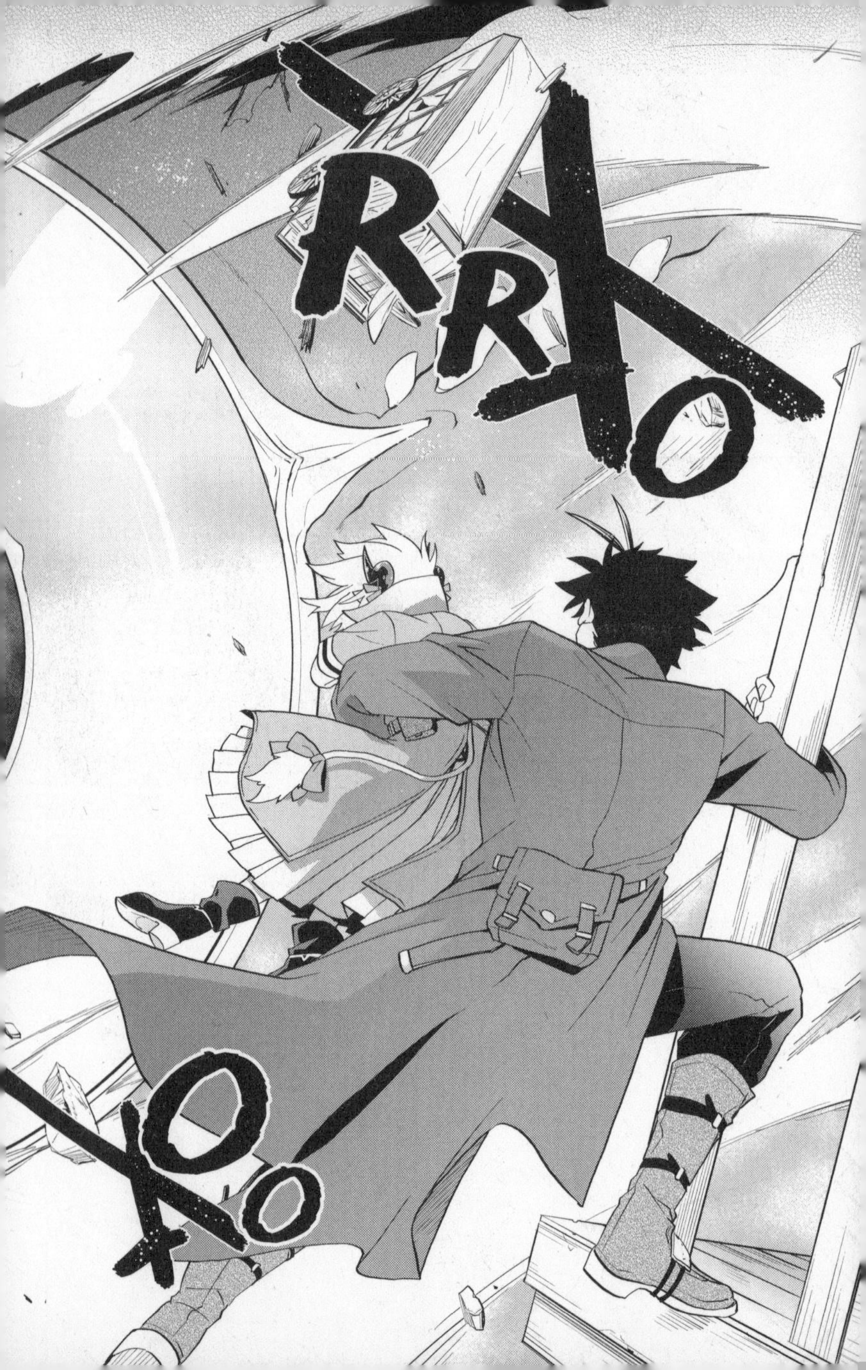
RRO
OO

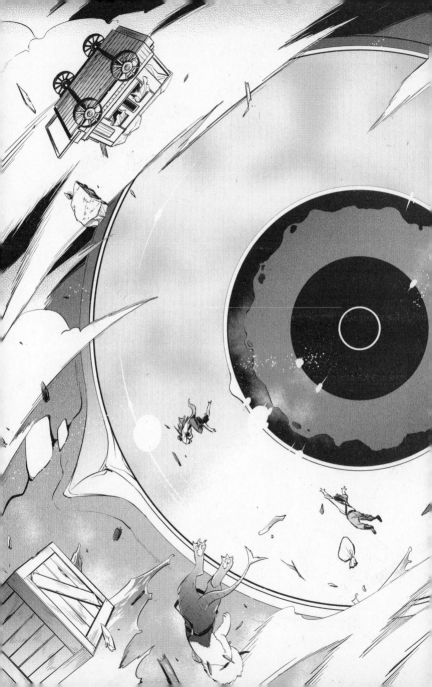

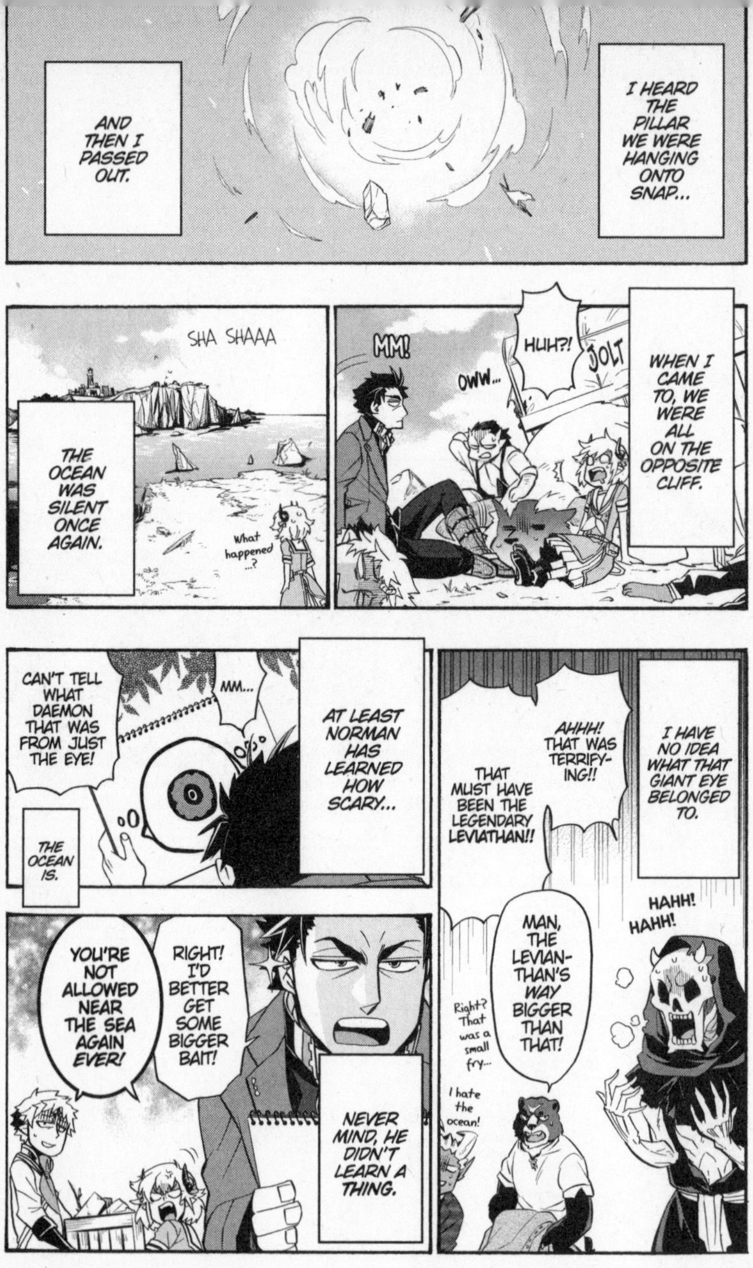
I HEARD THE PILLAR WE WERE HANGING ONTO SNAP...
AND THEN I PASSED OUT.
WHEN I CAME TO, WE WERE ALL ON THE OPPOSITE CLIFF.
HUH?!
JOLT
MM!
OWW...
SHA SHAAA
THE OCEAN WAS SILENT ONCE AGAIN.
What happened ...?
I HAVE NO IDEA WHAT THAT GIANT EYE BELONGED TO.
AHHH! THAT WAS TERRIFYING!!
THAT MUST HAVE BEEN THE LEGENDARY LEVIATHAN!!
HAHH! HAHH!
MAN, THE LEVIANTHAN'S WAY BIGGER THAN THAT!
Right? That was a small fry...
I hate the ocean!
AT LEAST NORMAN HAS LEARNED HOW SCARY...
MM...
CAN'T TELL WHAT DAEMON THAT WAS FROM JUST THE EYE!
THE OCEAN IS.
RIGHT! I'D BETTER GET SOME BIGGER BAIT!
YOU'RE NOT ALLOWED NEAR THE SEA AGAIN EVER!
NEVER MIND, HE DIDN'T LEARN A THING.

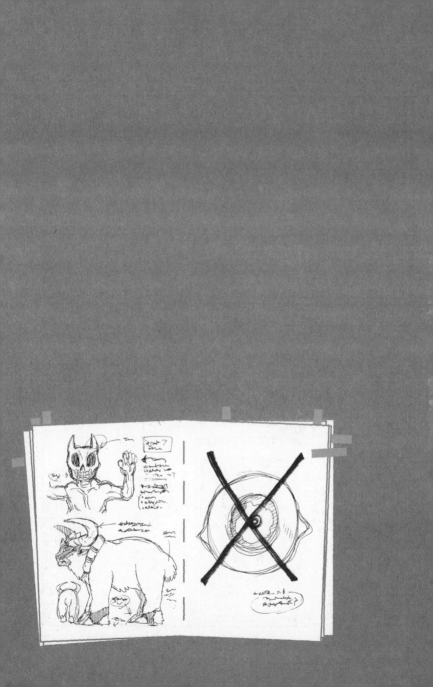

Sorry For My Familiar

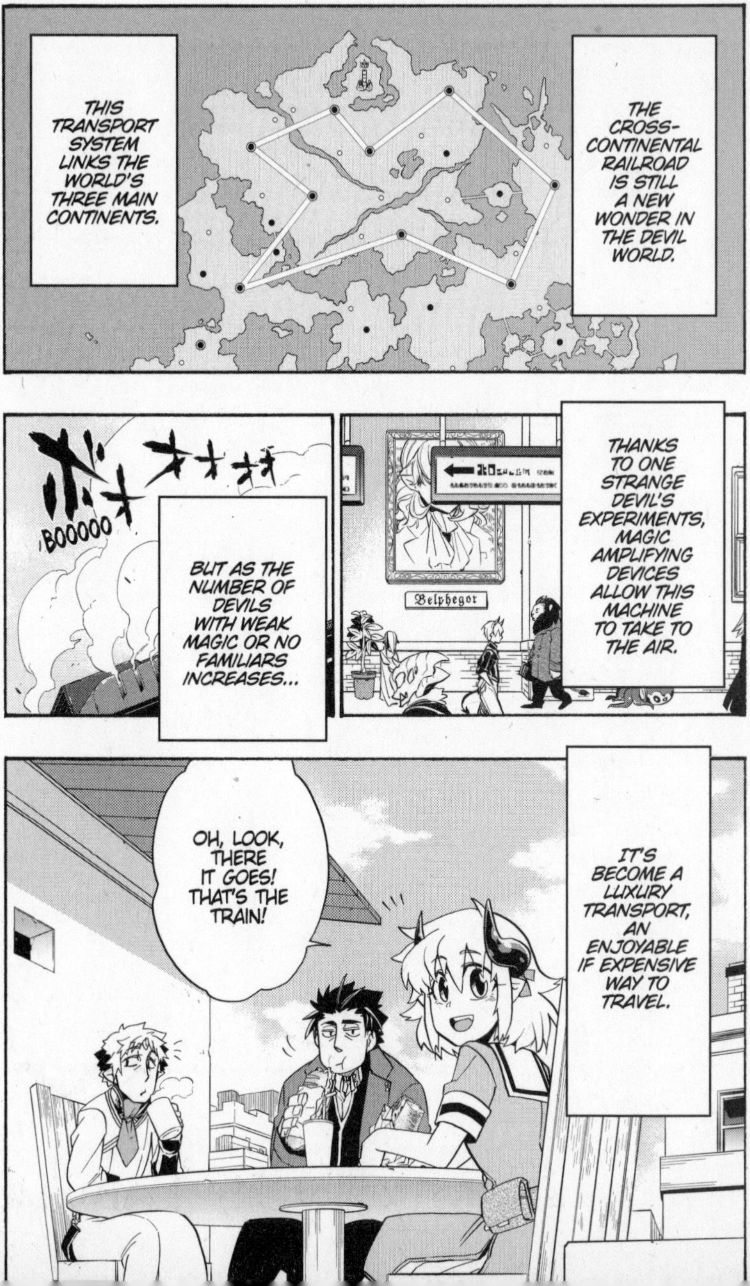
THE CROSS-CONTINENTAL RAILROAD IS STILL A NEW WONDER IN THE DEVIL WORLD.
THIS TRANSPORT SYSTEM LINKS THE WORLD'S THREE MAIN CONTINENTS.
THANKS TO ONE STRANGE DEVIL'S EXPERIMENTS, MAGIC AMPLIFYING DEVICES ALLOW THIS MACHINE TO TAKE TO THE AIR.
Belphegor
BUT AS THE NUMBER OF DEVILS WITH WEAK MAGIC OR NO FAMILIARS INCREASES...
ボォオオオ
BOOOOO
IT'S BECOME A LUXURY TRANSPORT, AN ENJOYABLE IF EXPENSIVE WAY TO TRAVEL.
OH, LOOK, THERE IT GOES! THAT'S THE TRAIN!

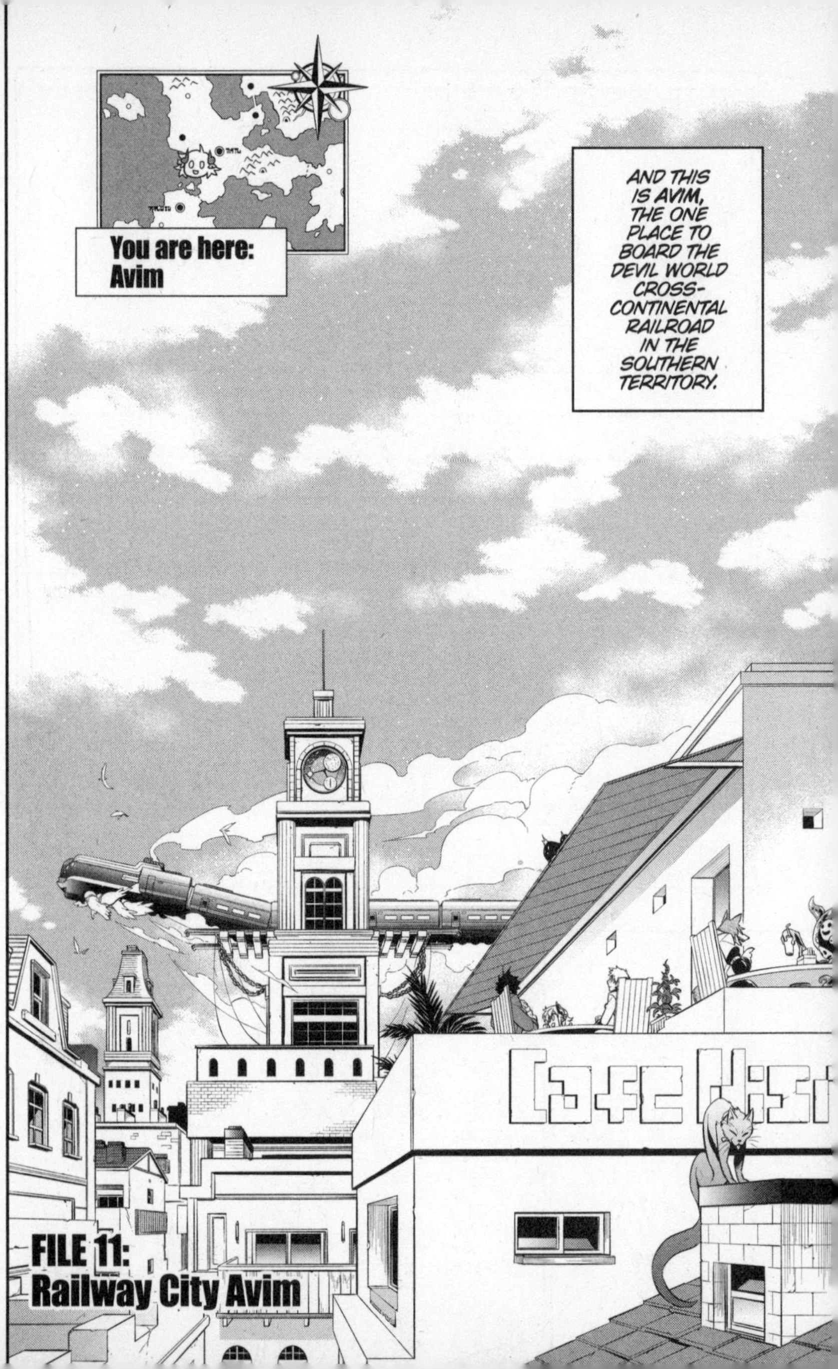
AND THIS IS AVIM, THE ONE PLACE TO BOARD THE DEVIL WORLD CROSS-CONTINENTAL RAILROAD IN THE SOUTHERN TERRITORY.
You are here: Avim
FILE 11: Railway City Avim

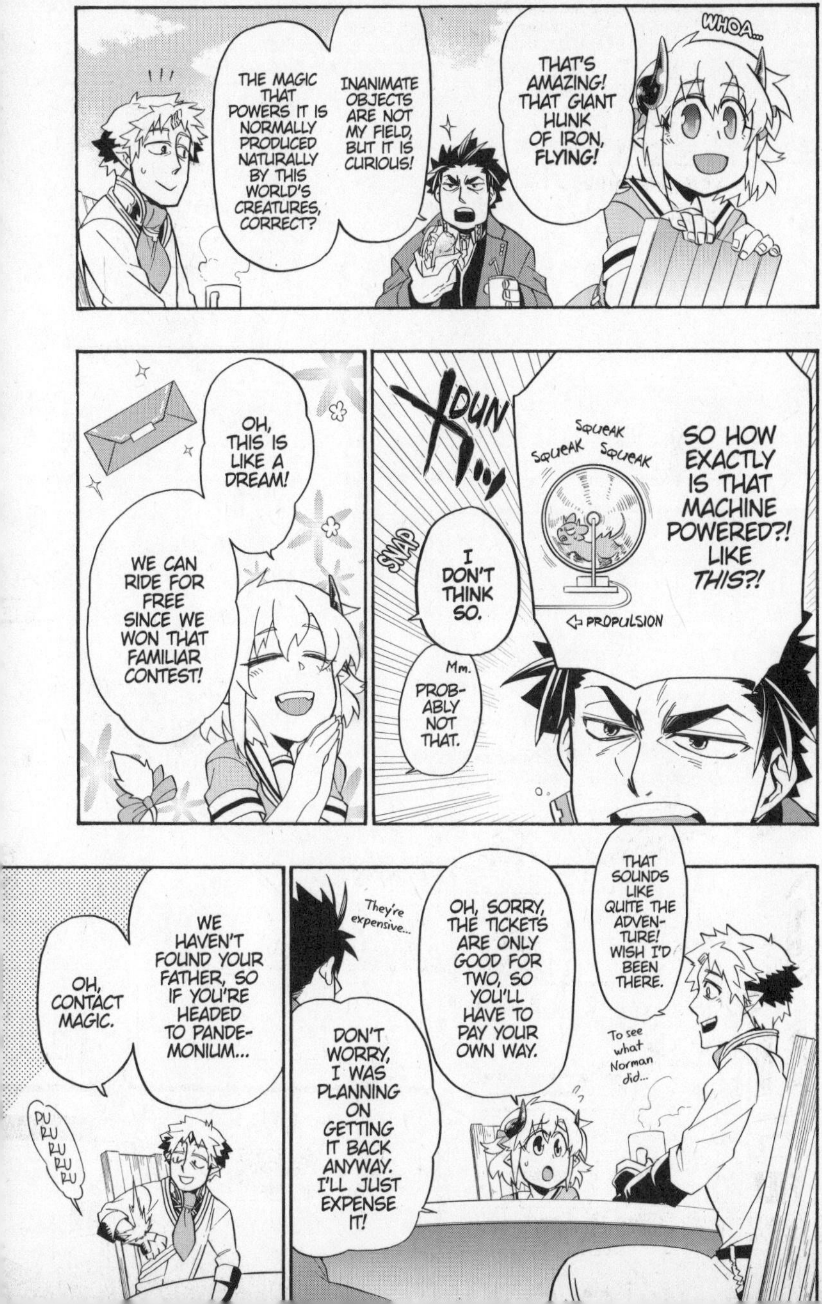
WHOA...
THAT'S AMAZING! THAT GIANT HUNK OF IRON, FLYING!
INANIMATE OBJECTS ARE NOT MY FIELD, BUT IT IS CURIOUS!
THE MAGIC THAT POWERS IT IS NORMALLY PRODUCED NATURALLY BY THIS WORLD'S CREATURES, CORRECT?
SO HOW EXACTLY IS THAT MACHINE POWERED?! LIKE *THIS?!*
SQUEAK SQUEAK SQUEAK
PROPULSION
DUN...
SNAP
I DON'T THINK SO.
Mm. PROBABLY NOT THAT.
OH, THIS IS LIKE A DREAM!
WE CAN RIDE FOR FREE SINCE WE WON THAT FAMILIAR CONTEST!
THAT SOUNDS LIKE QUITE THE ADVENTURE! WISH I'D BEEN THERE.
To see what Norman did...
OH, SORRY, THE TICKETS ARE ONLY GOOD FOR TWO, SO YOU'LL HAVE TO PAY YOUR OWN WAY.
They're expensive...
DON'T WORRY, I WAS PLANNING ON GETTING IT BACK ANYWAY. I'LL JUST EXPENSE IT!
WE HAVEN'T FOUND YOUR FATHER, SO IF YOU'RE HEADED TO PANDEMONIUM...
OH, CONTACT MAGIC.
PURURURURU

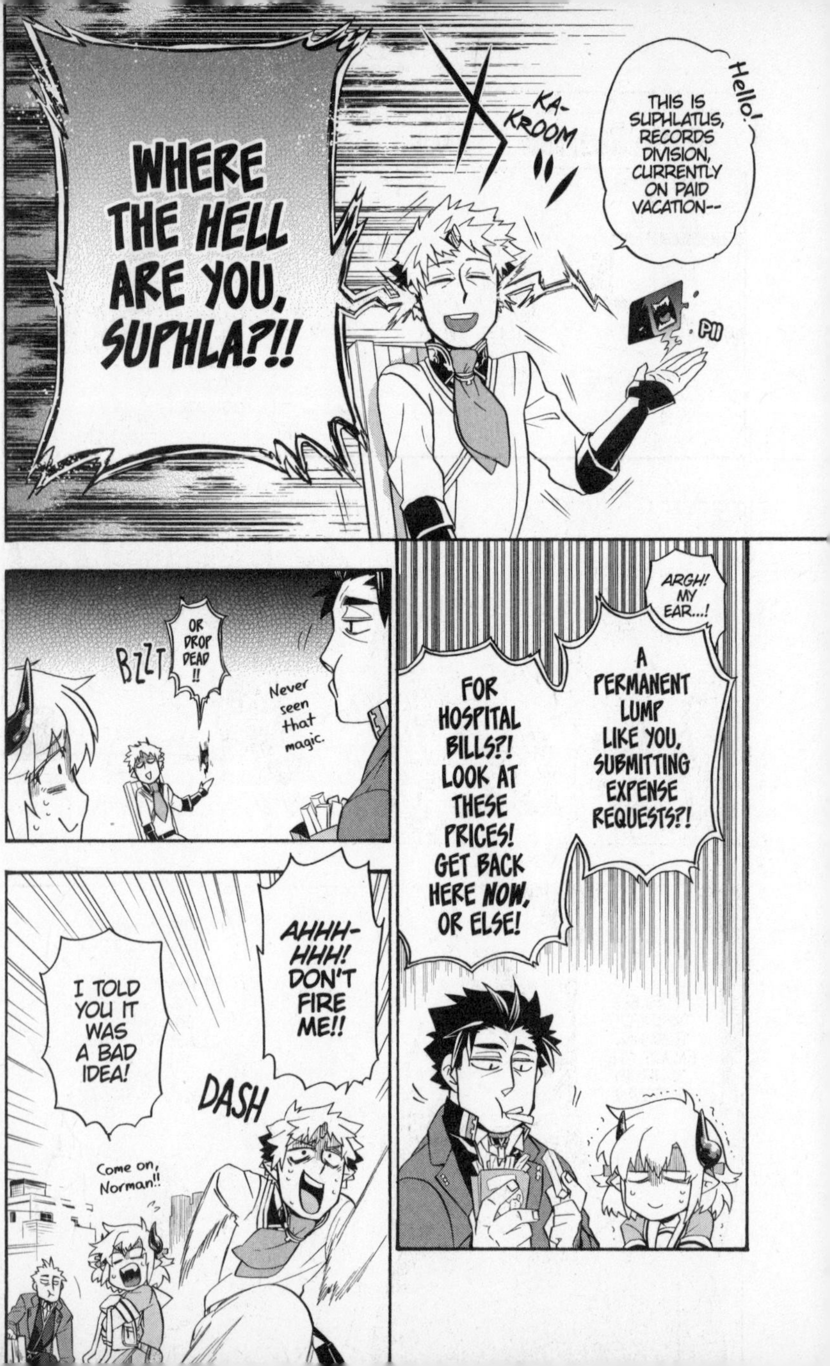
Hello!
THIS IS SUPHLATUS, RECORDS DIVISION, CURRENTLY ON PAID VACATION--
KA-KROOM
PII
WHERE THE HELL ARE YOU, SUPHLA?!!
ARGH! MY EAR...!
A PERMANENT LUMP LIKE YOU, SUBMITTING EXPENSE REQUESTS?!
FOR HOSPITAL BILLS?! LOOK AT THESE PRICES! GET BACK HERE NOW, OR ELSE!
OR DROP DEAD!!
BZZT
Never seen that magic.
AHHHHHH! DON'T FIRE ME!!
I TOLD YOU IT WAS A BAD IDEA!
DASH
Come on, Norman!!

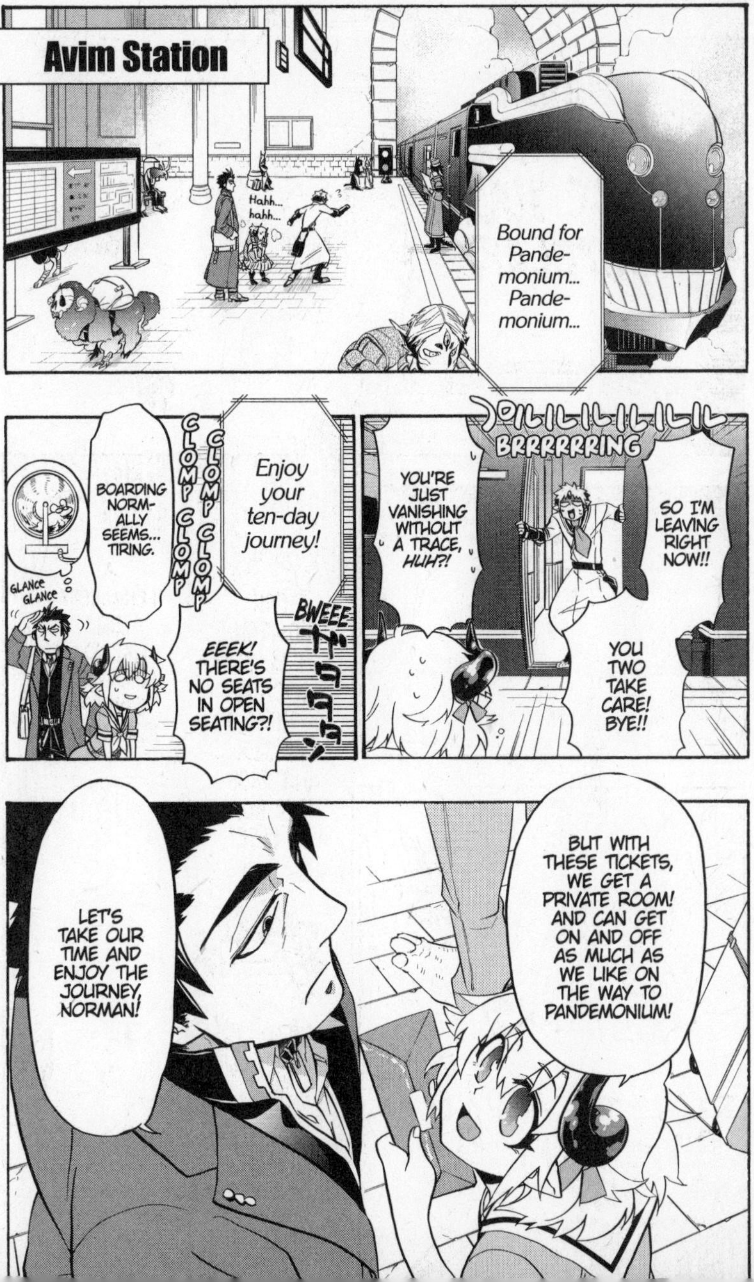

Avim Station
Bound for Pandemonium... Pandemonium...
Hahh... hahh...
BRRRRRRING
SO I'M LEAVING RIGHT NOW!!
YOU'RE JUST VANISHING WITHOUT A TRACE, HUH?!
YOU TWO TAKE CARE! BYE!!
Enjoy your ten-day journey!
CLOMP CLOMP
CLOMP CLOMP
BWEEE
EEEK! THERE'S NO SEATS IN OPEN SEATING?!
BOARDING NORMALLY SEEMS... TIRING.
GLANCE GLANCE
BUT WITH THESE TICKETS, WE GET A PRIVATE ROOM! AND CAN GET ON AND OFF AS MUCH AS WE LIKE ON THE WAY TO PANDEMONIUM!
LET'S TAKE OUR TIME AND ENJOY THE JOURNEY, NORMAN!

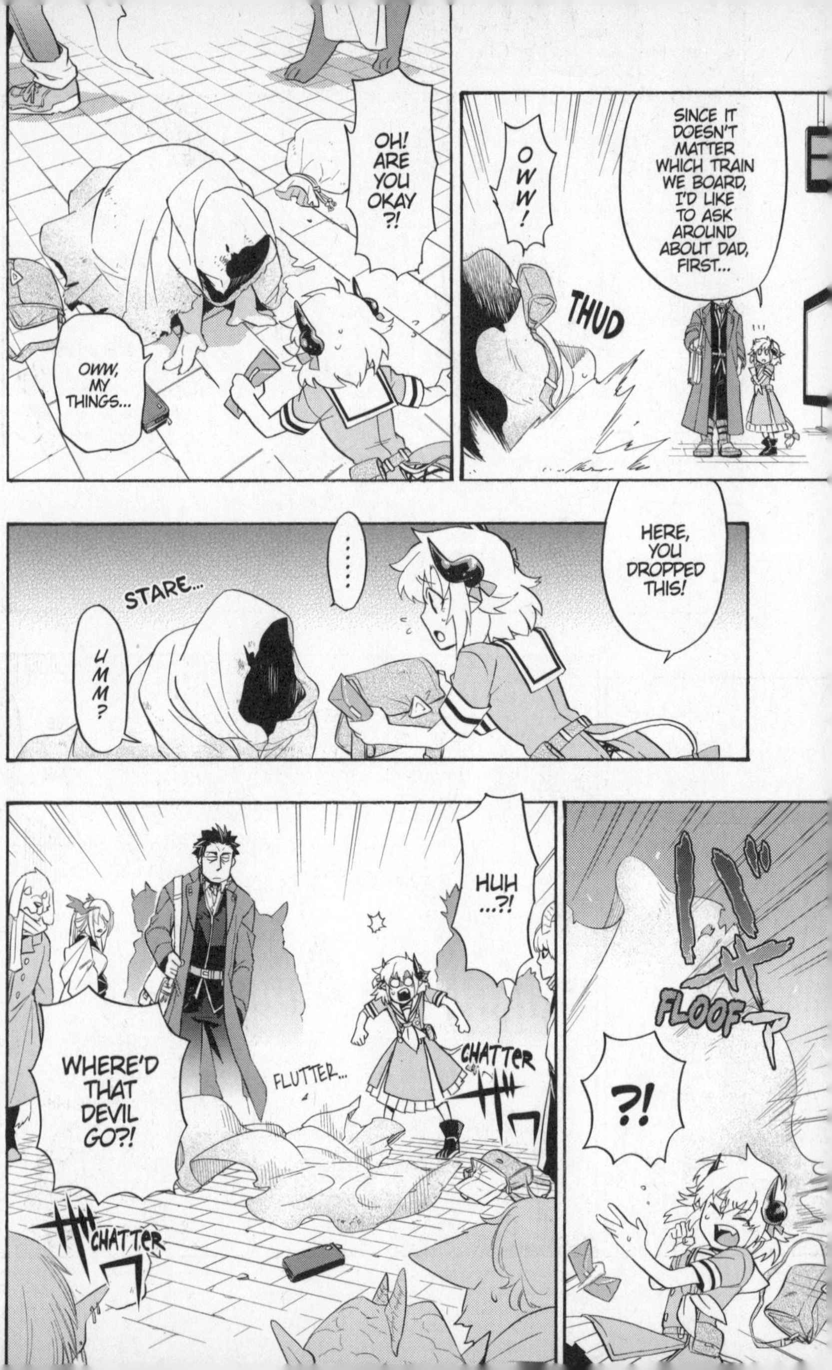
SINCE IT DOESN'T MATTER WHICH TRAIN WE BOARD, I'D LIKE TO ASK AROUND ABOUT DAD, FIRST...
OWW!
THUD
OH! ARE YOU OKAY?!
OWW, MY THINGS...
HERE, YOU DROPPED THIS!
......
STARE...
UMM?
FLOOF
?!
HUH...?!
CHATTER
FLUTTER...
WHERE'D THAT DEVIL GO?!
CHATTER

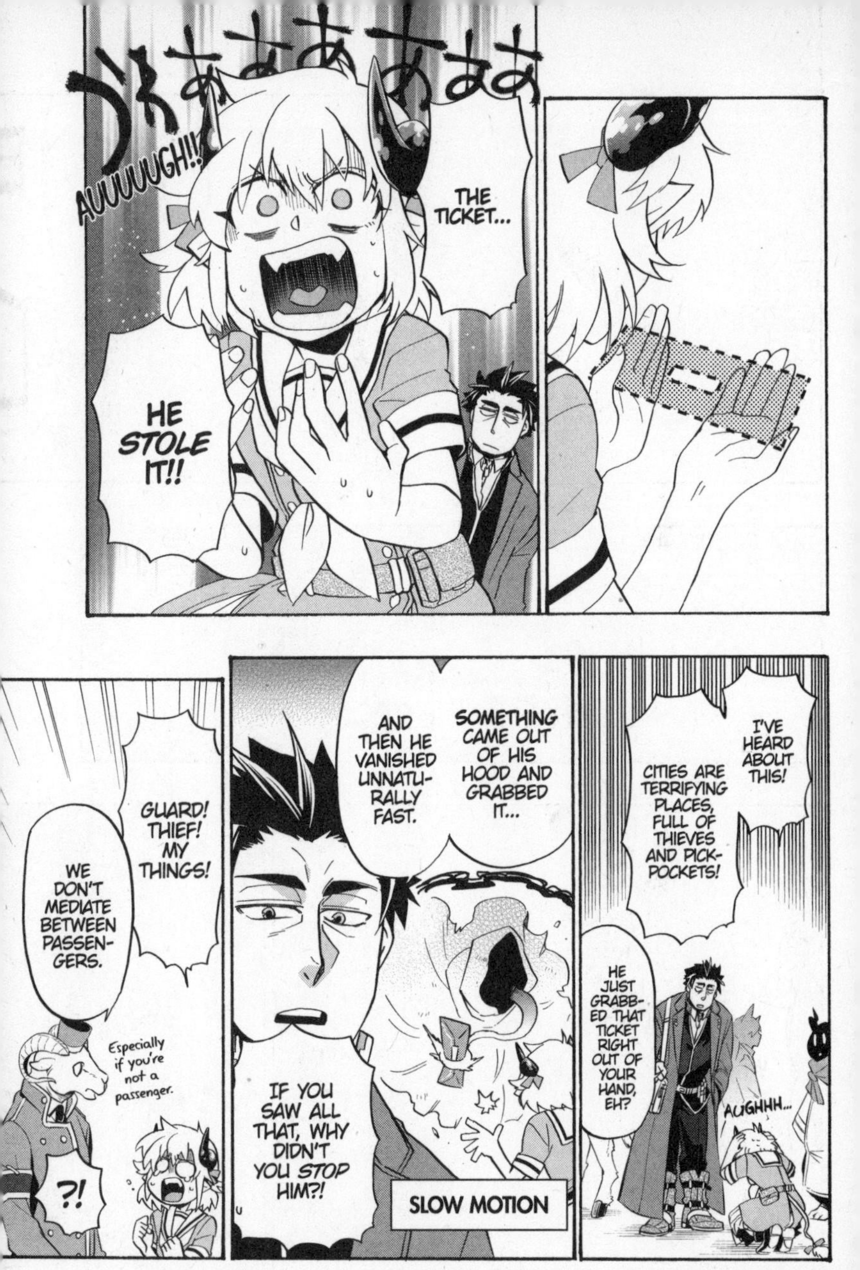
うわああああああ
AUUUUUGH!!
THE TICKET...
HE STOLE IT!!
I'VE HEARD ABOUT THIS!
CITIES ARE TERRIFYING PLACES, FULL OF THIEVES AND PICKPOCKETS!
HE JUST GRABBED THAT TICKET RIGHT OUT OF YOUR HAND, EH?
AUGHHH...
SOMETHING CAME OUT OF HIS HOOD AND GRABBED IT...
AND THEN HE VANISHED UNNATURALLY FAST.
IF YOU SAW ALL THAT, WHY DIDN'T YOU STOP HIM?!
SLOW MOTION
GUARD! THIEF! MY THINGS!
WE DON'T MEDIATE BETWEEN PASSENGERS.
Especially if you're not a passenger.
?!

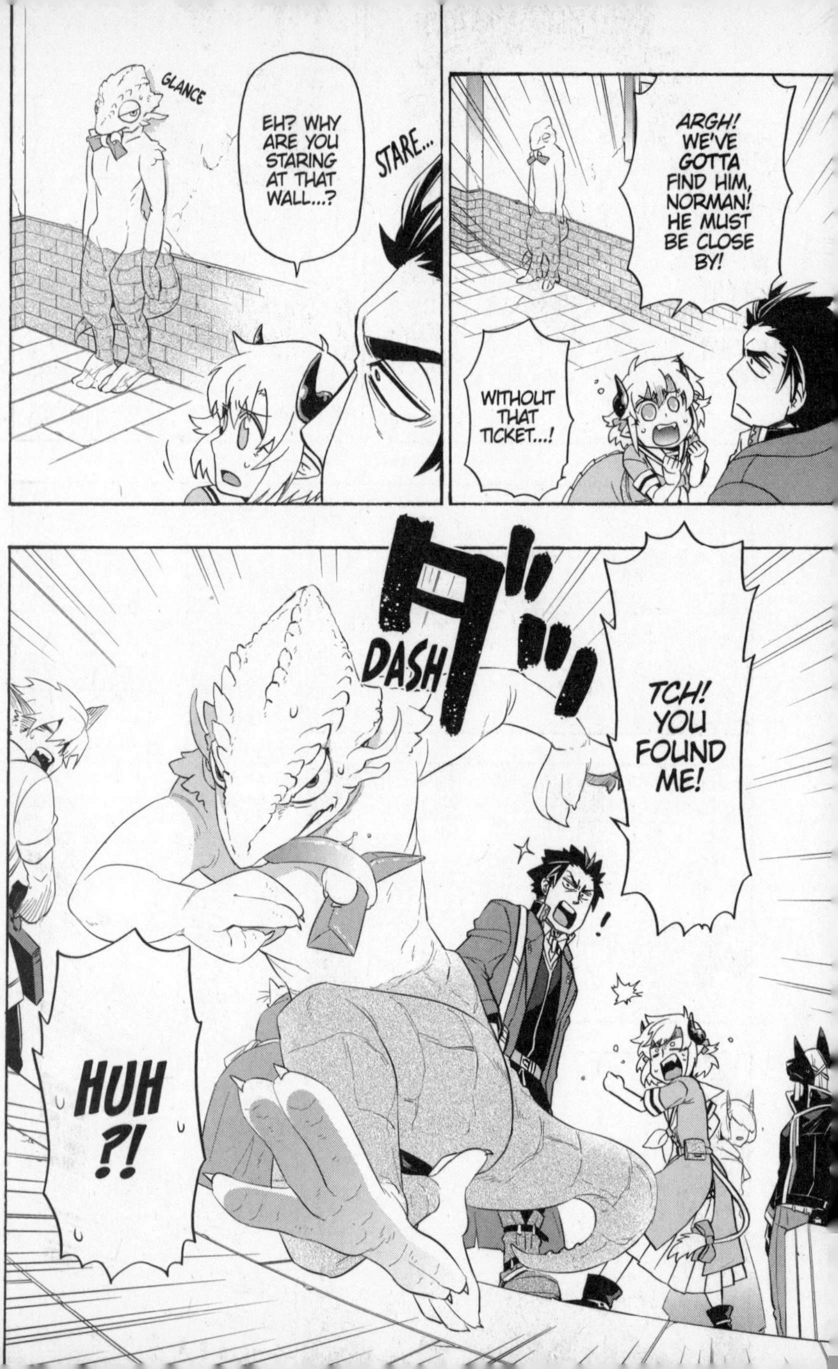
ARGH! WE'VE GOTTA FIND HIM, NORMAN! HE MUST BE CLOSE BY!
WITHOUT THAT TICKET...!
STARE...
EH? WHY ARE YOU STARING AT THAT WALL...?
GLANCE
TCH! YOU FOUND ME!
ダッ
DASH
HUH ?!

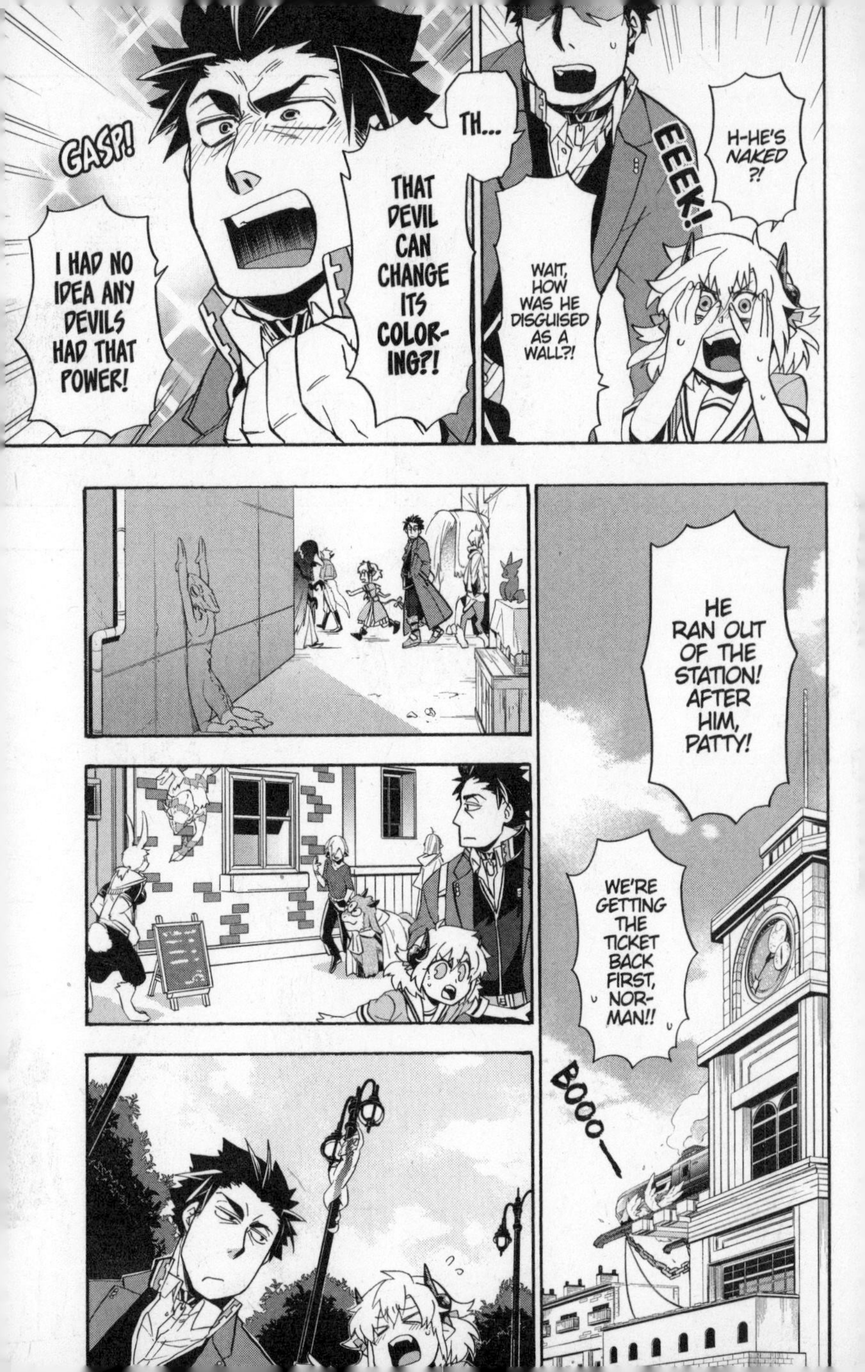
H-HE'S NAKED?!
EEEK!
WAIT, HOW WAS HE DISGUISED AS A WALL?!
TH...
THAT DEVIL CAN CHANGE ITS COLOR-ING?!
GASP!
I HAD NO IDEA ANY DEVILS HAD THAT POWER!
HE RAN OUT OF THE STATION! AFTER HIM, PATTY!
WE'RE GETTING THE TICKET BACK FIRST, NOR-MAN!!
BOOO—

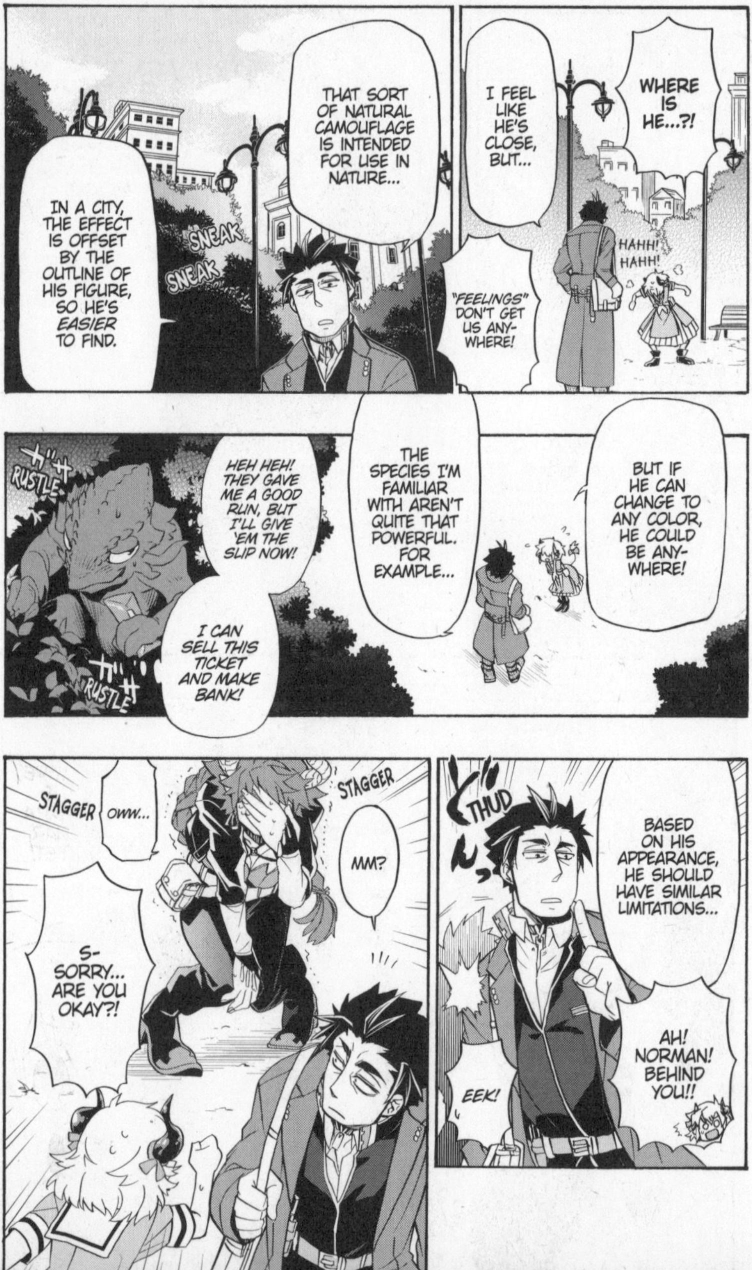
WHERE IS HE...?!
HAHH! HAHH!
I FEEL LIKE HE'S CLOSE, BUT...
"FEELINGS" DON'T GET US ANY-WHERE!
THAT SORT OF NATURAL CAMOUFLAGE IS INTENDED FOR USE IN NATURE...
SNEAK
SNEAK
IN A CITY, THE EFFECT IS OFFSET BY THE OUTLINE OF HIS FIGURE, SO HE'S *EASIER* TO FIND.
BUT IF HE CAN CHANGE TO ANY COLOR, HE COULD BE ANY-WHERE!
THE SPECIES I'M FAMILIAR WITH AREN'T QUITE THAT POWERFUL. FOR EXAMPLE...
HEH HEH! THEY GAVE ME A GOOD RUN, BUT I'LL GIVE 'EM THE SLIP NOW!
RUSTLE
I CAN SELL THIS TICKET AND MAKE BANK!
RUSTLE
THUD
BASED ON HIS APPEARANCE, HE SHOULD HAVE SIMILAR LIMITATIONS...
AH! NORMAN! BEHIND YOU!!
EEK!
STAGGER
MM?
STAGGER
OWW...
S-SORRY... ARE YOU OKAY?!

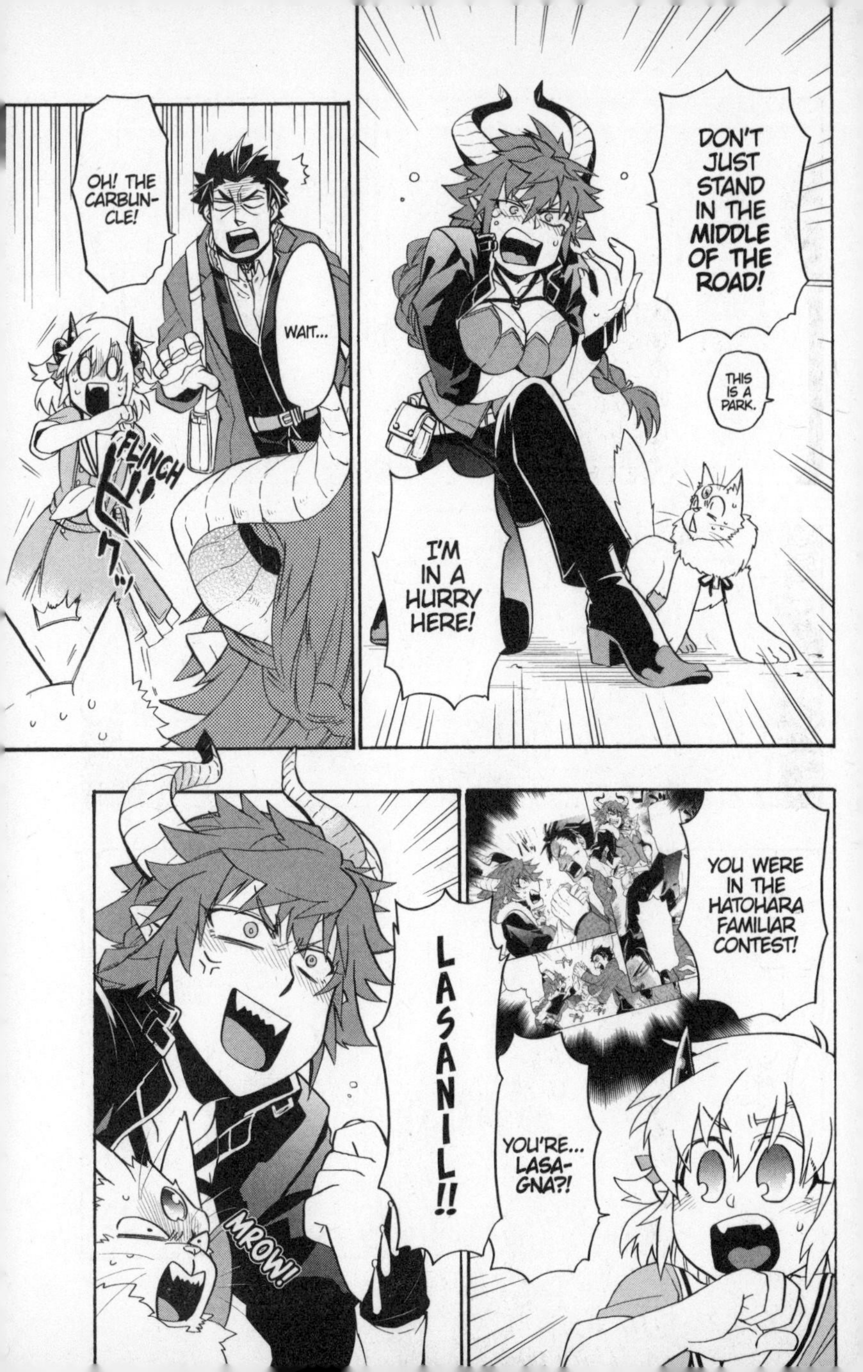
DON'T JUST STAND IN THE MIDDLE OF THE ROAD!
THIS IS A PARK.
I'M IN A HURRY HERE!
OH! THE CARBUN-CLE!
WAIT...
FLINCH
YOU WERE IN THE HATOHARA FAMILIAR CONTEST!
YOU'RE... LASA-GNA?!
LASANIL!!
MROW!

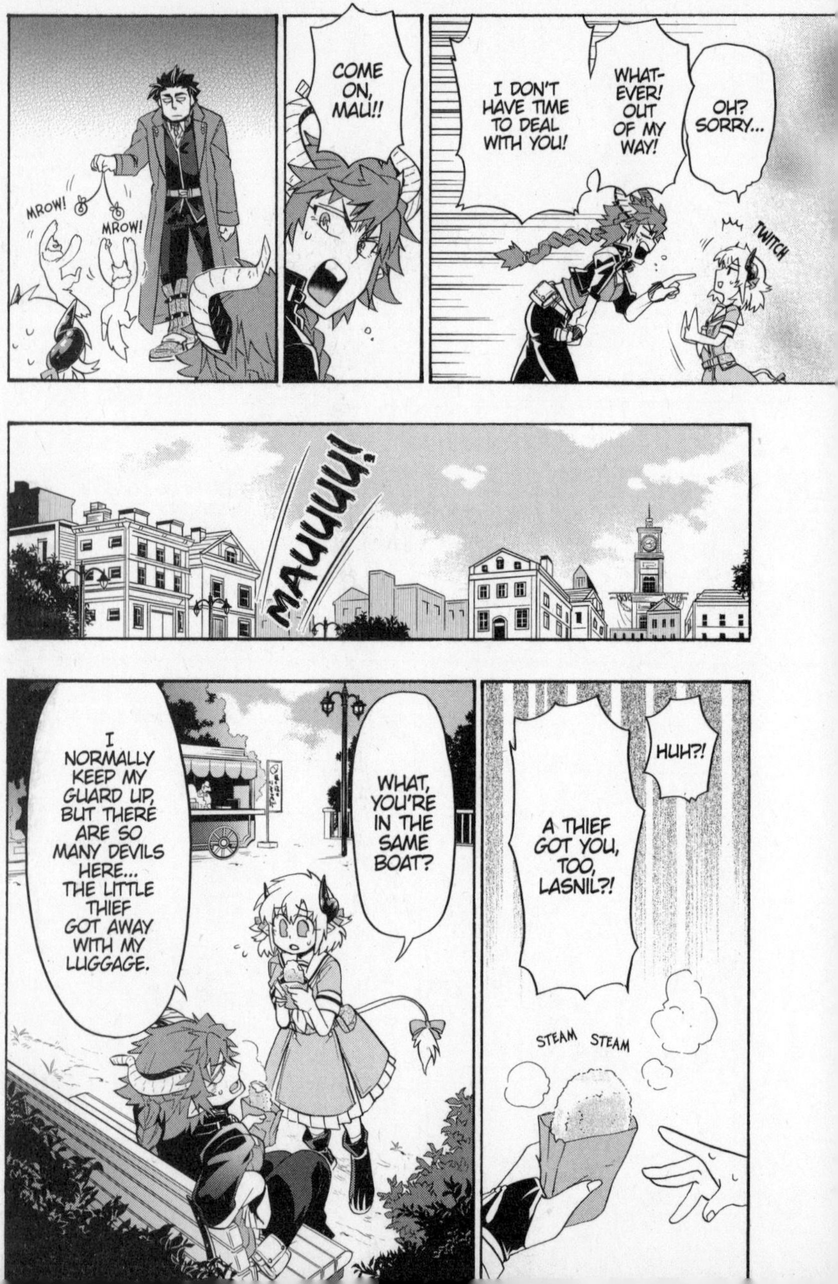
OH? SORRY...
WHAT-EVER! OUT OF MY WAY!
I DON'T HAVE TIME TO DEAL WITH YOU!
TWITCH
COME ON, MAU!!
MROW!
MROW!
MAUUUU!
HUH?!
A THIEF GOT YOU, TOO, LASNIL?!
STEAM STEAM
WHAT, YOU'RE IN THE SAME BOAT?
I NORMALLY KEEP MY GUARD UP, BUT THERE ARE SO MANY DEVILS HERE... THE LITTLE THIEF GOT AWAY WITH MY LUGGAGE.

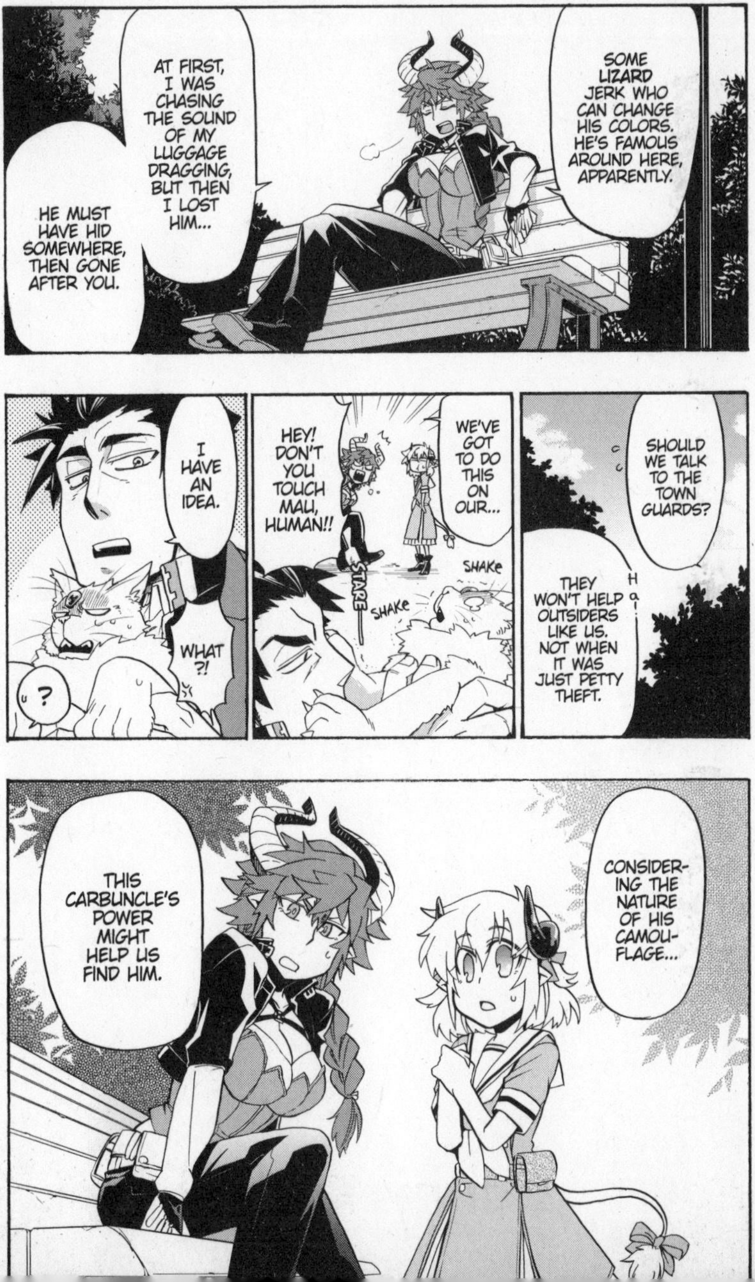
SOME LIZARD JERK WHO CAN CHANGE HIS COLORS. HE'S FAMOUS AROUND HERE, APPARENTLY.
AT FIRST, I WAS CHASING THE SOUND OF MY LUGGAGE DRAGGING, BUT THEN I LOST HIM...
HE MUST HAVE HID SOMEWHERE, THEN GONE AFTER YOU.
SHOULD WE TALK TO THE TOWN GUARDS?
Ha!
THEY WON'T HELP OUTSIDERS LIKE US. NOT WHEN IT WAS JUST PETTY THEFT.
WE'VE GOT TO DO THIS ON OUR...
HEY! DON'T YOU TOUCH MAU, HUMAN!!
SHAKE
STARE
SHAKE
I HAVE AN IDEA.
WHAT?!
?
CONSIDER-ING THE NATURE OF HIS CAMOU-FLAGE...
THIS CARBUNCLE'S POWER MIGHT HELP US FIND HIM.

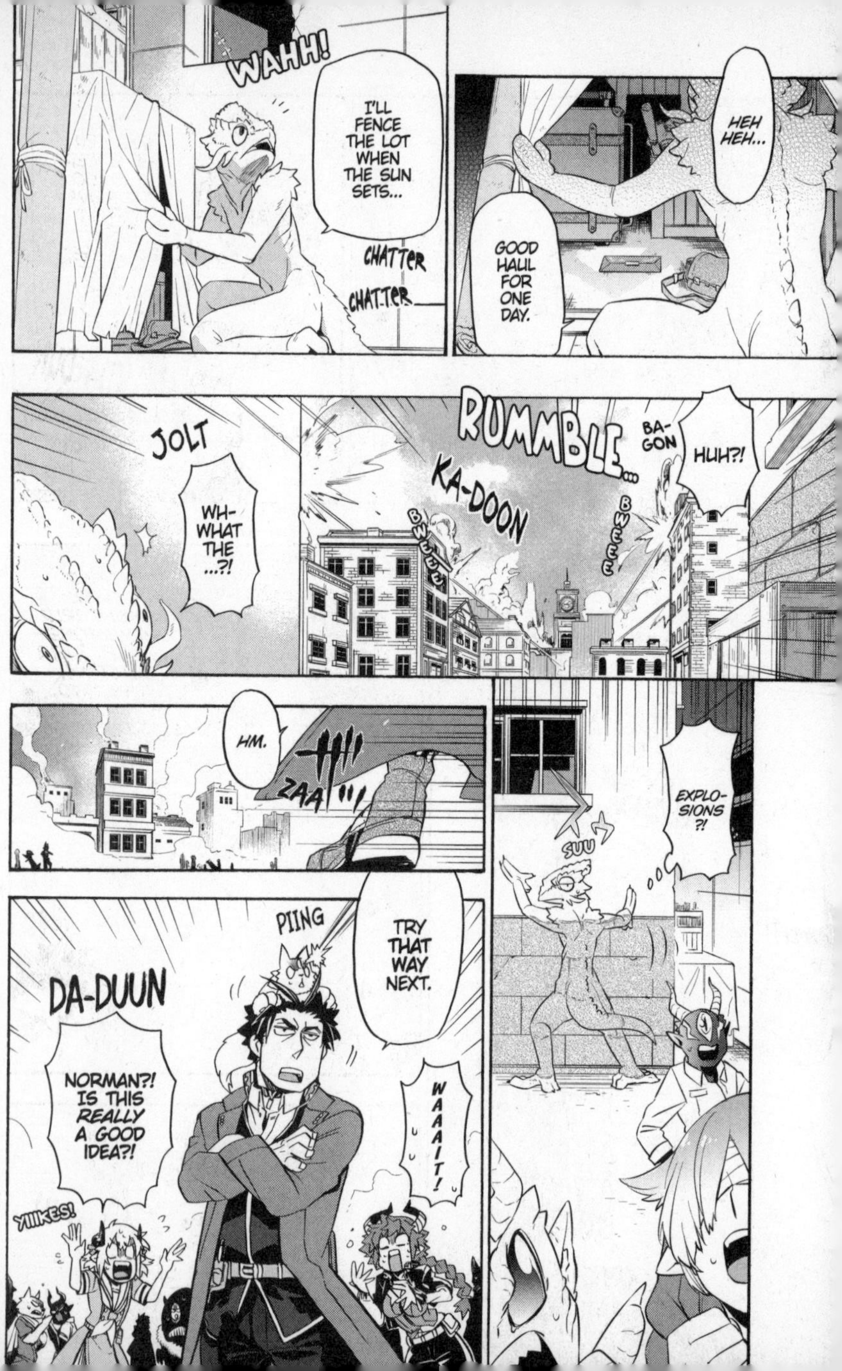
HEH HEH...
GOOD HAUL FOR ONE DAY.
WAHH!
I'LL FENCE THE LOT WHEN THE SUN SETS...
CHATTER
CHATTER
HUH?!
BA-GON
RUMMBLE...
KA-DOON
BWEEE
BWEEE
JOLT
WH-WHAT THE ...?!
EXPLOSIONS?!
SUU
HM.
ZAA
TRY THAT WAY NEXT.
PIING
DA-DUUN
NORMAN?! IS THIS *REALLY* A GOOD IDEA?!
WAAAAIT!
YIIIKES!

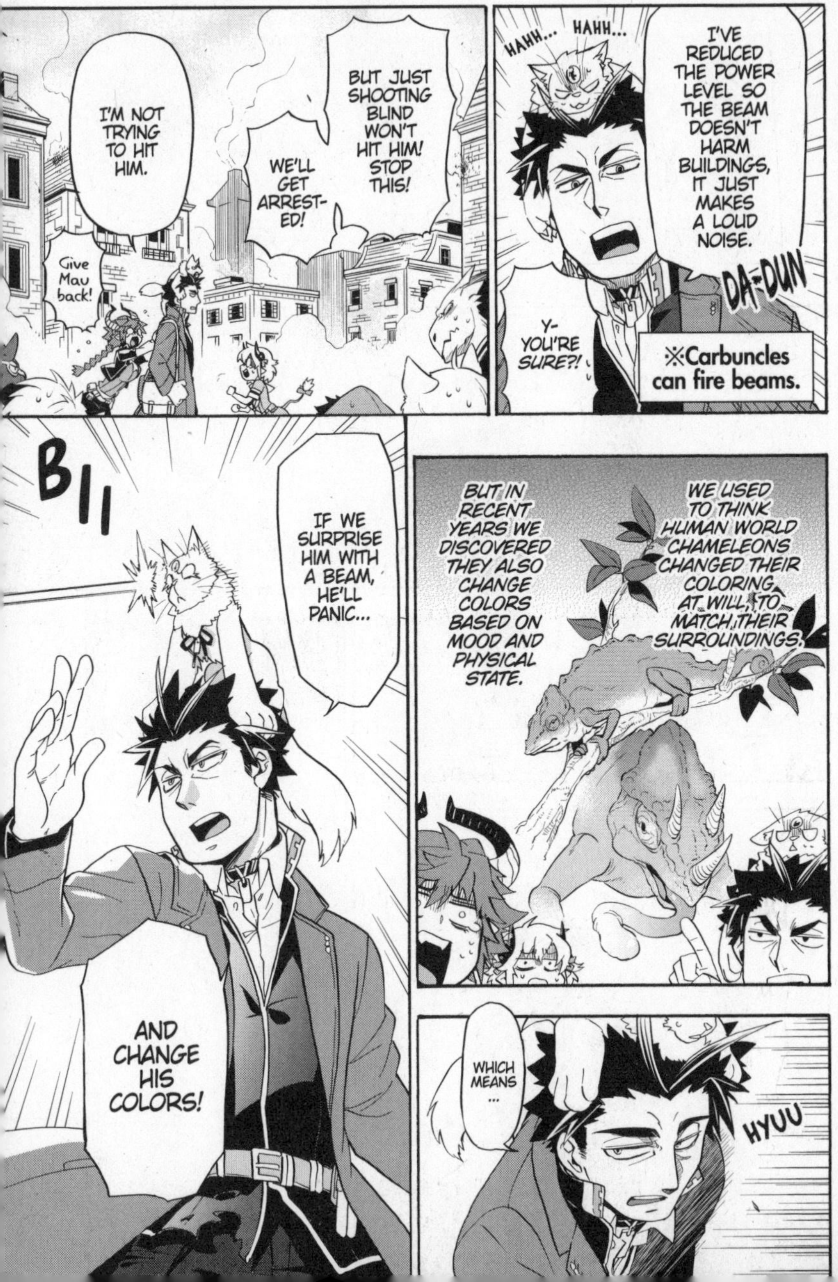
HAHH... HAHH...
I'VE REDUCED THE POWER LEVEL SO THE BEAM DOESN'T HARM BUILDINGS, IT JUST MAKES A LOUD NOISE.
DA-DUN
Y-YOU'RE SURE?!
※Carbuncles can fire beams.
BUT JUST SHOOTING BLIND WON'T HIT HIM! STOP THIS!
WE'LL GET ARREST-ED!
I'M NOT TRYING TO HIT HIM.
Give Mau back!
WE USED TO THINK HUMAN WORLD CHAMELEONS CHANGED THEIR COLORING AT WILL, TO MATCH THEIR SURROUNDINGS.
BUT IN RECENT YEARS WE DISCOVERED THEY ALSO CHANGE COLORS BASED ON MOOD AND PHYSICAL STATE.
WHICH MEANS ...
HYUU
BII
IF WE SURPRISE HIM WITH A BEAM, HE'LL PANIC...
AND CHANGE HIS COLORS!

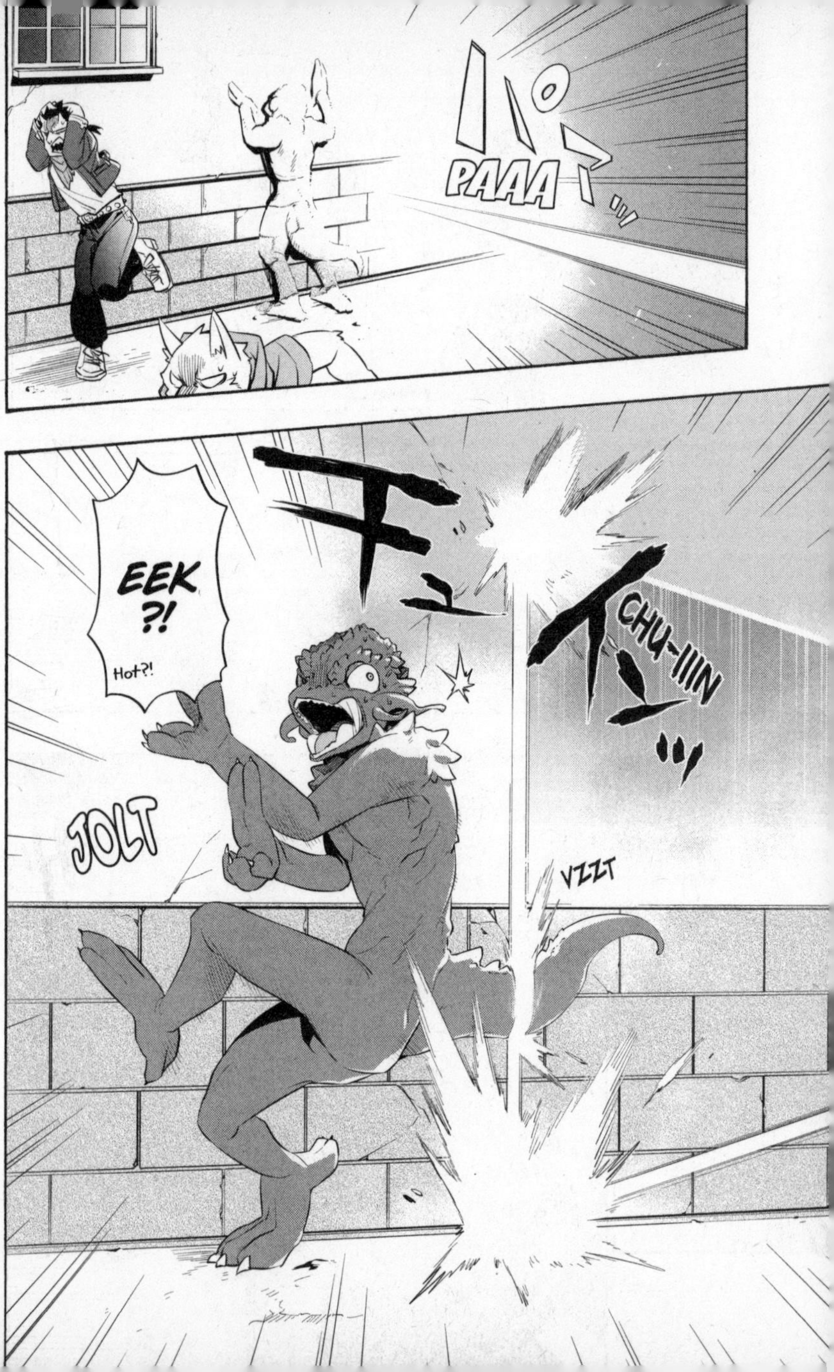
PAAA
CHU-IIIN
EEK ?!
Hot?!
VZZT
JOLT

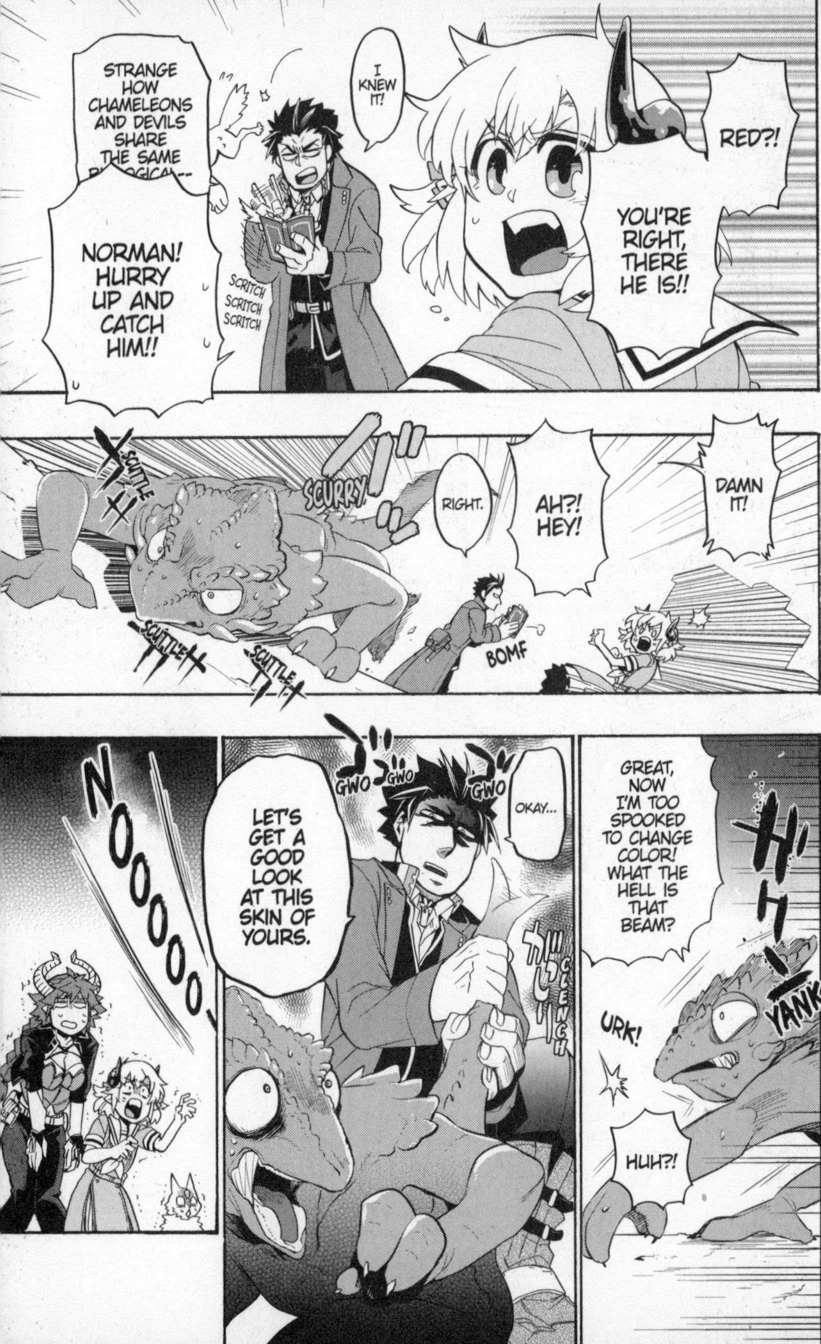
RED?!
YOU'RE RIGHT, THERE HE IS!!
I KNEW IT!
STRANGE HOW CHAMELEONS AND DEVILS SHARE THE SAME
NORMAN! HURRY UP AND CATCH HIM!!
SCRITCH SCRITCH SCRITCH
DAMN IT!
AH?! HEY!
RIGHT.
SCURRY
SCUTTLE
SCUTTLE
SCUTTLE
BOMF
GREAT, NOW I'M TOO SPOOKED TO CHANGE COLOR! WHAT THE HELL IS THAT BEAM?
YANK
URK!
HUH?!
OKAY...
GWO GWO GWO
LET'S GET A GOOD LOOK AT THIS SKIN OF YOURS.
CLENCH
NOOOOOO

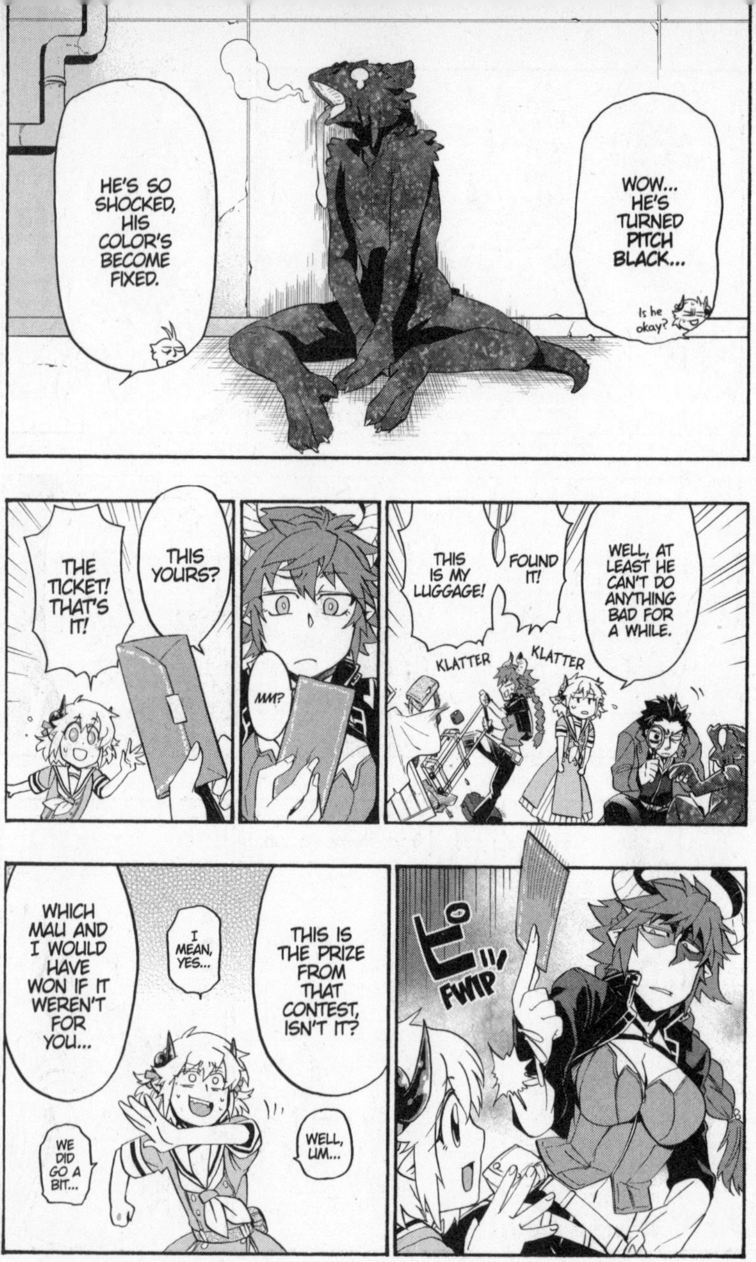
WOW... HE'S TURNED PITCH BLACK...
Is he okay?
HE'S SO SHOCKED, HIS COLOR'S BECOME FIXED.
WELL, AT LEAST HE CAN'T DO ANYTHING BAD FOR A WHILE.
FOUND IT!
THIS IS MY LUGGAGE!
KLATTER
KLATTER
MM?
THIS YOURS?
THE TICKET! THAT'S IT!
ピ
FWIP
THIS IS THE PRIZE FROM THAT CONTEST, ISN'T IT?
I MEAN, YES...
WHICH MAU AND I WOULD HAVE WON IF IT WEREN'T FOR YOU...
WELL, UM...
WE DID GO A BIT...

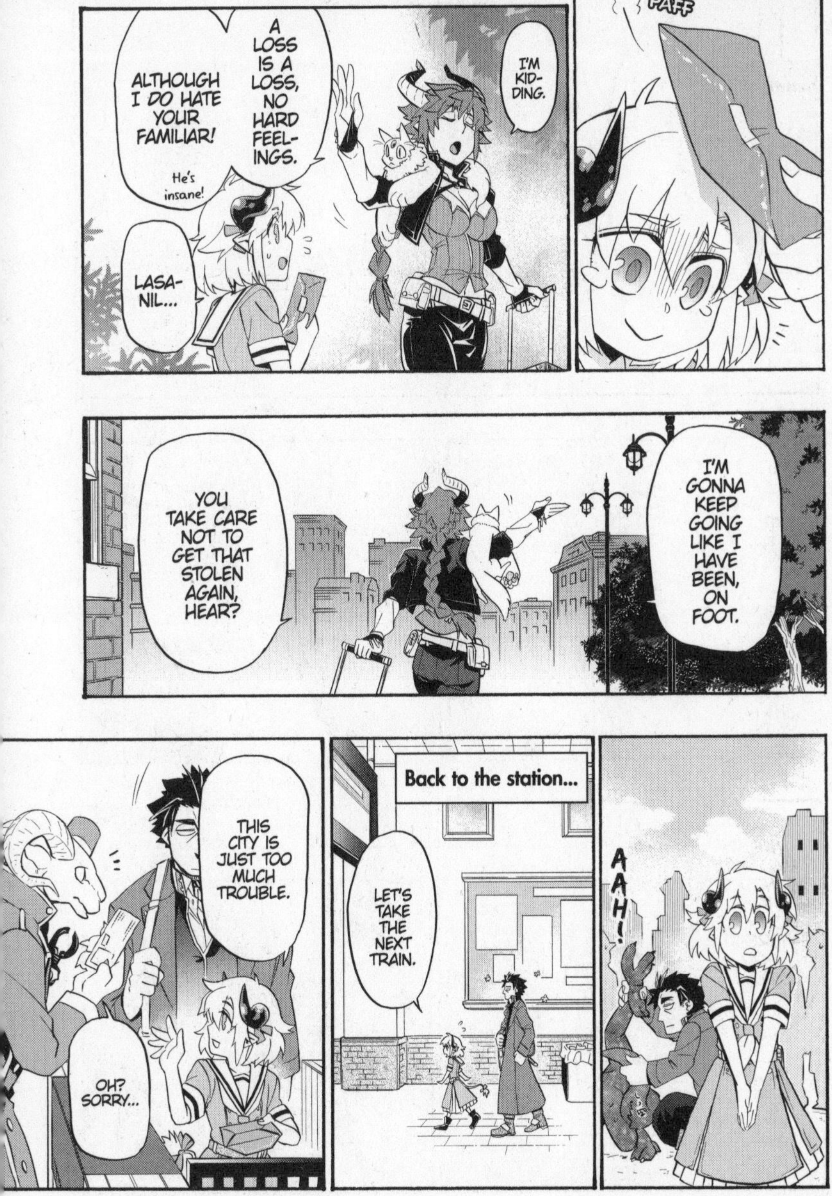
PAFF
I'M KID-DING.
A LOSS IS A LOSS, NO HARD FEEL-INGS.
ALTHOUGH I DO HATE YOUR FAMILIAR!
He's insane!
LASA-NIL...
I'M GONNA KEEP GOING LIKE I HAVE BEEN, ON FOOT.
YOU TAKE CARE NOT TO GET THAT STOLEN AGAIN, HEAR?
AAH!
Back to the station...
LET'S TAKE THE NEXT TRAIN.
THIS CITY IS JUST TOO MUCH TROUBLE.
OH? SORRY...

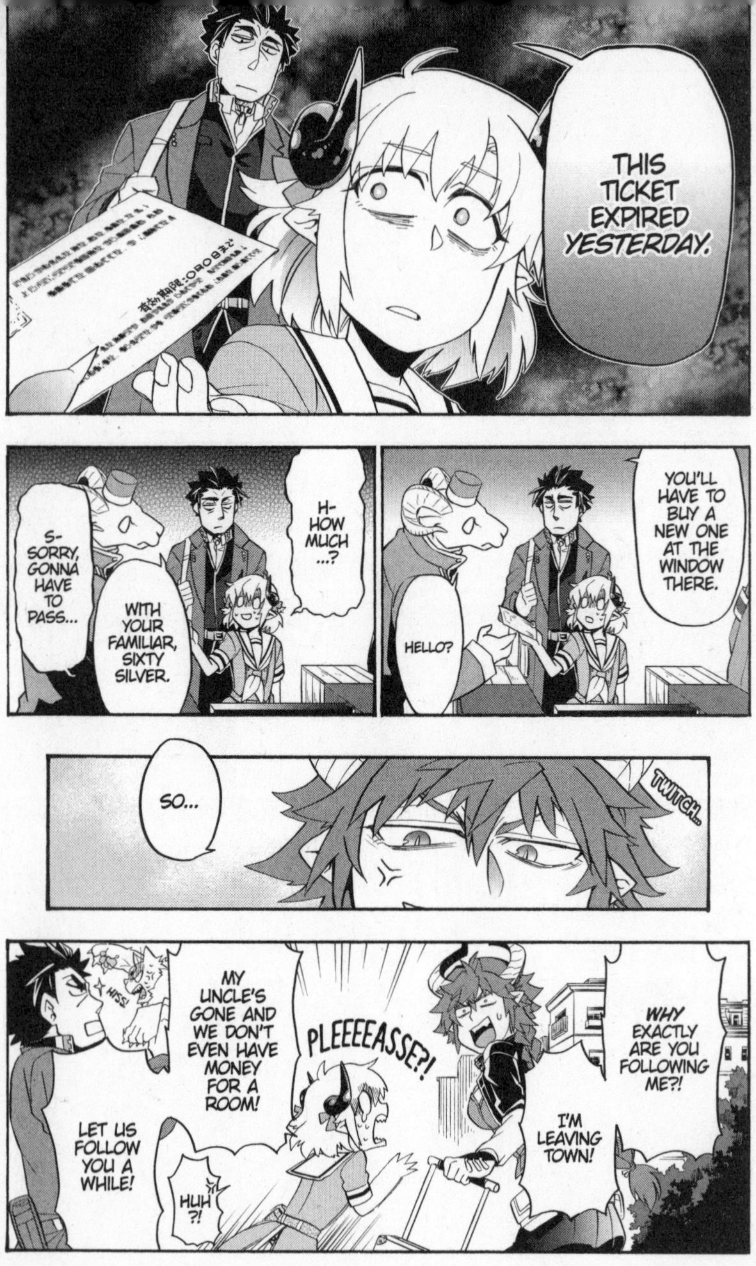
THIS TICKET EXPIRED YESTERDAY.
YOU'LL HAVE TO BUY A NEW ONE AT THE WINDOW THERE.
HELLO?
H-HOW MUCH ...?
WITH YOUR FAMILIAR, SIXTY SILVER.
S-SORRY, GONNA HAVE TO PASS...
TWITCH...
SO...
WHY EXACTLY ARE YOU FOLLOWING ME?!
I'M LEAVING TOWN!
PLEEEEASSE?!
MY UNCLE'S GONE AND WE DON'T EVEN HAVE MONEY FOR A ROOM!
HISS!
LET US FOLLOW YOU A WHILE!
HUH ?!

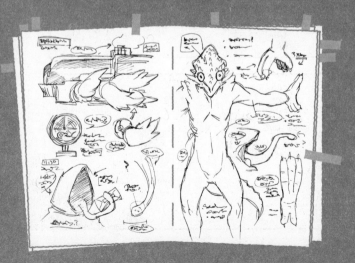

Sorry For My Familiar

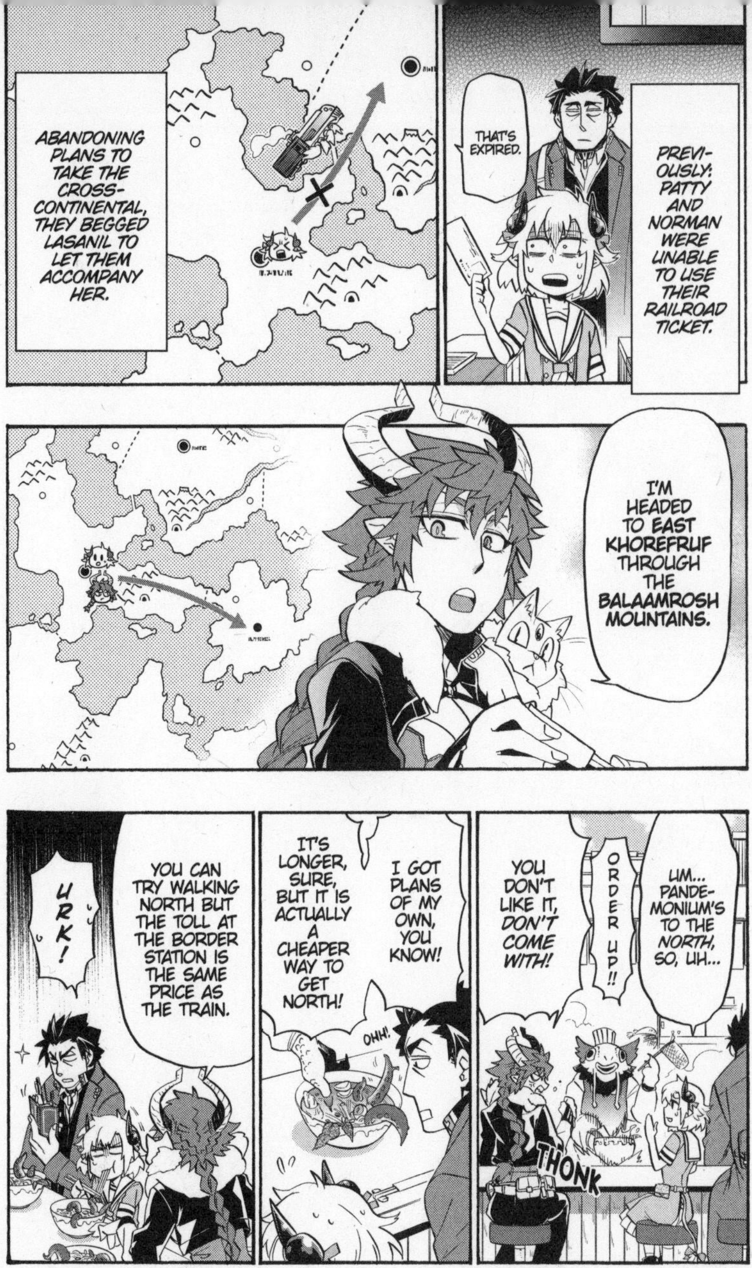
PREVIOUSLY: PATTY AND NORMAN WERE UNABLE TO USE THEIR RAILROAD TICKET.
THAT'S EXPIRED.
ABANDONING PLANS TO TAKE THE CROSS-CONTINENTAL, THEY BEGGED LASANIL TO LET THEM ACCOMPANY HER.
I'M HEADED TO EAST KHOREFRUF THROUGH THE BALAAMROSH MOUNTAINS.
UM... PANDEMONIUM'S TO THE NORTH, SO, UH...
ORDER UP!!
YOU DON'T LIKE IT, DON'T COME WITH!
THONK
I GOT PLANS OF MY OWN, YOU KNOW!
IT'S LONGER, SURE, BUT IT IS ACTUALLY A CHEAPER WAY TO GET NORTH!
OHH!
YOU CAN TRY WALKING NORTH BUT THE TOLL AT THE BORDER STATION IS THE SAME PRICE AS THE TRAIN.
URK!

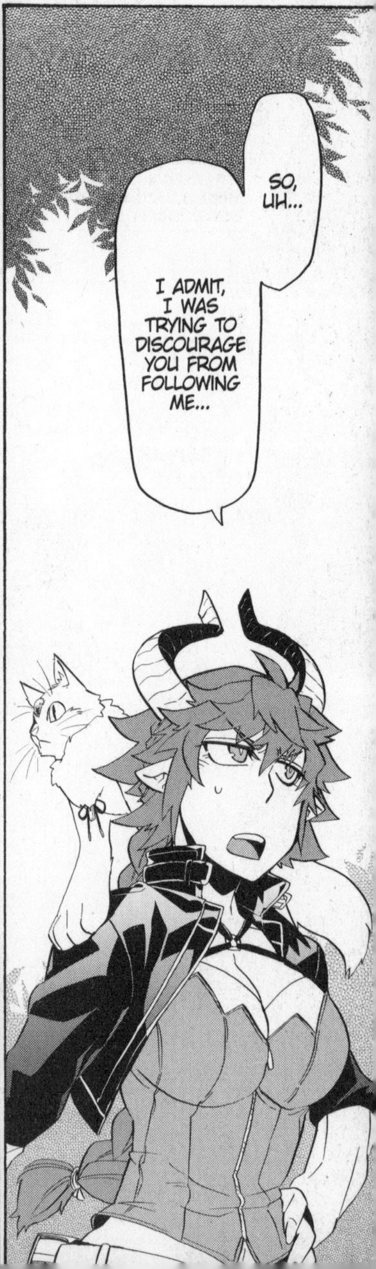
SO, UH...
I ADMIT, I WAS TRYING TO DISCOURAGE YOU FROM FOLLOWING ME...
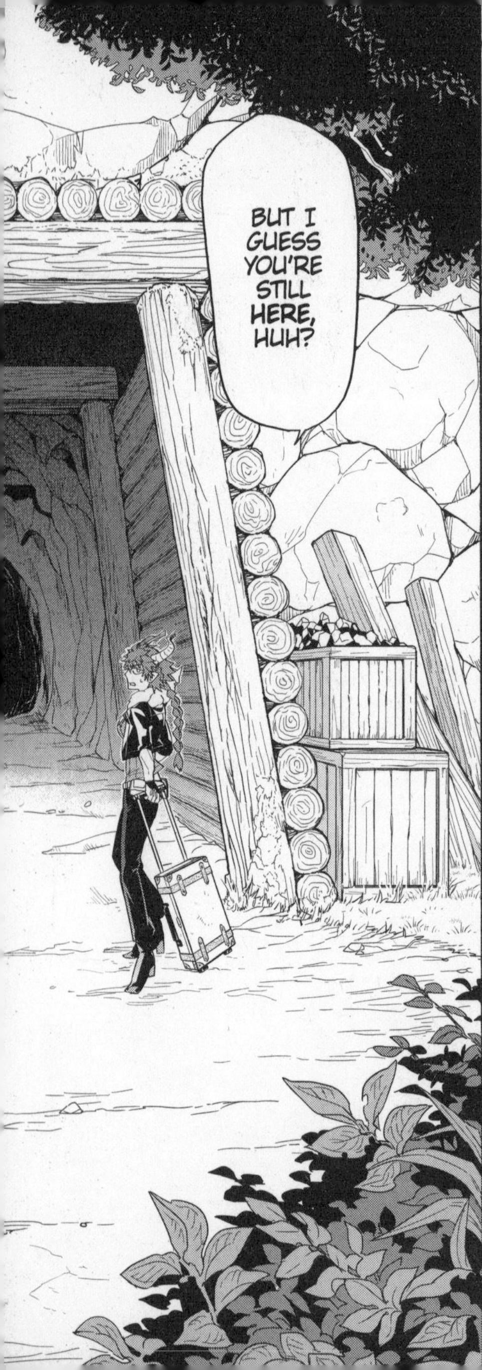
BUT I GUESS YOU'RE STILL HERE, HUH?

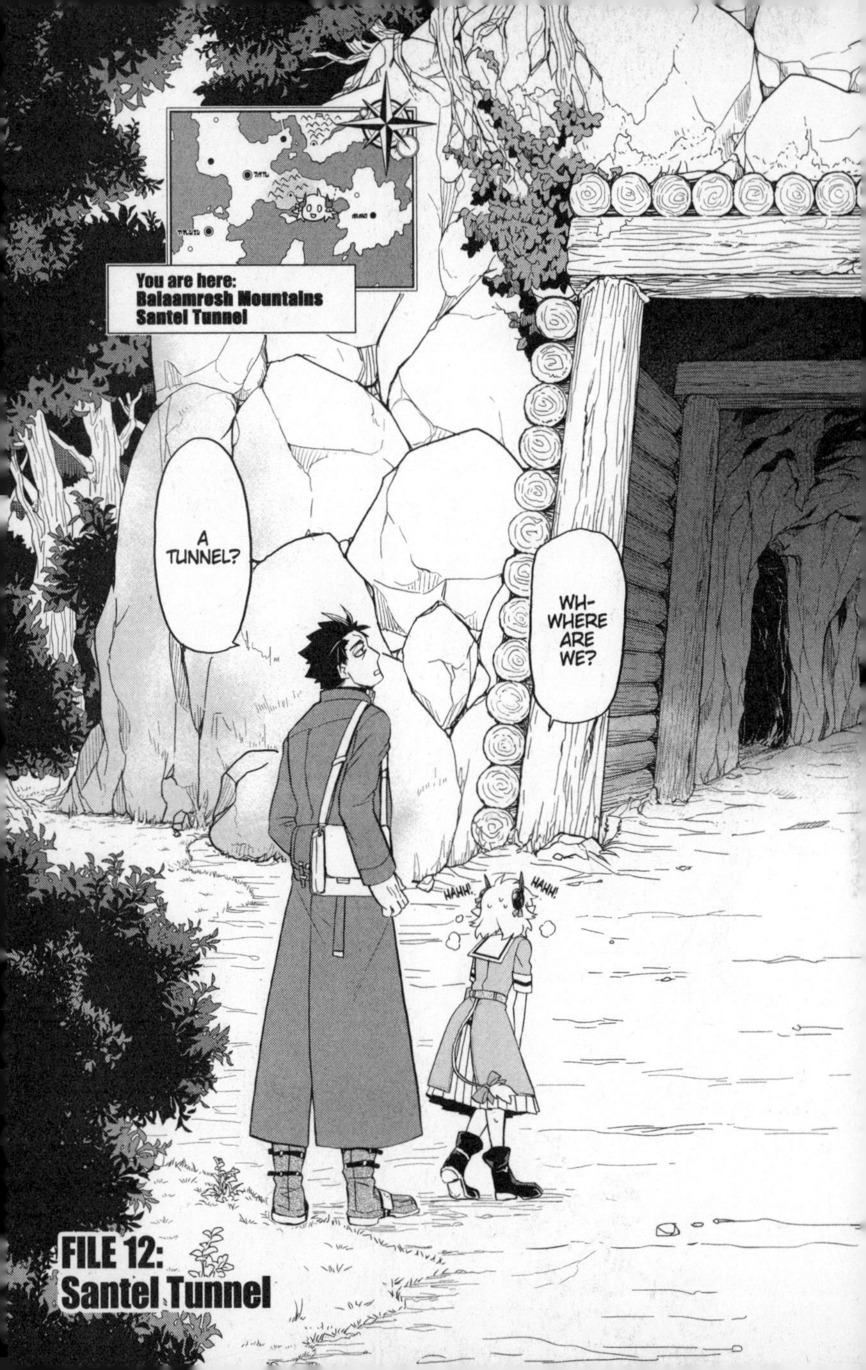
You are here:
Balaamresh Mountains
Santel Tunnel
WH-WHERE ARE WE?
A TUNNEL?
HAHH!
HAHH!

FILE 12: Santel Tunnel

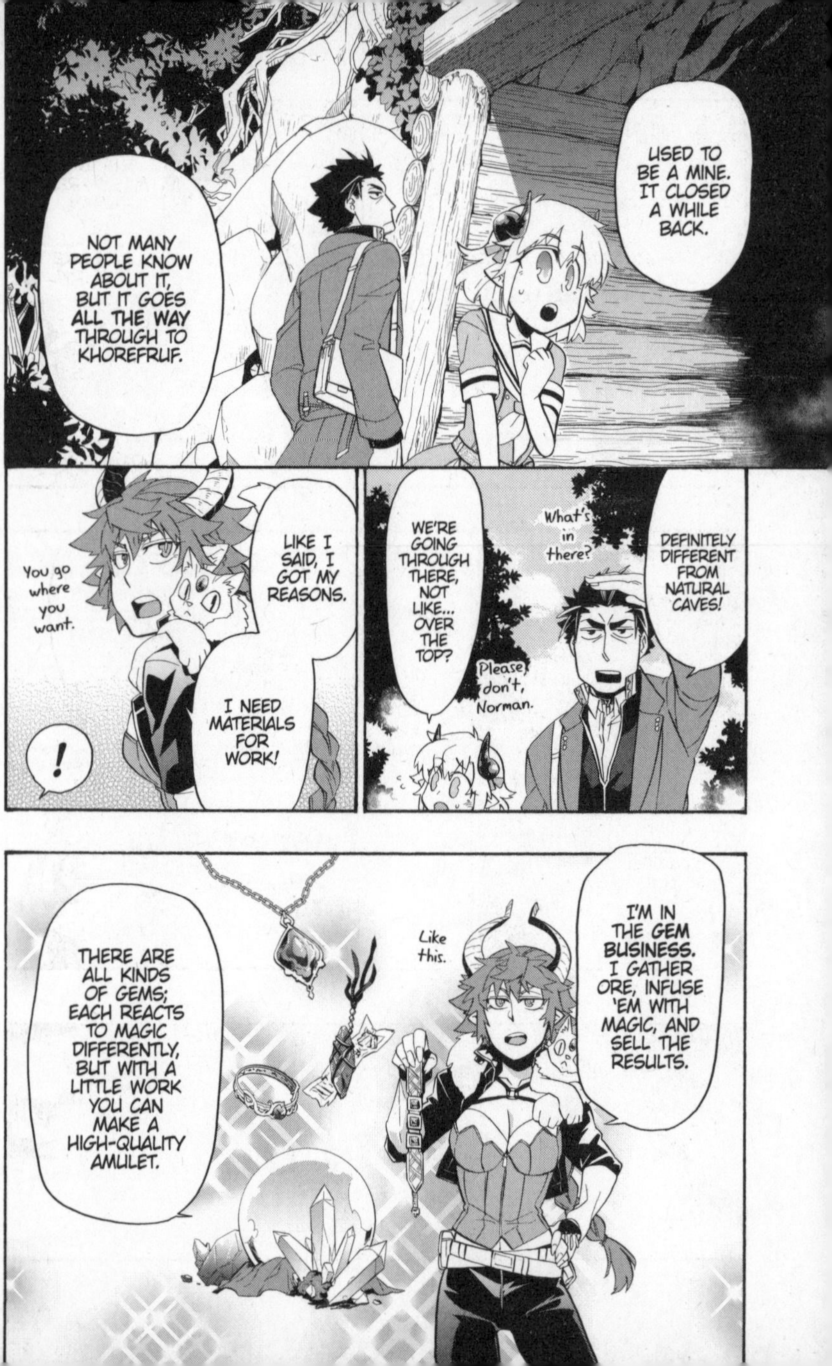
USED TO BE A MINE. IT CLOSED A WHILE BACK.
NOT MANY PEOPLE KNOW ABOUT IT, BUT IT GOES ALL THE WAY THROUGH TO KHOREFRUF.
DEFINITELY DIFFERENT FROM NATURAL CAVES!
What's in there?
WE'RE GOING THROUGH THERE, NOT LIKE... OVER THE TOP?
Please, don't, Norman.
LIKE I SAID, I GOT MY REASONS.
You go where you want.
I NEED MATERIALS FOR WORK!
!
I'M IN THE GEM BUSINESS. I GATHER ORE, INFUSE 'EM WITH MAGIC, AND SELL THE RESULTS.
Like this.
THERE ARE ALL KINDS OF GEMS; EACH REACTS TO MAGIC DIFFERENTLY, BUT WITH A LITTLE WORK YOU CAN MAKE A HIGH-QUALITY AMULET.

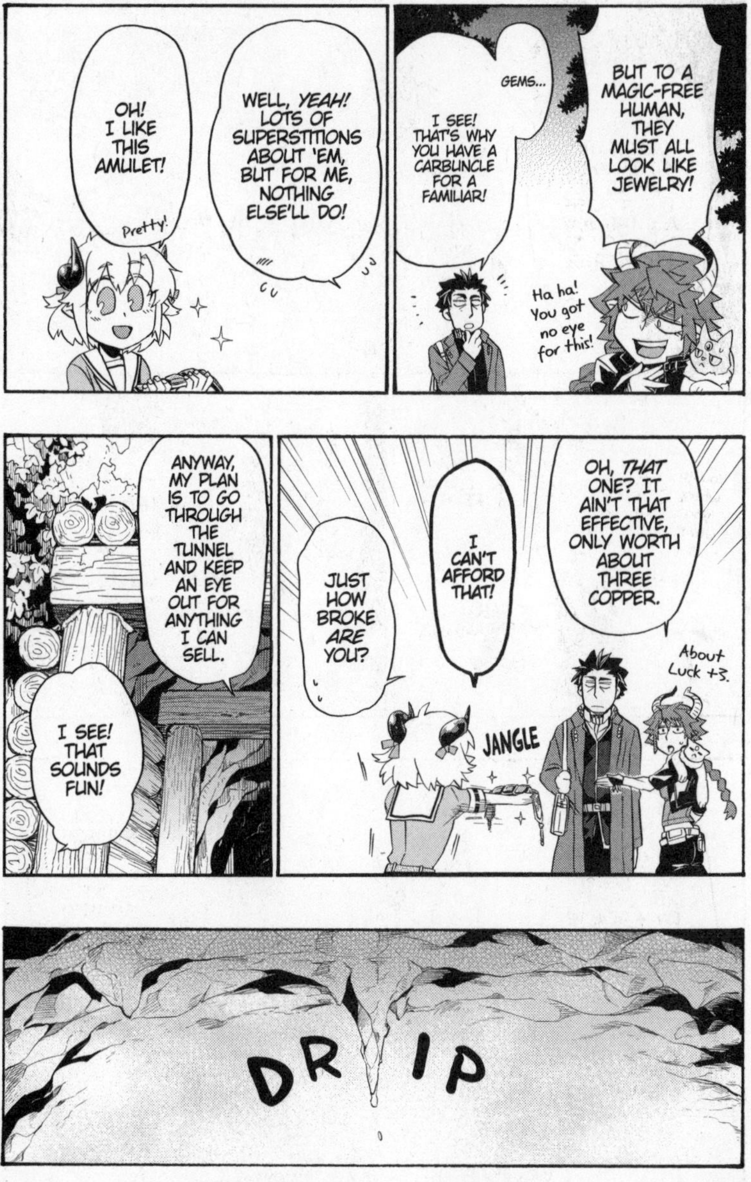
GEMS...
BUT TO A MAGIC-FREE HUMAN, THEY MUST ALL LOOK LIKE JEWELRY!
I SEE! THAT'S WHY YOU HAVE A CARBUNCLE FOR A FAMILIAR!
Ha ha! You got no eye for this!
WELL, YEAH! LOTS OF SUPERSTITIONS ABOUT 'EM, BUT FOR ME, NOTHING ELSE'LL DO!
OH! I LIKE THIS AMULET!
Pretty!
OH, THAT ONE? IT AIN'T THAT EFFECTIVE, ONLY WORTH ABOUT THREE COPPER.
About Luck +3.
I CAN'T AFFORD THAT!
JUST HOW BROKE ARE YOU?
JANGLE
ANYWAY, MY PLAN IS TO GO THROUGH THE TUNNEL AND KEEP AN EYE OUT FOR ANYTHING I CAN SELL.
I SEE! THAT SOUNDS FUN!
DRIP

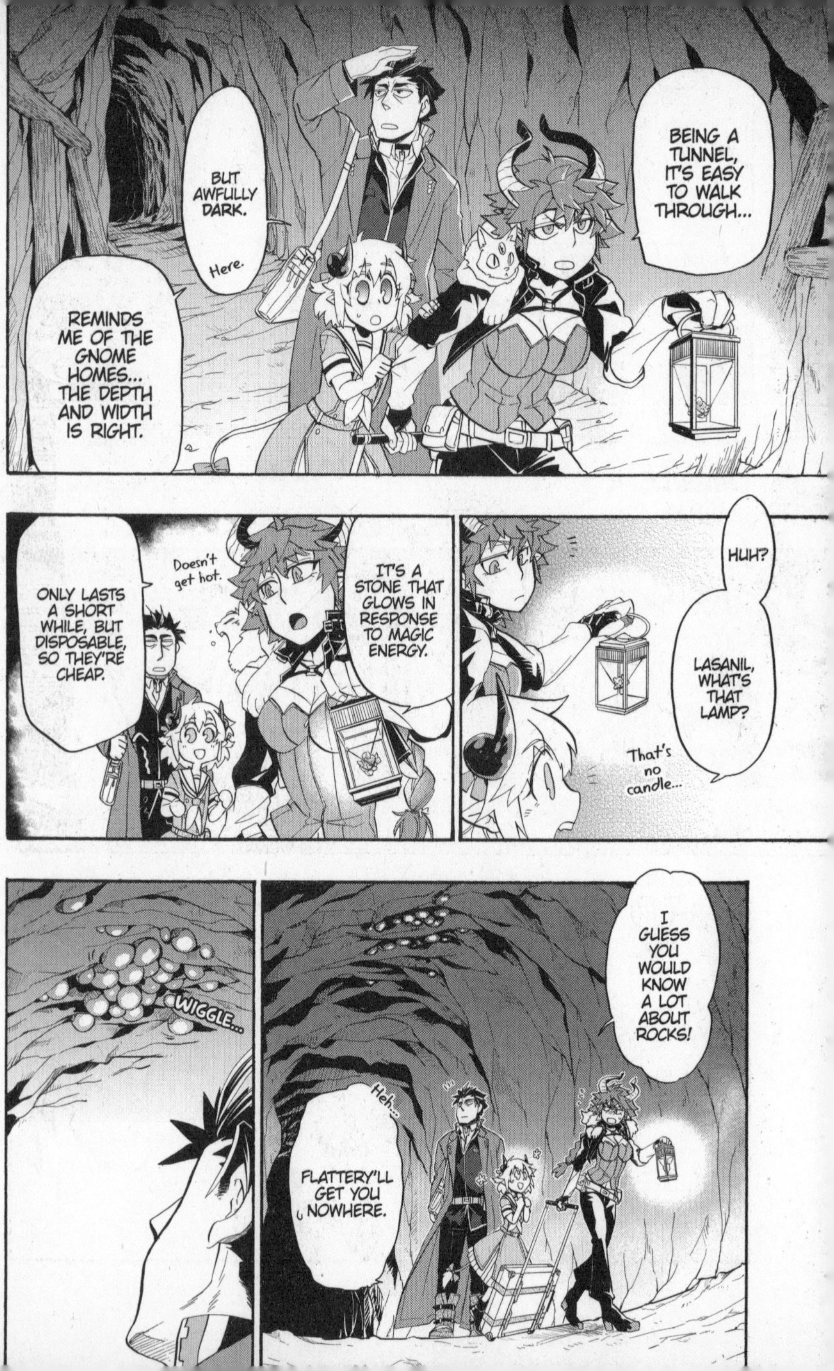
BEING A TUNNEL, IT'S EASY TO WALK THROUGH...
BUT AWFULLY DARK.
Here.
REMINDS ME OF THE GNOME HOMES... THE DEPTH AND WIDTH IS RIGHT.
HUH?
LASANIL, WHAT'S THAT LAMP?
That's no candle...
IT'S A STONE THAT GLOWS IN RESPONSE TO MAGIC ENERGY.
Doesn't get hot.
ONLY LASTS A SHORT WHILE, BUT DISPOSABLE, SO THEY'RE CHEAP.
I GUESS YOU WOULD KNOW A LOT ABOUT ROCKS!
Heh...
FLATTERY'LL GET YOU NOWHERE.
WIGGLE...

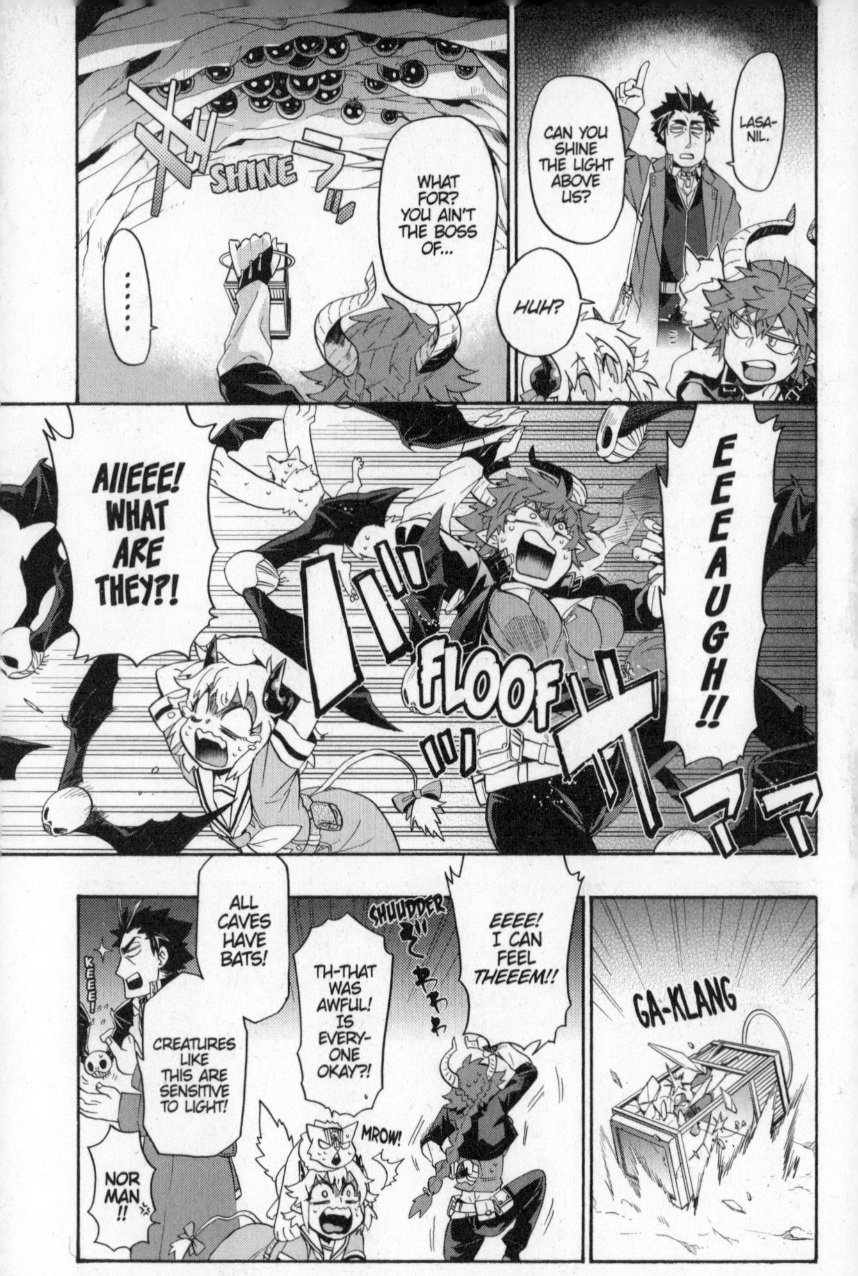
LASA-NIL.
CAN YOU SHINE THE LIGHT ABOVE US?
HUH?
WHAT FOR? YOU AIN'T THE BOSS OF...
SHINE
......
EEEAUGH!!
AIIEEE! WHAT ARE THEY?!
FLOOF
GA-KLANG
EEEE! I CAN FEEL THEEEM!!
SHUUDDER
TH-THAT WAS AWFUL! IS EVERY-ONE OKAY?!
ALL CAVES HAVE BATS!
CREATURES LIKE THIS ARE SENSITIVE TO LIGHT!
KEEE!
MROW!
NOR MAN!!

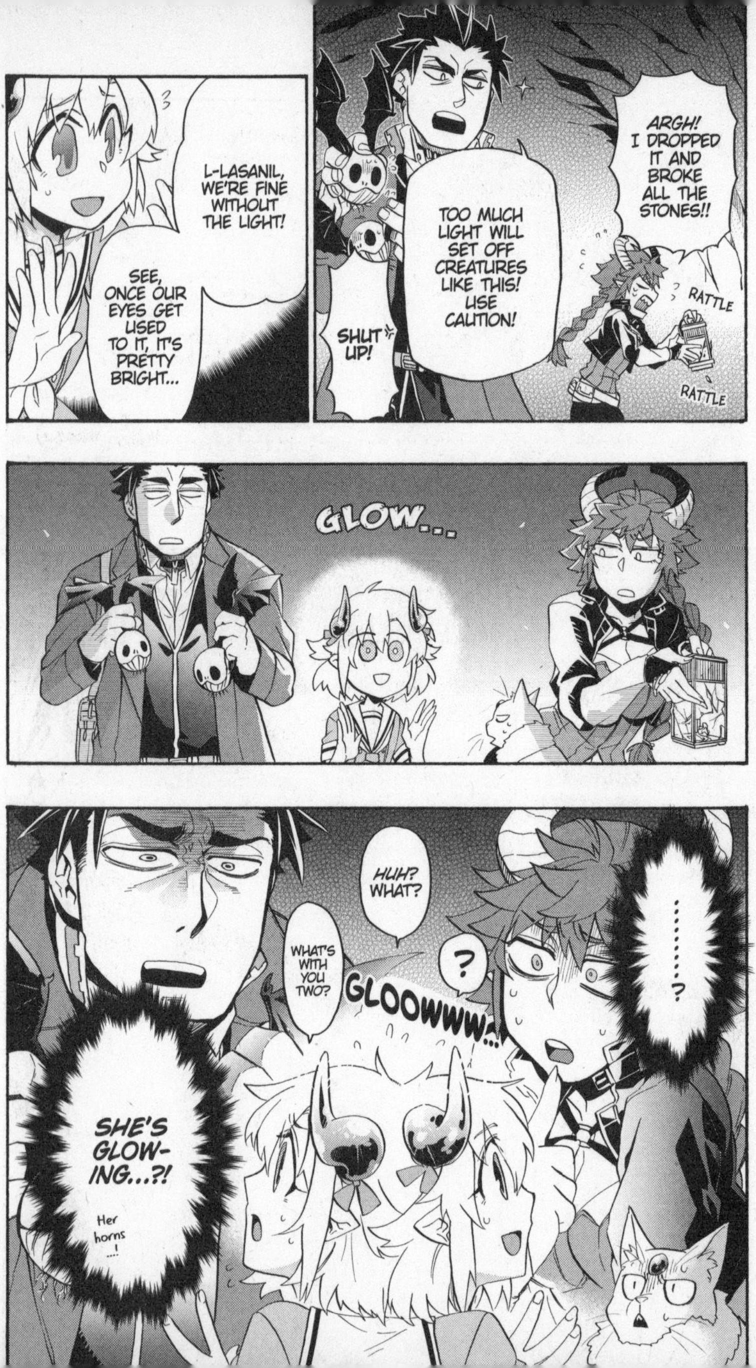
ARGH! I DROPPED IT AND BROKE ALL THE STONES!!
RATTLE
RATTLE
TOO MUCH LIGHT WILL SET OFF CREATURES LIKE THIS! USE CAUTION!
SHUT UP!
L-LASANIL, WE'RE FINE WITHOUT THE LIGHT!
SEE, ONCE OUR EYES GET USED TO IT, IT'S PRETTY BRIGHT...
GLOW...
......?
HUH? WHAT?
?
GLOOWWW...
WHAT'S WITH YOU TWO?
SHE'S GLOW-ING...?!
Her horns...!

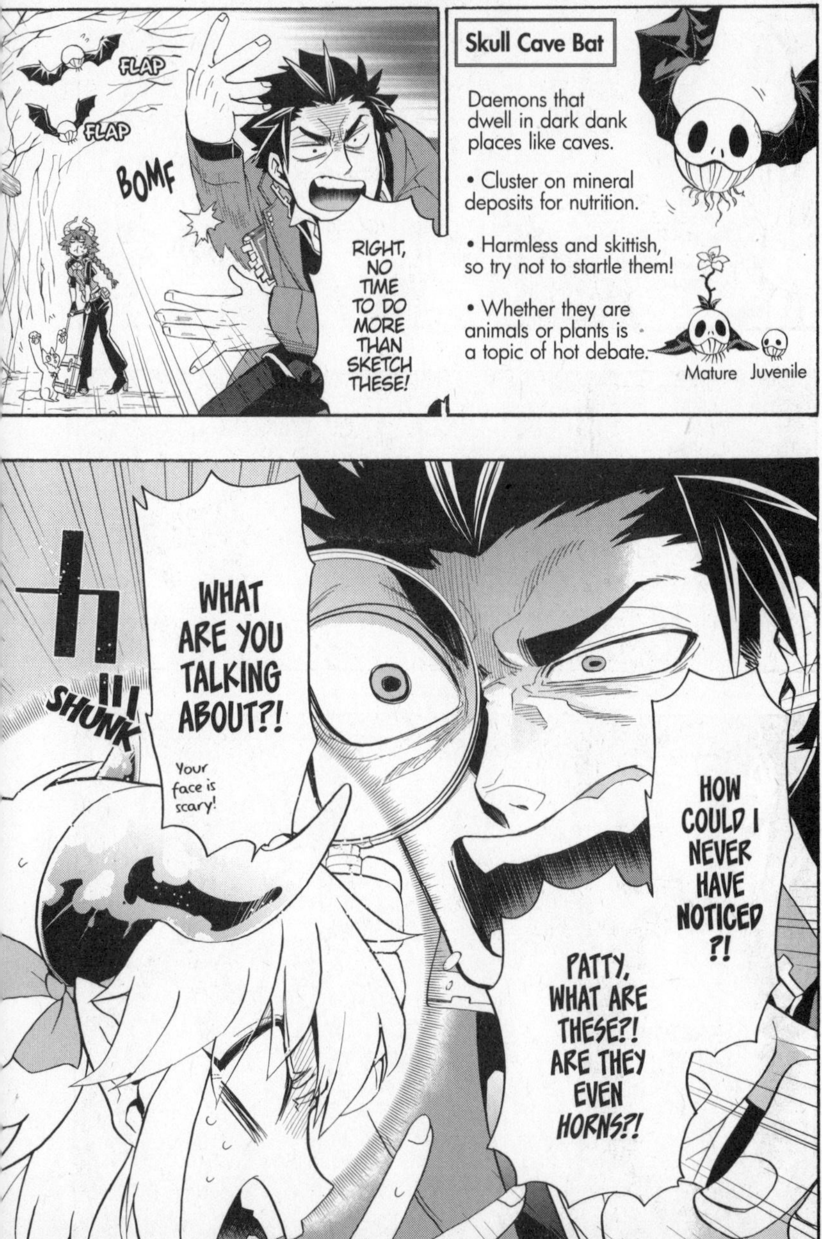
Skull Cave Bat
Daemons that dwell in dark dank places like caves.
• Cluster on mineral deposits for nutrition.
• Harmless and skittish, so try not to startle them!
• Whether they are animals or plants is a topic of hot debate.
Mature
Juvenile
RIGHT, NO TIME TO DO MORE THAN SKETCH THESE!
FLAP
FLAP
BOMF
HOW COULD I NEVER HAVE NOTICED?!
PATTY, WHAT ARE THESE?! ARE THEY EVEN HORNS?!
WHAT ARE YOU TALKING ABOUT?!
Your face is scary!
SHUNK

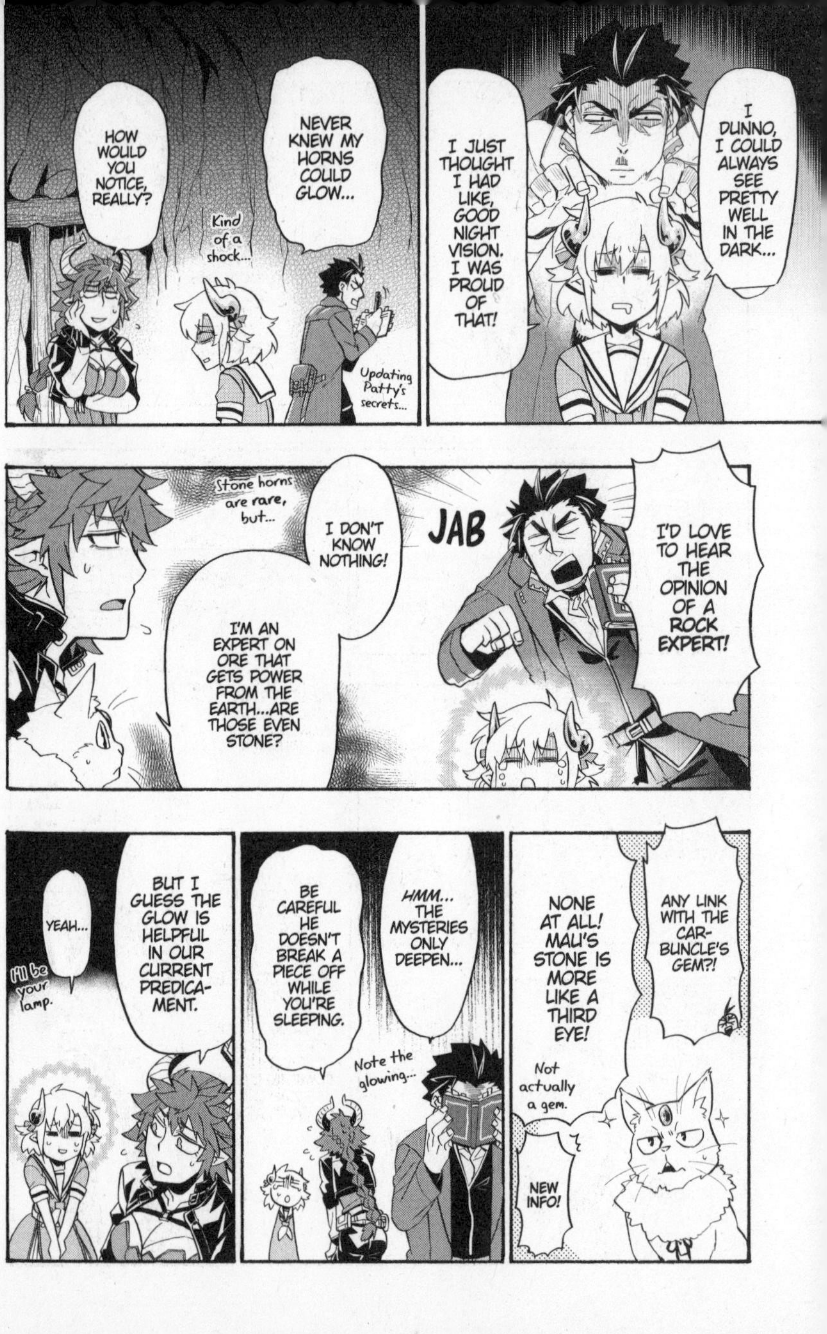
I DUNNO, I COULD ALWAYS SEE PRETTY WELL IN THE DARK...
I JUST THOUGHT I HAD LIKE, GOOD NIGHT VISION. I WAS PROUD OF THAT!
NEVER KNEW MY HORNS COULD GLOW...
Kind of a shock...
HOW WOULD YOU NOTICE, REALLY?
Updating Patty's secrets...
I'D LOVE TO HEAR THE OPINION OF A ROCK EXPERT!
JAB
I DON'T KNOW NOTHING!
Stone horns are rare, but...
I'M AN EXPERT ON ORE THAT GETS POWER FROM THE EARTH...ARE THOSE EVEN STONE?
ANY LINK WITH THE CAR-BUNCLE'S GEM?!
NONE AT ALL! MAU'S STONE IS MORE LIKE A THIRD EYE!
Not actually a gem.
NEW INFO!
HMM... THE MYSTERIES ONLY DEEPEN...
BE CAREFUL HE DOESN'T BREAK A PIECE OFF WHILE YOU'RE SLEEPING.
Note the glowing...
BUT I GUESS THE GLOW IS HELPFUL IN OUR CURRENT PREDICA-MENT.
YEAH...
I'll be your lamp.

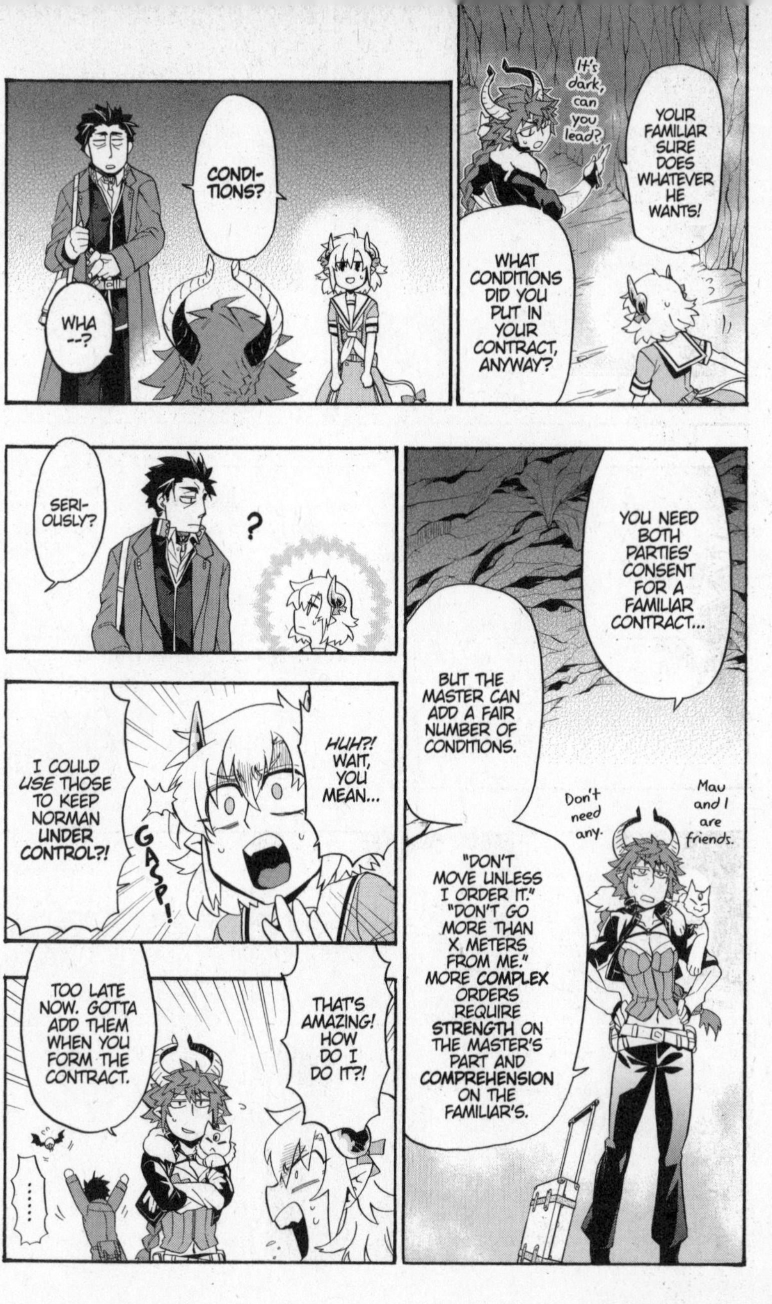
It's dark, can you lead?
YOUR FAMILIAR SURE DOES WHATEVER HE WANTS!
WHAT CONDITIONS DID YOU PUT IN YOUR CONTRACT, ANYWAY?
CONDITIONS?
WHA--?
YOU NEED BOTH PARTIES' CONSENT FOR A FAMILIAR CONTRACT...
BUT THE MASTER CAN ADD A FAIR NUMBER OF CONDITIONS.
Mau and I are friends.
Don't need any.
"DON'T MOVE UNLESS I ORDER IT." "DON'T GO MORE THAN X METERS FROM ME." MORE COMPLEX ORDERS REQUIRE STRENGTH ON THE MASTER'S PART AND COMPREHENSION ON THE FAMILIAR'S.
SERI-OUSLY?
?
HUH?! WAIT, YOU MEAN...
I COULD USE THOSE TO KEEP NORMAN UNDER CONTROL?!
GASP!
THAT'S AMAZING! HOW DO I DO IT?!
TOO LATE NOW. GOTTA ADD THEM WHEN YOU FORM THE CONTRACT.
......

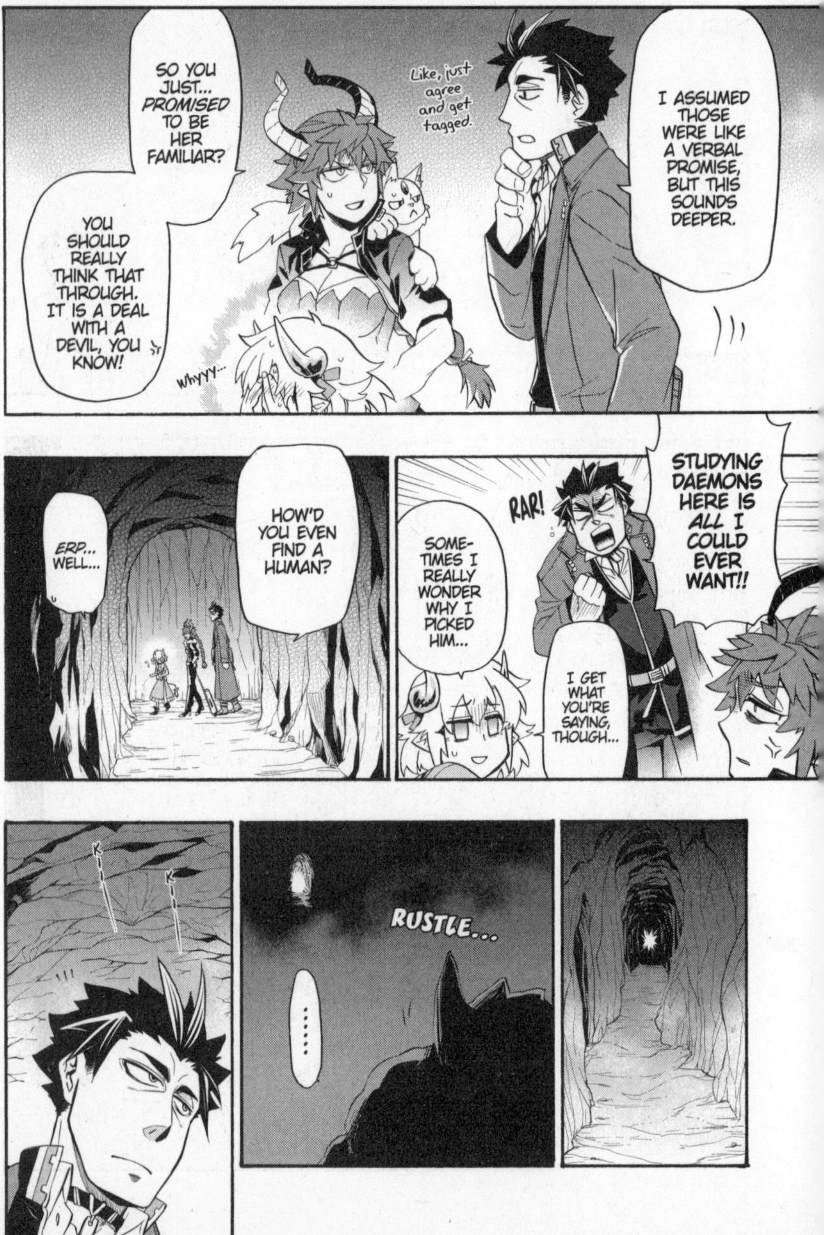
I ASSUMED THOSE WERE LIKE A VERBAL PROMISE, BUT THIS SOUNDS DEEPER.
Like, just agree and get tagged.
SO YOU JUST... PROMISED TO BE HER FAMILIAR?
YOU SHOULD REALLY THINK THAT THROUGH. IT IS A DEAL WITH A DEVIL, YOU KNOW!
Whyyy...
STUDYING DAEMONS HERE IS ALL I COULD EVER WANT!!
RAR!
SOME-TIMES I REALLY WONDER WHY I PICKED HIM...
I GET WHAT YOU'RE SAYING, THOUGH...
HOW'D YOU EVEN FIND A HUMAN?
ERP... WELL...
RUSTLE...
......

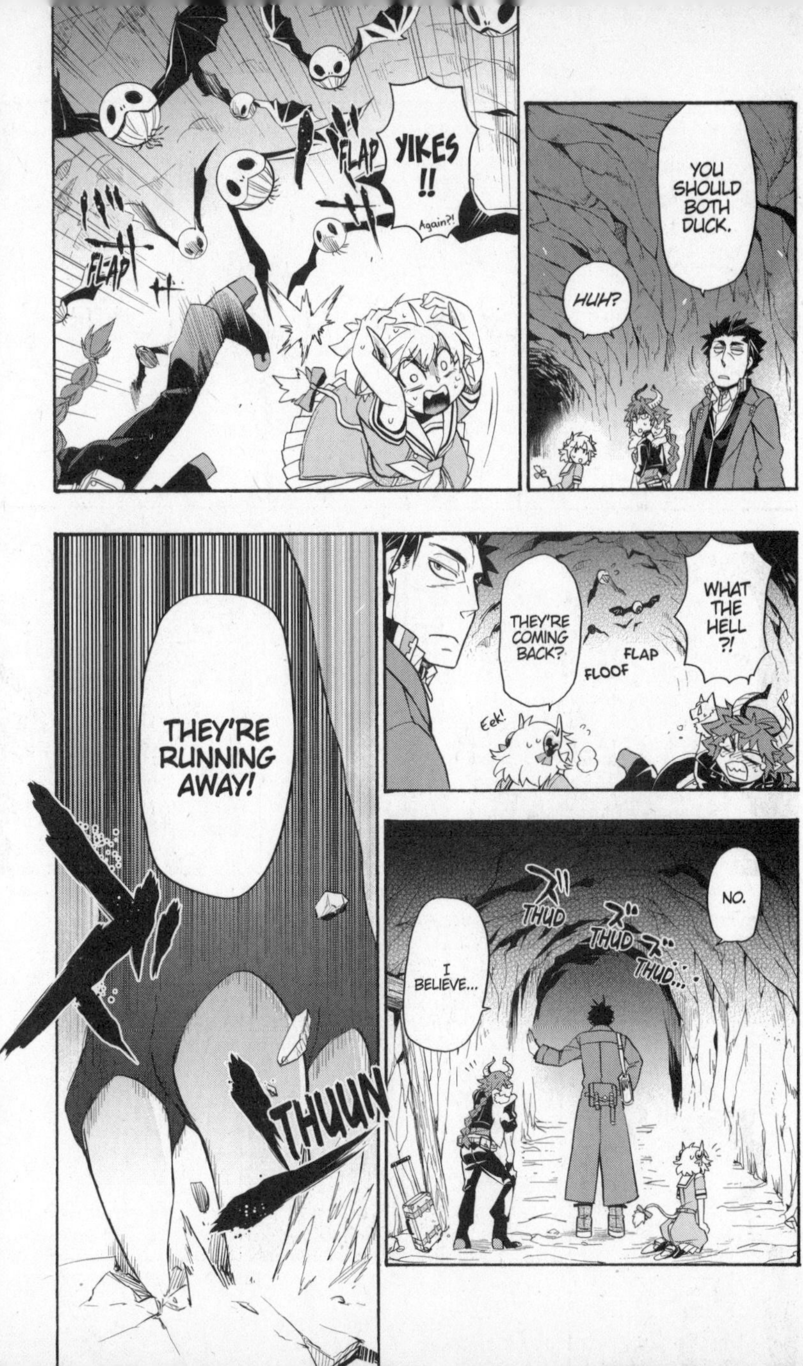
YOU SHOULD BOTH DUCK.
HUH?
YIKES!!
Again?!
FLAP
FLAP
WHAT THE HELL?!
THEY'RE COMING BACK?
FLAP
FLOOF
Eek!
NO.
I BELIEVE...
THUD
THUD
THUD...
THEY'RE RUNNING AWAY!
THUUN

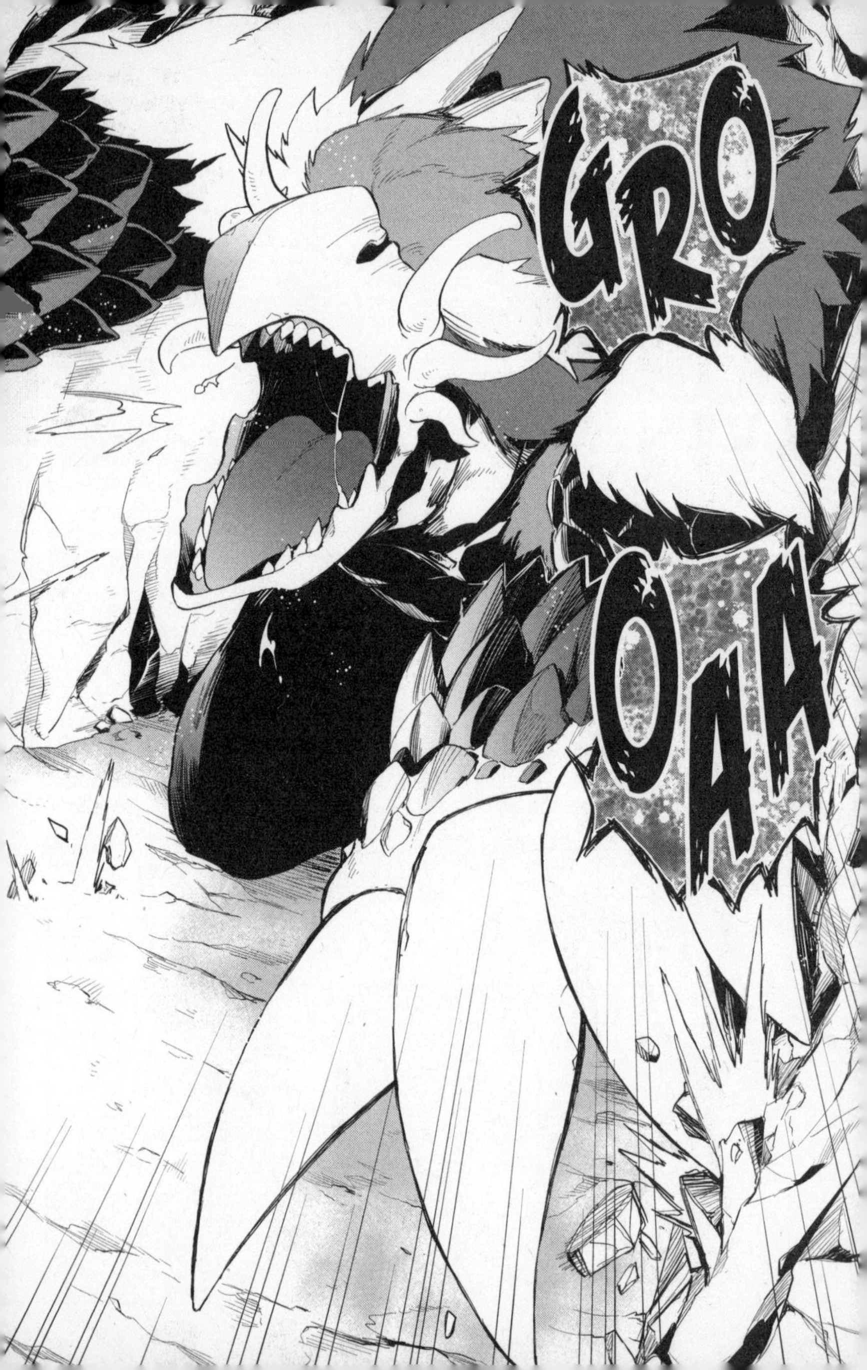
GROOAA

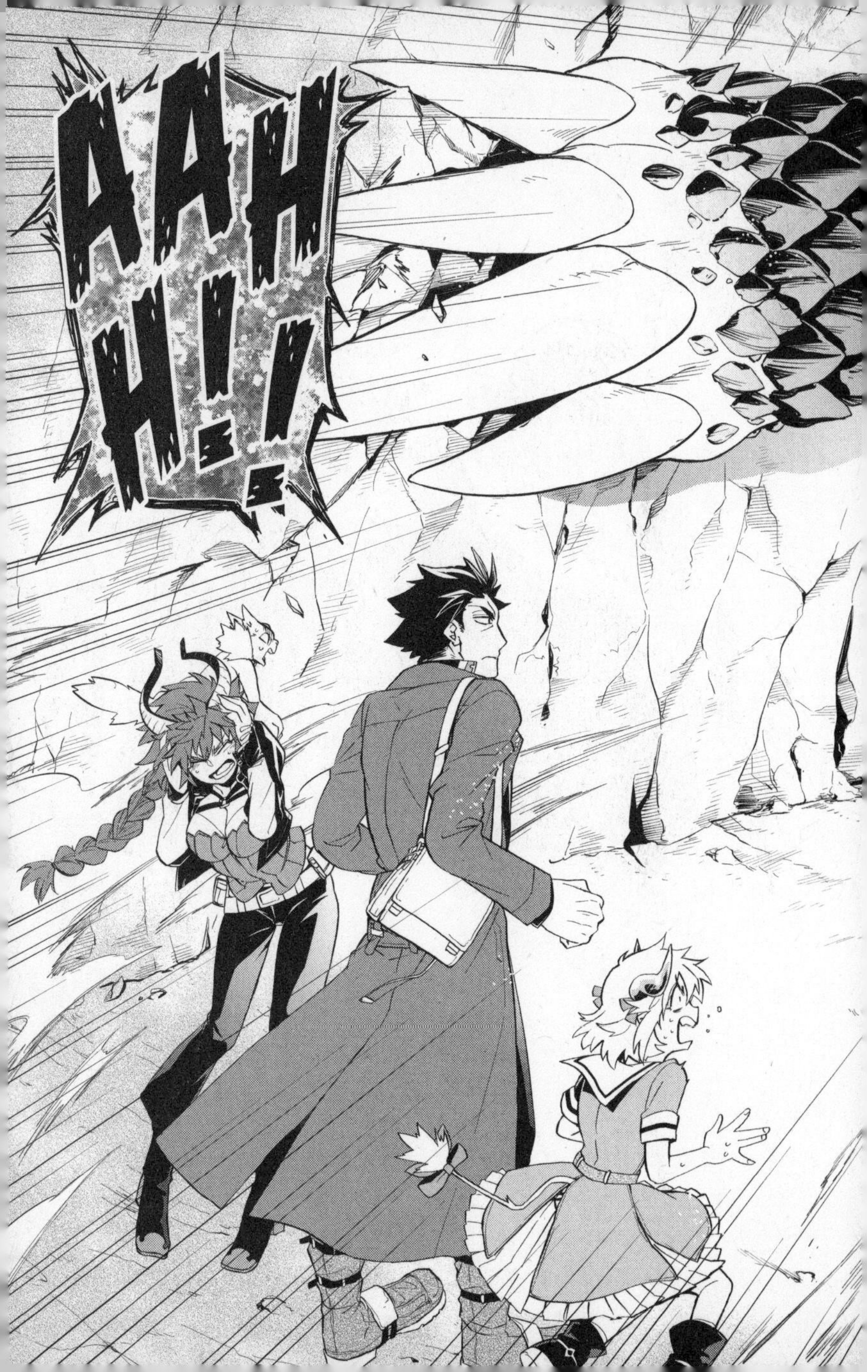
AAHH!!

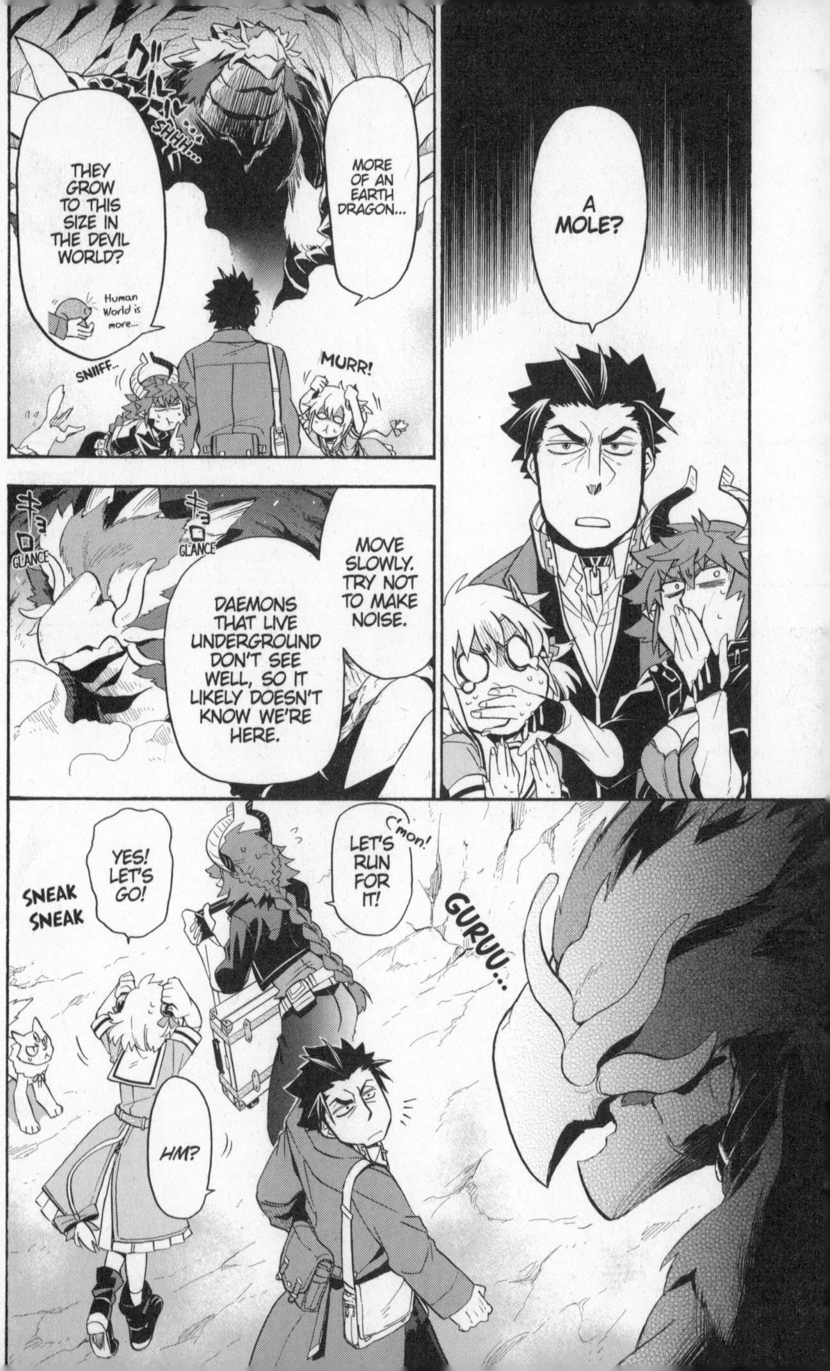
A MOLE?
MORE OF AN EARTH DRAGON...
SHHH...
THEY GROW TO THIS SIZE IN THE DEVIL WORLD?
Human World is more...
MURR!
SNIIFF...
MOVE SLOWLY. TRY NOT TO MAKE NOISE.
DAEMONS THAT LIVE UNDERGROUND DON'T SEE WELL, SO IT LIKELY DOESN'T KNOW WE'RE HERE.
GLANCE
GLANCE
GURUU...
C'mon!
LET'S RUN FOR IT!
YES! LET'S GO!
SNEAK SNEAK
HM?

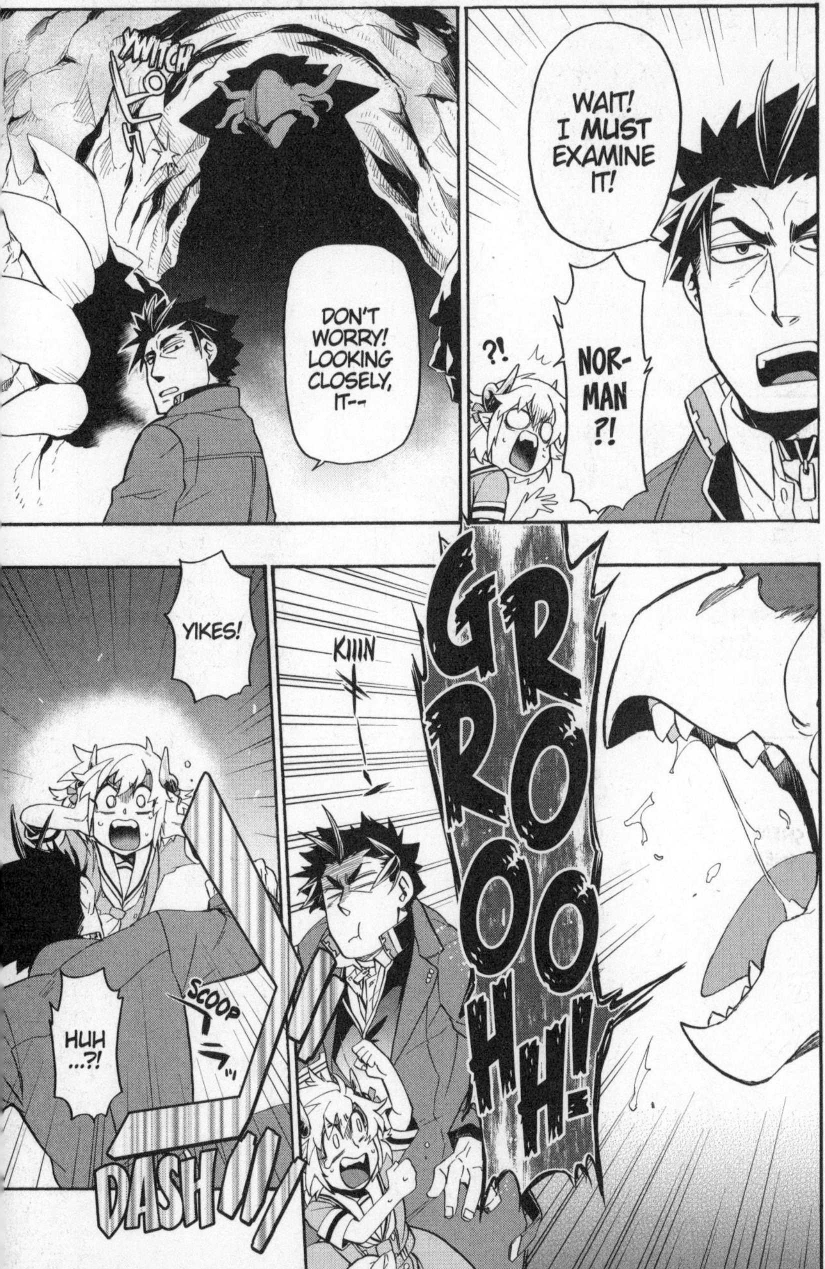
WAIT! I MUST EXAMINE IT!
?!
NOR-MAN?!
YWITCH
DON'T WORRY! LOOKING CLOSELY, IT--
GRROOOOHH!
KIIIN
YIKES!
SCOOP
HUH...?!
DASH!!

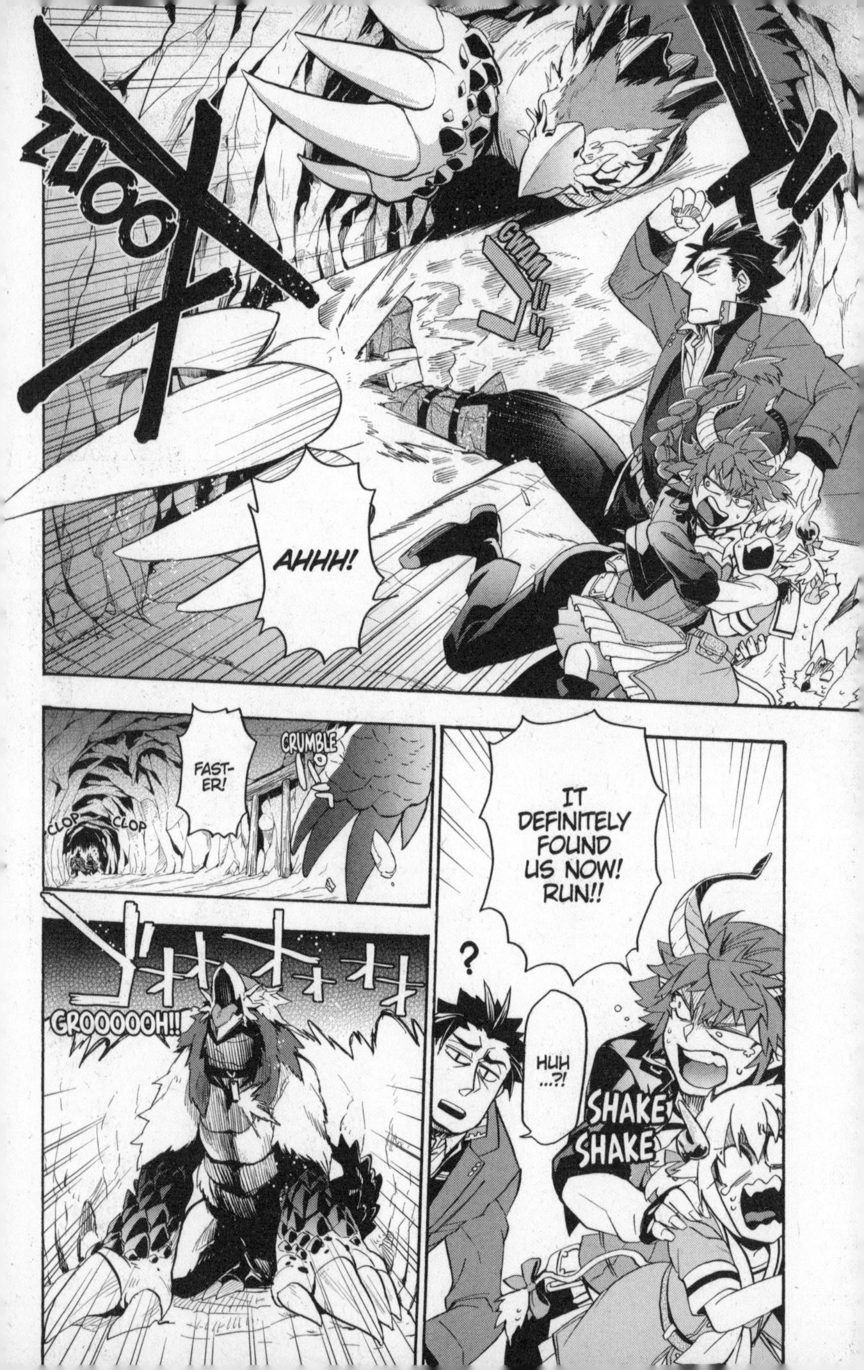
ZUOOO
GWAN
AHHH!
IT DEFINITELY FOUND US NOW! RUN!!
?
HUH ...?!
SHAKE SHAKE
FAST-ER!
CRUMBLE
CLOP CLOP
GROOOOOH!!

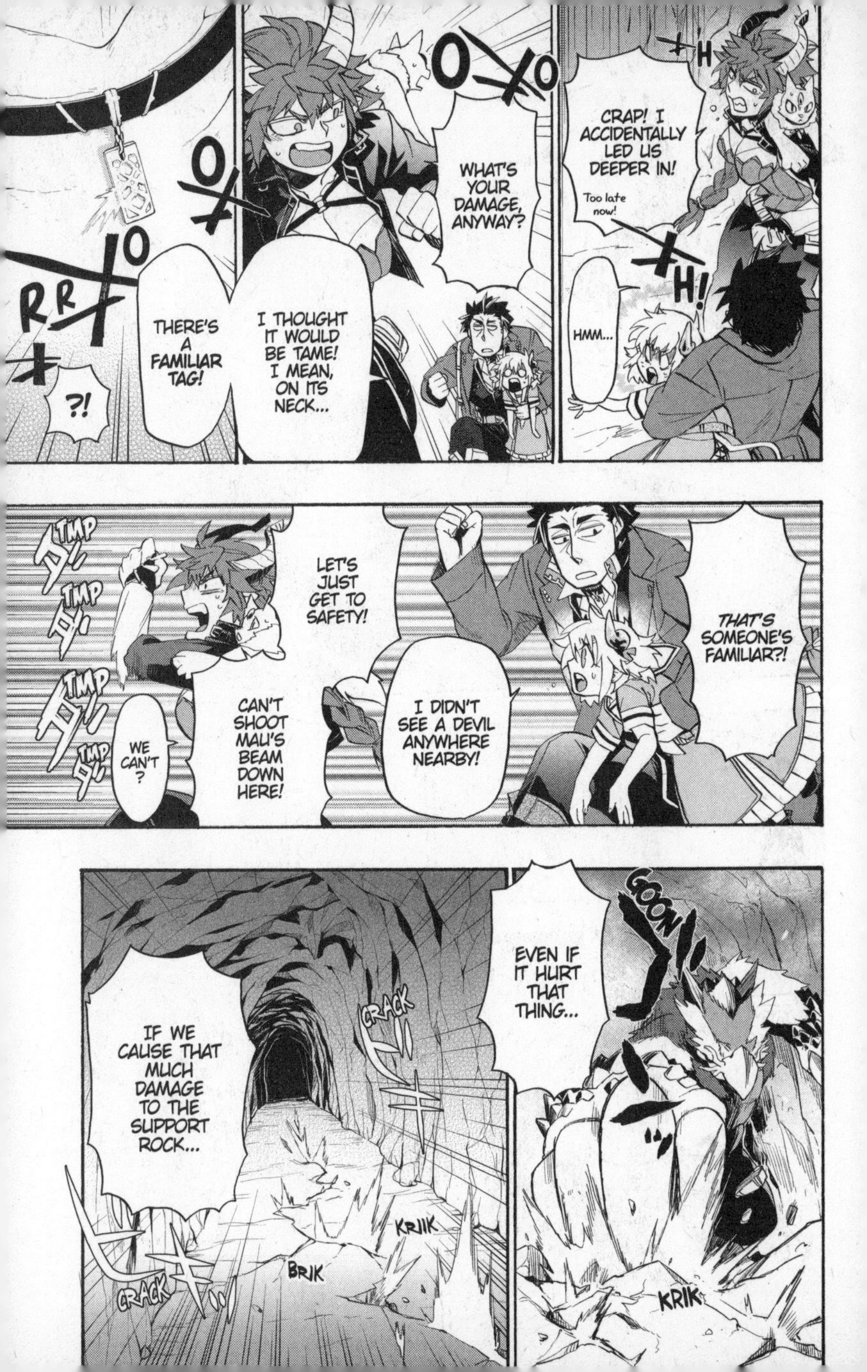
H
CRAP! I ACCIDENTALLY LED US DEEPER IN!
Too late now!
H!
HMM...
O
O
WHAT'S YOUR DAMAGE, ANYWAY?
I THOUGHT IT WOULD BE TAME! I MEAN, ON ITS NECK...
O
THERE'S A FAMILIAR TAG!
O
RR
?!
THAT'S SOMEONE'S FAMILIAR?!
I DIDN'T SEE A DEVIL ANYWHERE NEARBY!
LET'S JUST GET TO SAFETY!
CAN'T SHOOT MAU'S BEAM DOWN HERE!
TMP
TMP
TMP
WE CAN'T ?
TMP
GOOON
EVEN IF IT HURT THAT THING...
KRIK
CRACK
IF WE CAUSE THAT MUCH DAMAGE TO THE SUPPORT ROCK...
KRIIK
BRIK
CRACK

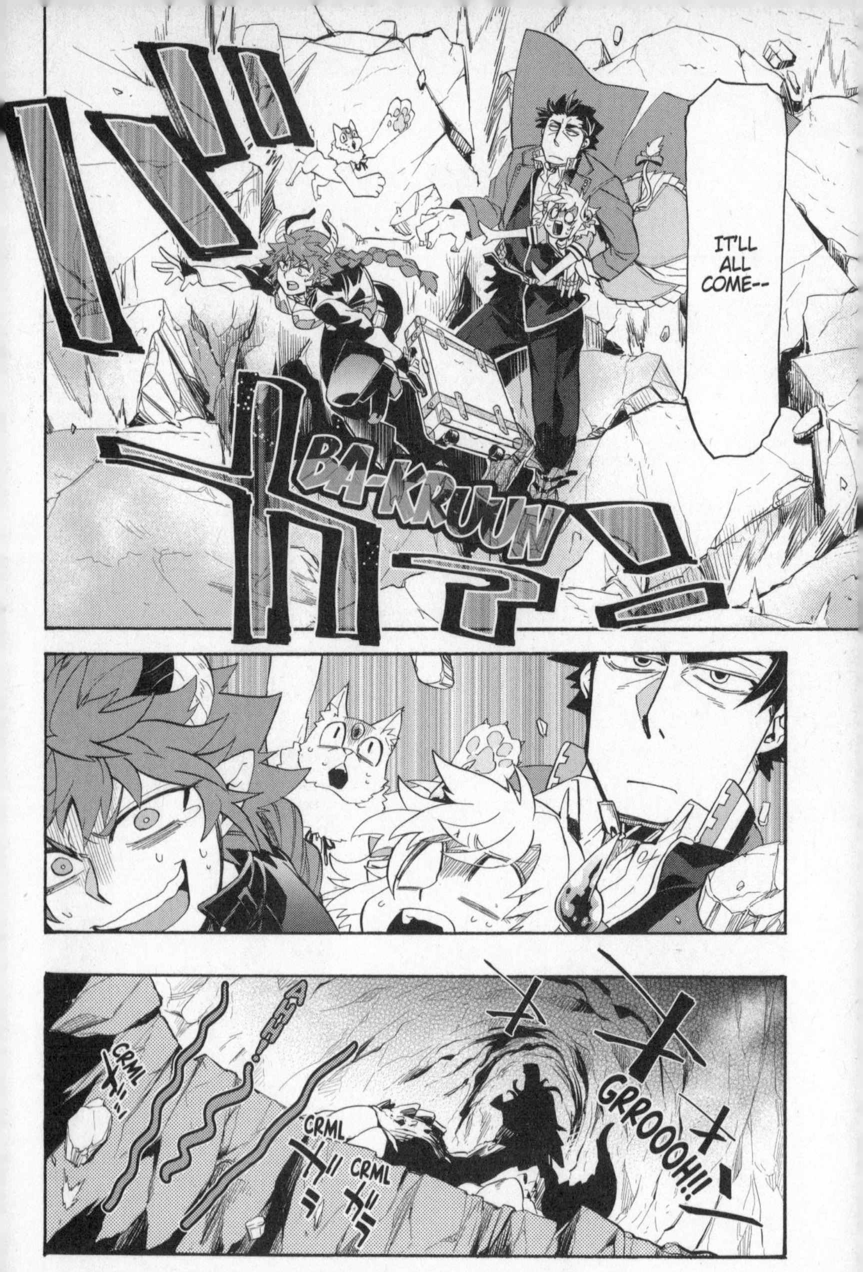
IT'LL ALL COME--
BA-KRUUN
GRROOOH!!
CRML
CRML
CRML

Sorry For My Familiar

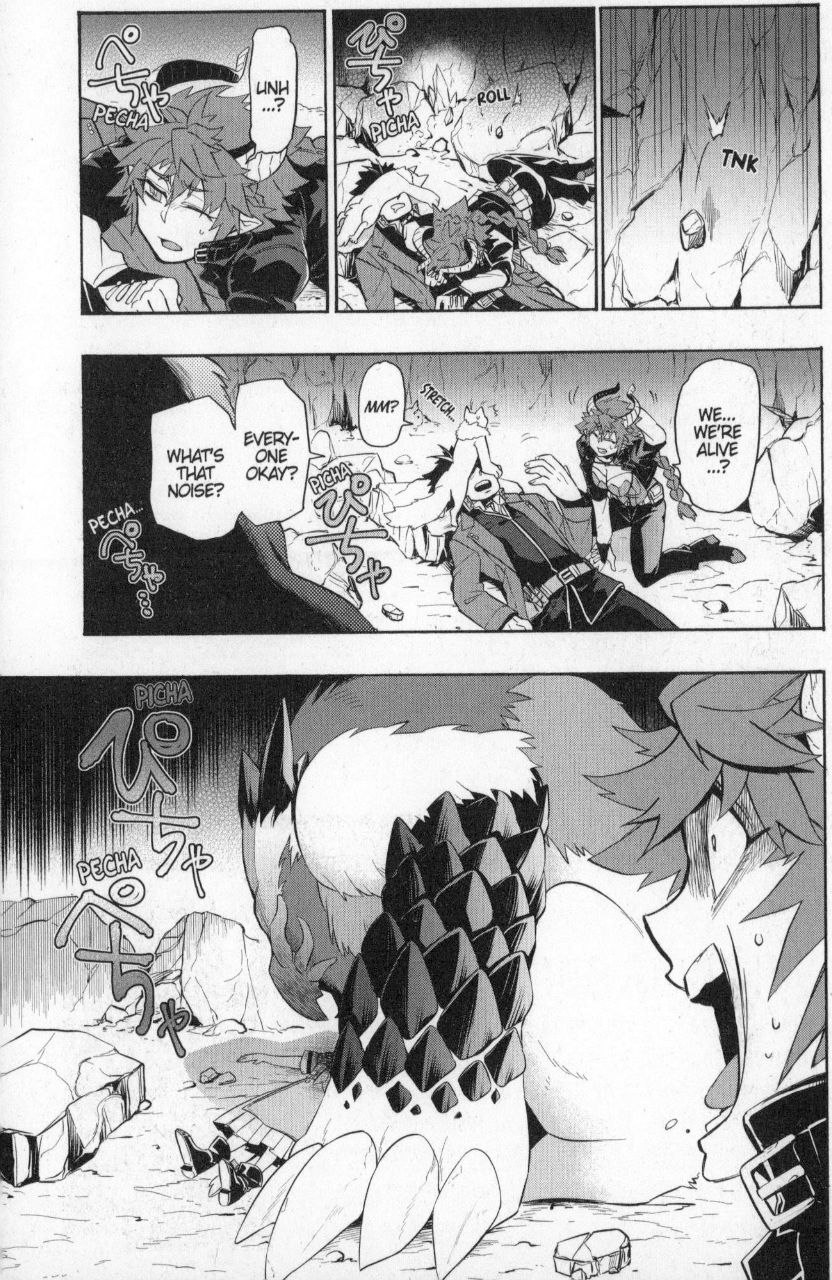
TNK
ぴちゃ
PICHA
ROLL
ぺちゃ
PECHA
UNH ...?
WE... WE'RE ALIVE ...?
STRETCH...
MM?
PICHA
ぴちゃ
EVERY-ONE OKAY?
WHAT'S THAT NOISE?
PECHA...
ぺちゃ...
PICHA
ぴちゃ
PECHA
ぺちゃ

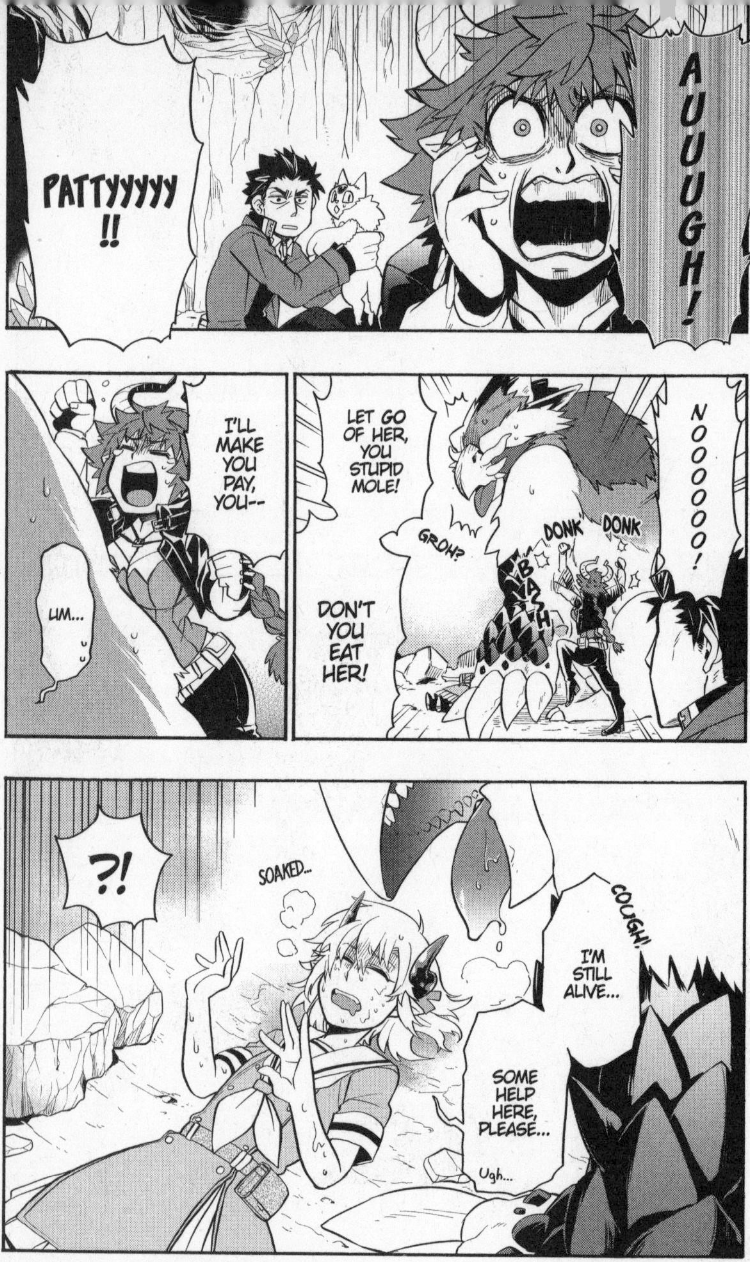
AUUUGH!
PATTYYYYY!!
NOOOOOOO!
LET GO OF HER, YOU STUPID MOLE!
DONK
DONK
BASH
GROH?
DON'T YOU EAT HER!
I'LL MAKE YOU PAY, YOU--
UM...
COUGH!
I'M STILL ALIVE...
SOAKED...
?!
SOME HELP HERE, PLEASE...
Ugh...

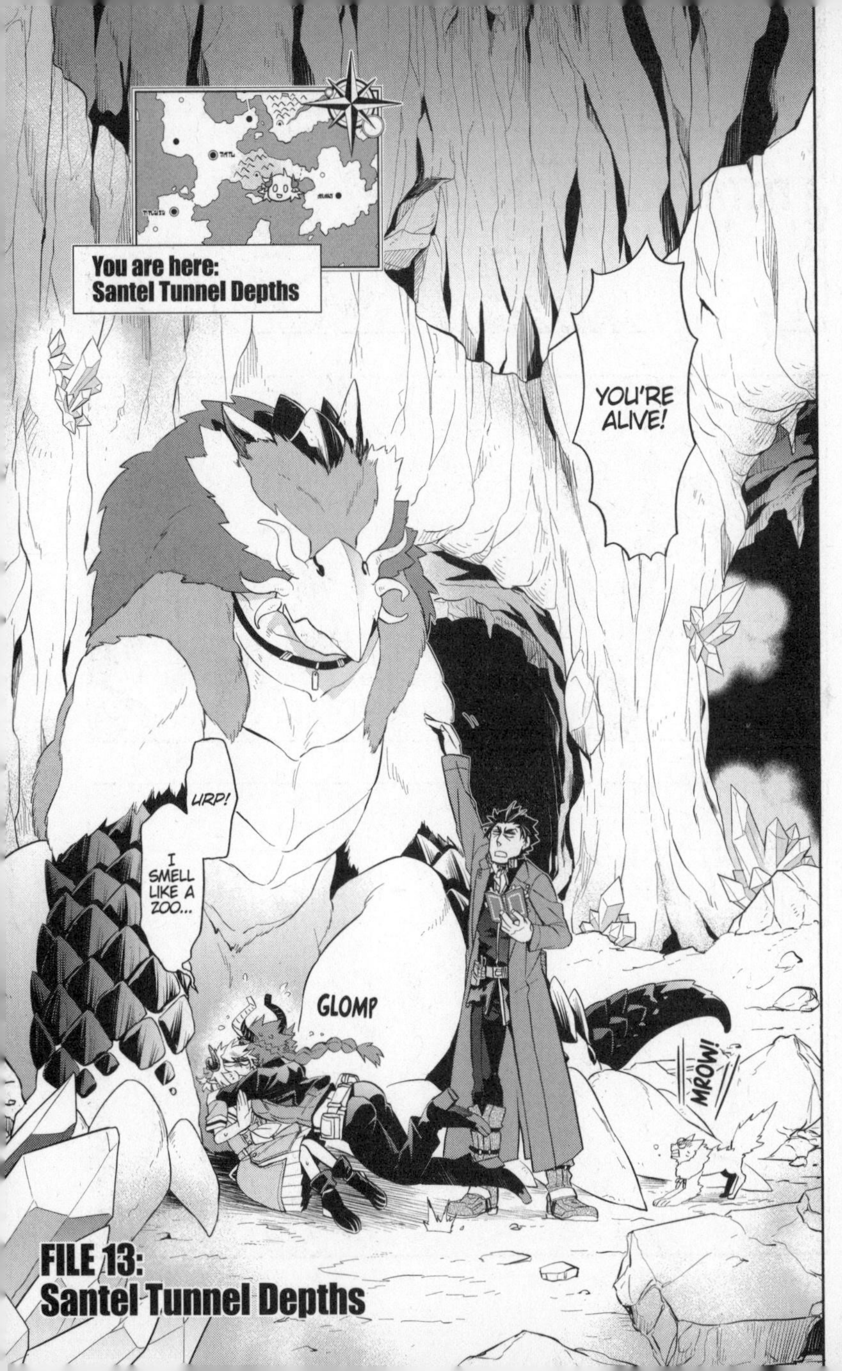
You are here:
Santel Tunnel Depths
YOU'RE ALIVE!
URP!
I SMELL LIKE A ZOO...
GLOMP
MROW!
FILE 13:
Santel Tunnel Depths

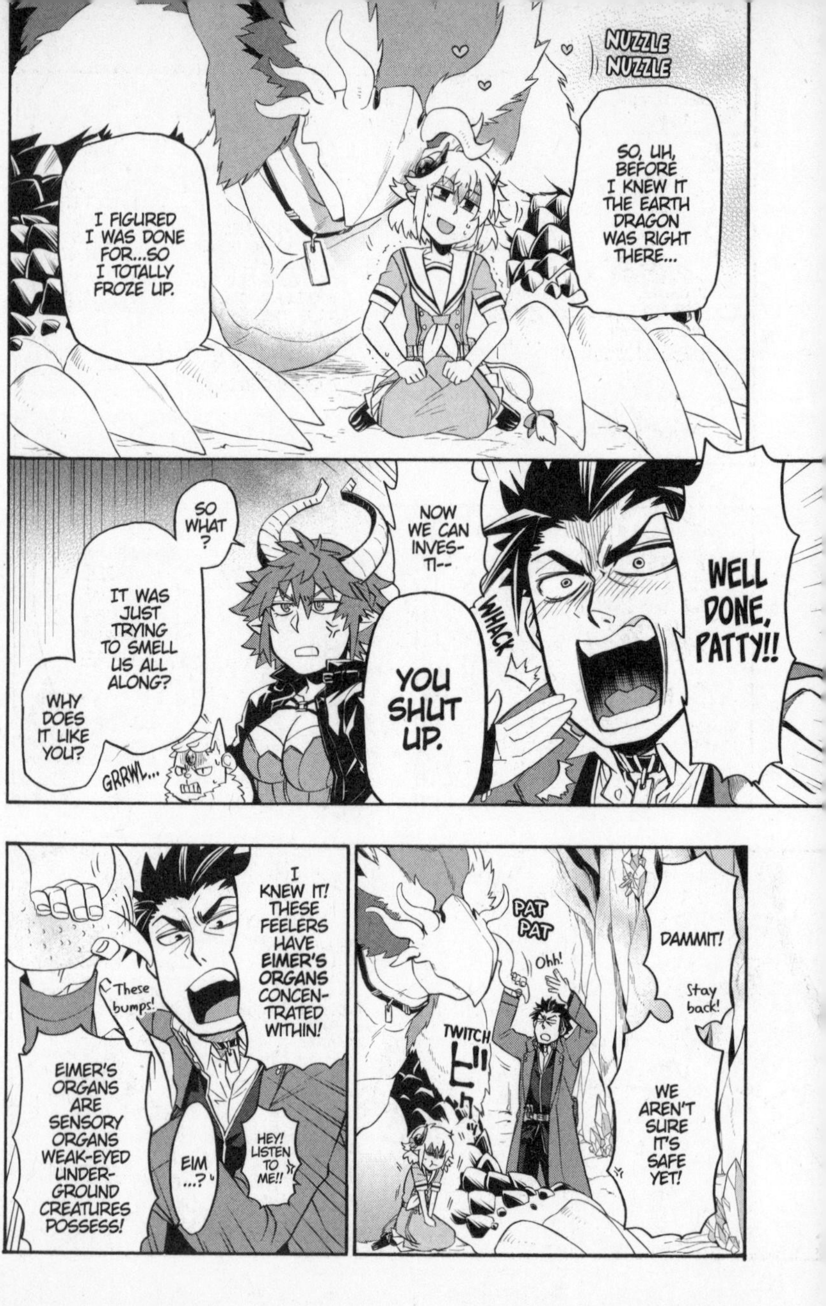
NUZZLE NUZZLE
SO, UH, BEFORE I KNEW IT THE EARTH DRAGON WAS RIGHT THERE...
I FIGURED I WAS DONE FOR...SO I TOTALLY FROZE UP.
WELL DONE, PATTY!!
NOW WE CAN INVESTI--
WHACK
YOU SHUT UP.
SO WHAT?
IT WAS JUST TRYING TO SMELL US ALL ALONG?
WHY DOES IT LIKE YOU?
GRRWL...
DAMMIT!
Stay back!
WE AREN'T SURE IT'S SAFE YET!
PAT PAT
Oh!
TWITCH
I KNEW IT! THESE FEELERS HAVE EIMER'S ORGANS CONCENTRATED WITHIN!
These bumps!
EIMER'S ORGANS ARE SENSORY ORGANS WEAK-EYED UNDERGROUND CREATURES POSSESS!
HEY! LISTEN TO ME!!
EIM...?

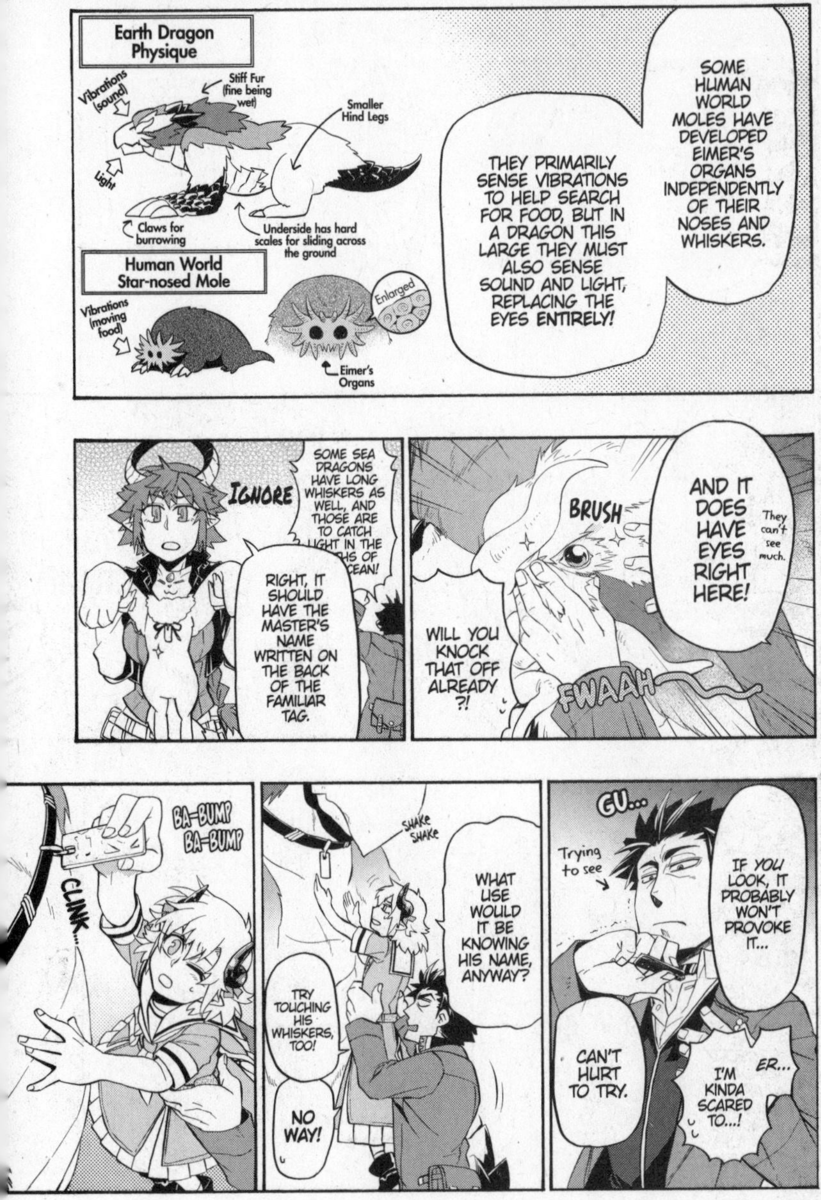
SOME HUMAN WORLD MOLES HAVE DEVELOPED EIMER'S ORGANS INDEPENDENTLY OF THEIR NOSES AND WHISKERS.
THEY PRIMARILY SENSE VIBRATIONS TO HELP SEARCH FOR FOOD, BUT IN A DRAGON THIS LARGE THEY MUST ALSO SENSE SOUND AND LIGHT, REPLACING THE EYES ENTIRELY!
Earth Dragon Physique
Vibrations (sound)
Stiff Fur (fine being wet)
Smaller Hind Legs
Light
Claws for burrowing
Underside has hard scales for sliding across the ground
Human World Star-nosed Mole
Vibrations (moving food)
Enlarged
Eimer's Organs
AND IT DOES HAVE EYES RIGHT HERE!
They can't see much.
BRUSH
WILL YOU KNOCK THAT OFF ALREADY?!
FWAAH
SOME SEA DRAGONS HAVE LONG WHISKERS AS WELL, AND THOSE ARE TO CATCH LIGHT IN THE ...THS OF ...CEAN!
IGNORE
RIGHT, IT SHOULD HAVE THE MASTER'S NAME WRITTEN ON THE BACK OF THE FAMILIAR TAG.
GU...
IF YOU LOOK, IT PROBABLY WON'T PROVOKE IT...
Trying to see
ER...
I'M KINDA SCARED TO...!
CAN'T HURT TO TRY.
SHAKE SHAKE
WHAT USE WOULD IT BE KNOWING HIS NAME, ANYWAY?
TRY TOUCHING HIS WHISKERS, TOO!
NO WAY!
BA-BUMP BA-BUMP
CLINK...

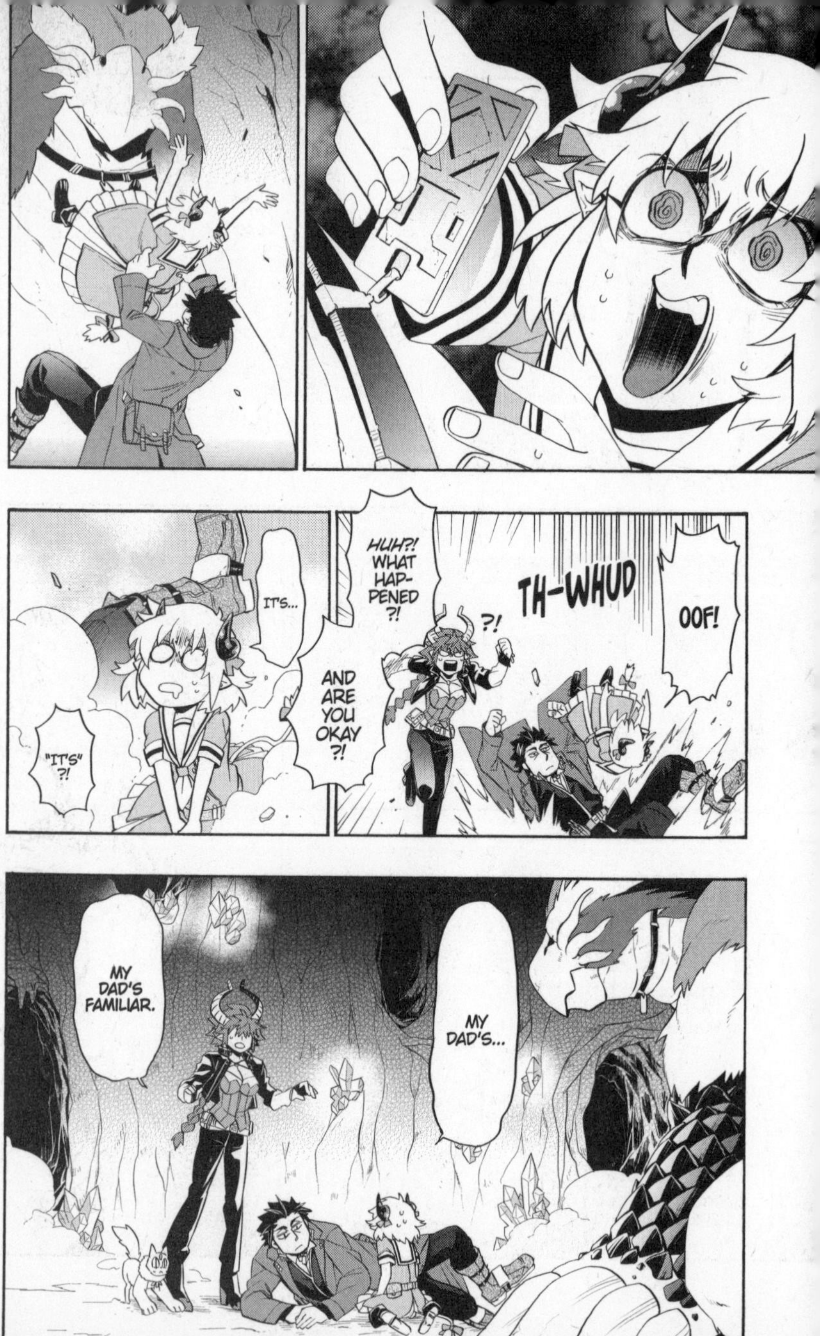
OOF!
TH-WHUD
?!
HUH?! WHAT HAP-PENED ?!
AND ARE YOU OKAY ?!
IT'S...
"IT'S" ?!
MY DAD'S...
MY DAD'S FAMILIAR.

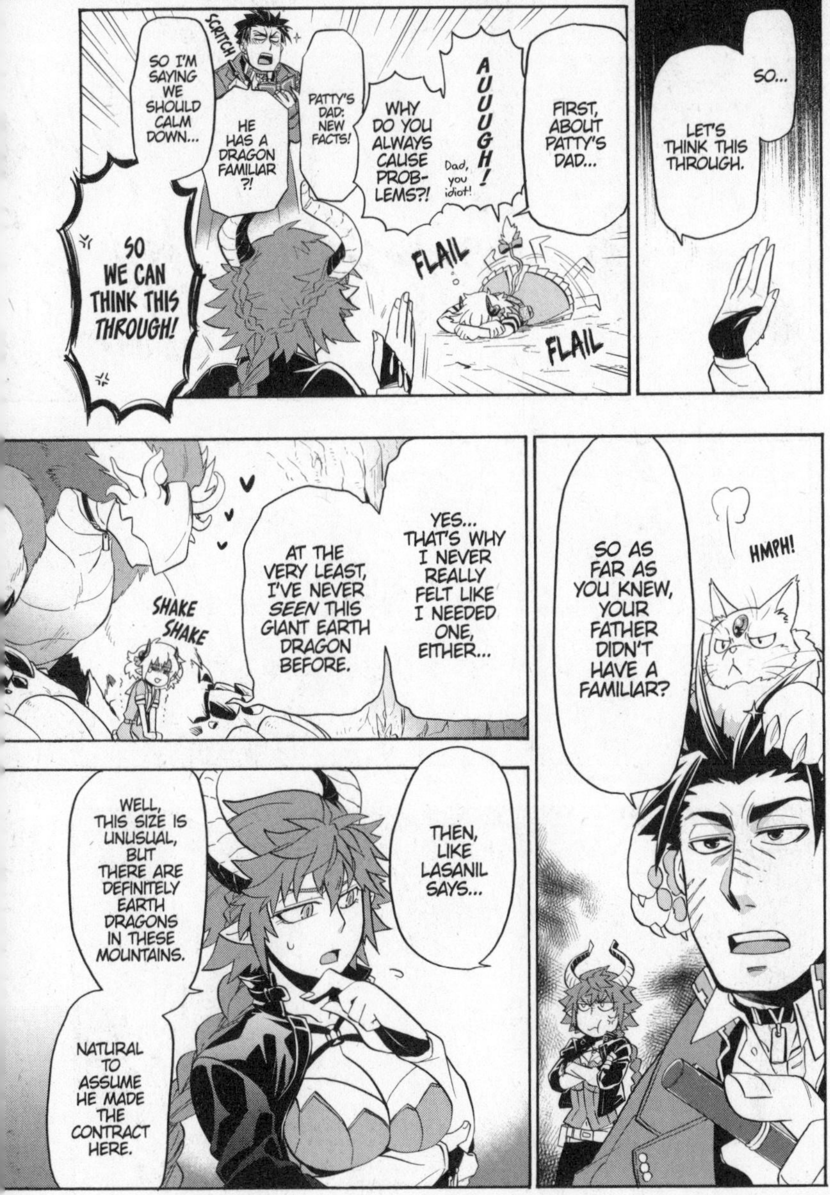
SO...
LET'S THINK THIS THROUGH.
FIRST, ABOUT PATTY'S DAD...
AUUUGH!
Dad, you idiot!
WHY DO YOU ALWAYS CAUSE PROB-LEMS?!
PATTY'S DAD: NEW FACTS!
HE HAS A DRAGON FAMILIAR?!
SCRITCH
SO I'M SAYING WE SHOULD CALM DOWN...
SO WE CAN THINK THIS THROUGH!
FLAIL
FLAIL
SO AS FAR AS YOU KNEW, YOUR FATHER DIDN'T HAVE A FAMILIAR?
HMPH!
YES... THAT'S WHY I NEVER REALLY FELT LIKE I NEEDED ONE, EITHER...
AT THE VERY LEAST, I'VE NEVER SEEN THIS GIANT EARTH DRAGON BEFORE.
SHAKE SHAKE
THEN, LIKE LASANIL SAYS...
WELL, THIS SIZE IS UNUSUAL, BUT THERE ARE DEFINITELY EARTH DRAGONS IN THESE MOUNTAINS.
NATURAL TO ASSUME HE MADE THE CONTRACT HERE.

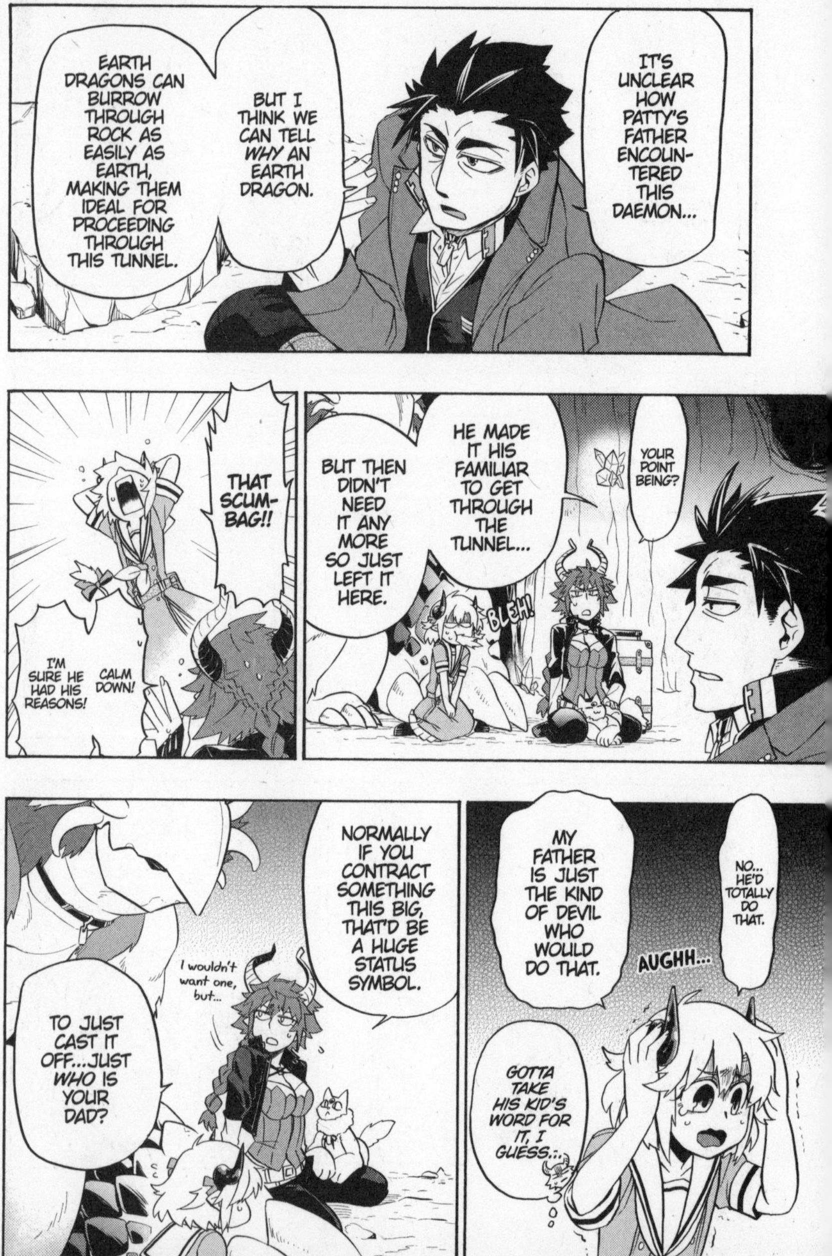
IT'S UNCLEAR HOW PATTY'S FATHER ENCOUNTERED THIS DAEMON...
BUT I THINK WE CAN TELL *WHY* AN EARTH DRAGON.
EARTH DRAGONS CAN BURROW THROUGH ROCK AS EASILY AS EARTH, MAKING THEM IDEAL FOR PROCEEDING THROUGH THIS TUNNEL.
YOUR POINT BEING?
HE MADE IT HIS FAMILIAR TO GET THROUGH THE TUNNEL...
BUT THEN DIDN'T NEED IT ANY MORE SO JUST LEFT IT HERE.
BLEH!
THAT SCUM-BAG!!
CALM DOWN!
I'M SURE HE HAD HIS REASONS!
NO... HE'D TOTALLY DO THAT.
MY FATHER IS JUST THE KIND OF DEVIL WHO WOULD DO THAT.
AUGHH...
GOTTA TAKE HIS KID'S WORD FOR IT, I GUESS...
NORMALLY IF YOU CONTRACT SOMETHING THIS BIG, THAT'D BE A HUGE STATUS SYMBOL.
I wouldn't want one, but...
TO JUST CAST IT OFF...JUST *WHO* IS YOUR DAD?

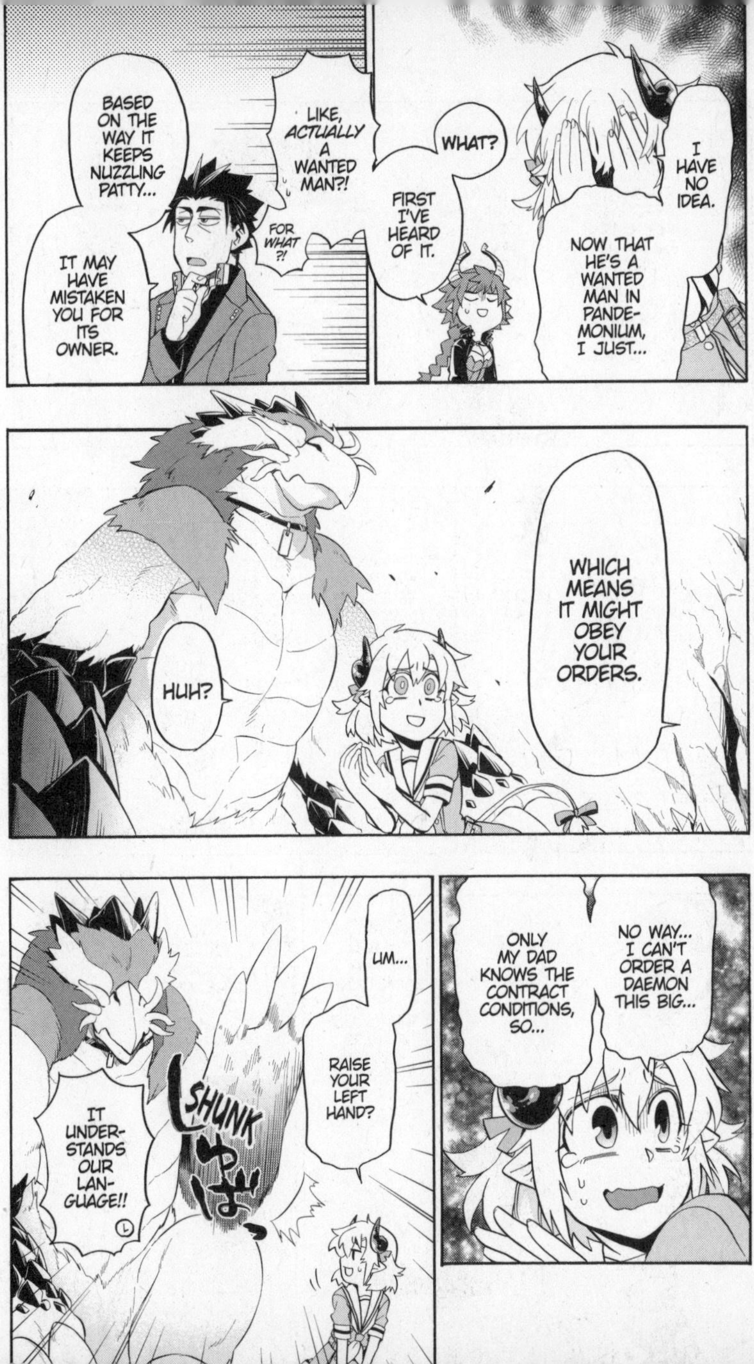
I HAVE NO IDEA.
NOW THAT HE'S A WANTED MAN IN PANDE-MONIUM, I JUST...
WHAT?
FIRST I'VE HEARD OF IT.
LIKE, *ACTUALLY* A WANTED MAN?!
FOR WHAT ?!
BASED ON THE WAY IT KEEPS NUZZLING PATTY...
IT MAY HAVE MISTAKEN YOU FOR ITS OWNER.
WHICH MEANS IT MIGHT OBEY YOUR ORDERS.
HUH?
NO WAY... I CAN'T ORDER A DAEMON THIS BIG...
ONLY MY DAD KNOWS THE CONTRACT CONDITIONS, SO...
UM...
RAISE YOUR LEFT HAND?
SHUNK
IT UNDER-STANDS OUR LAN-GUAGE!!

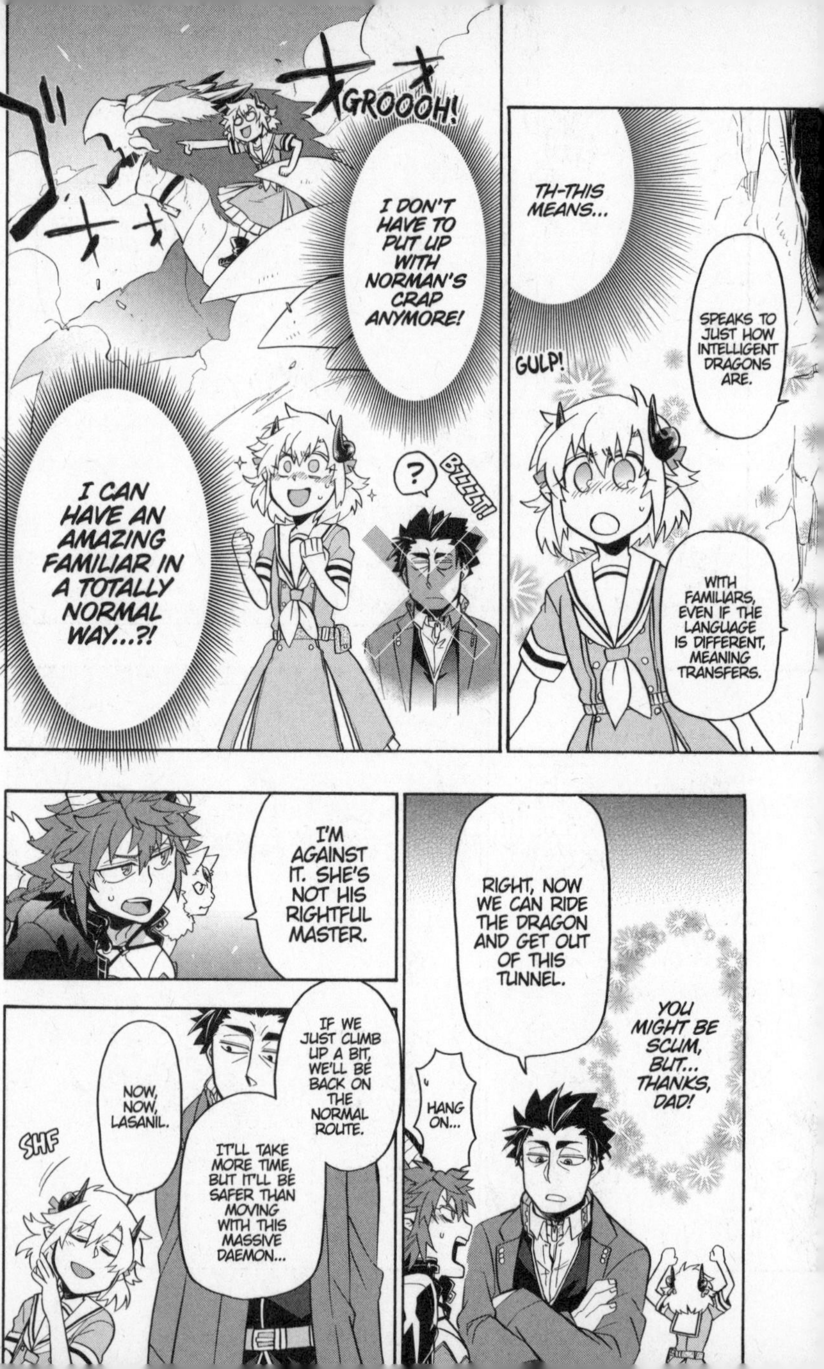
WITH FAMILIARS, EVEN IF THE LANGUAGE IS DIFFERENT, MEANING TRANSFERS.
SPEAKS TO JUST HOW INTELLIGENT DRAGONS ARE.
GULP!
TH-THIS MEANS...
GROOOH!
I DON'T HAVE TO PUT UP WITH NORMAN'S CRAP ANYMORE!
I CAN HAVE AN AMAZING FAMILIAR IN A TOTALLY NORMAL WAY...?!
?
BZZZT!
RIGHT, NOW WE CAN RIDE THE DRAGON AND GET OUT OF THIS TUNNEL.
YOU MIGHT BE SCUM, BUT... THANKS, DAD!
HANG ON...
I'M AGAINST IT. SHE'S NOT HIS RIGHTFUL MASTER.
SHF
NOW, NOW, LASANIL.
IF WE JUST CLIMB UP A BIT, WE'LL BE BACK ON THE NORMAL ROUTE.
IT'LL TAKE MORE TIME, BUT IT'LL BE SAFER THAN MOVING WITH THIS MASSIVE DAEMON...

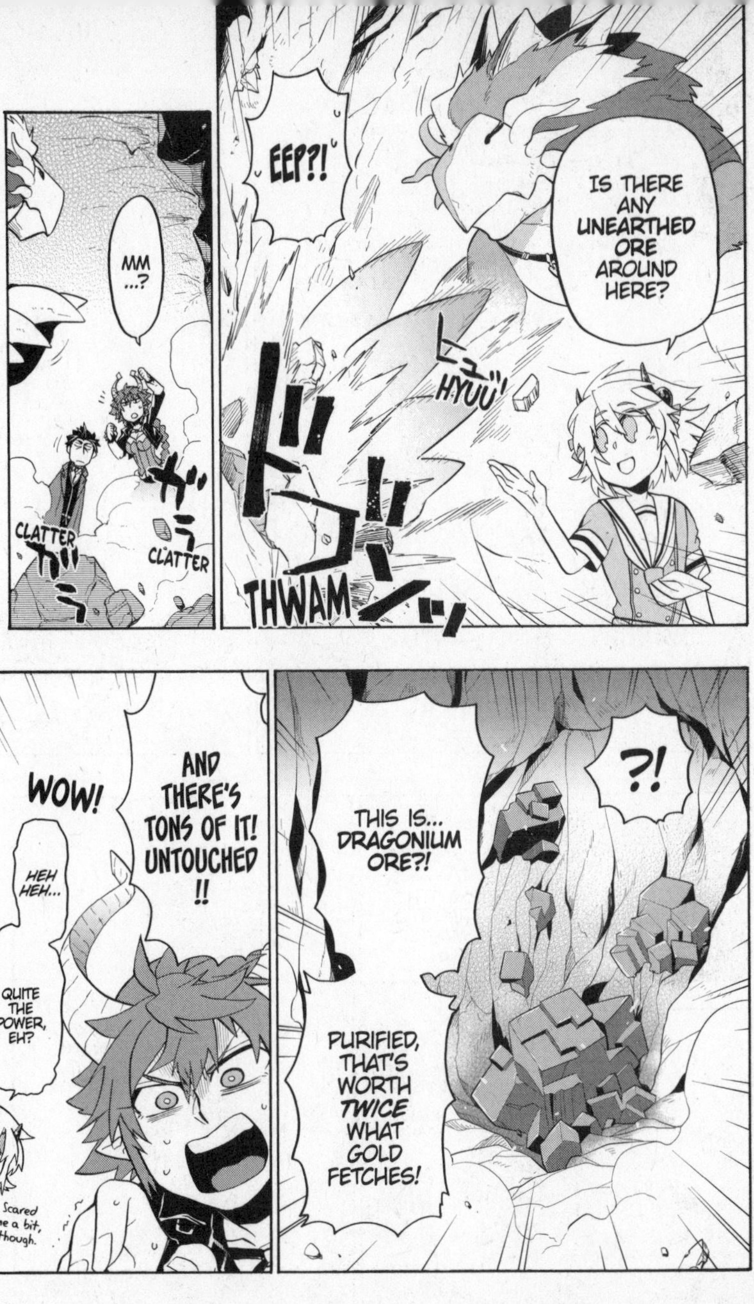
IS THERE ANY UNEARTHED ORE AROUND HERE?
EEP?!
HYUU
THWAM
MM ...?
CLATTER
CLATTER
?!
THIS IS... DRAGONIUM ORE?!
PURIFIED, THAT'S WORTH *TWICE* WHAT GOLD FETCHES!
AND THERE'S TONS OF IT! UNTOUCHED!!
WOW!
HEH HEH...
QUITE THE POWER, EH?
Scared me a bit, though.

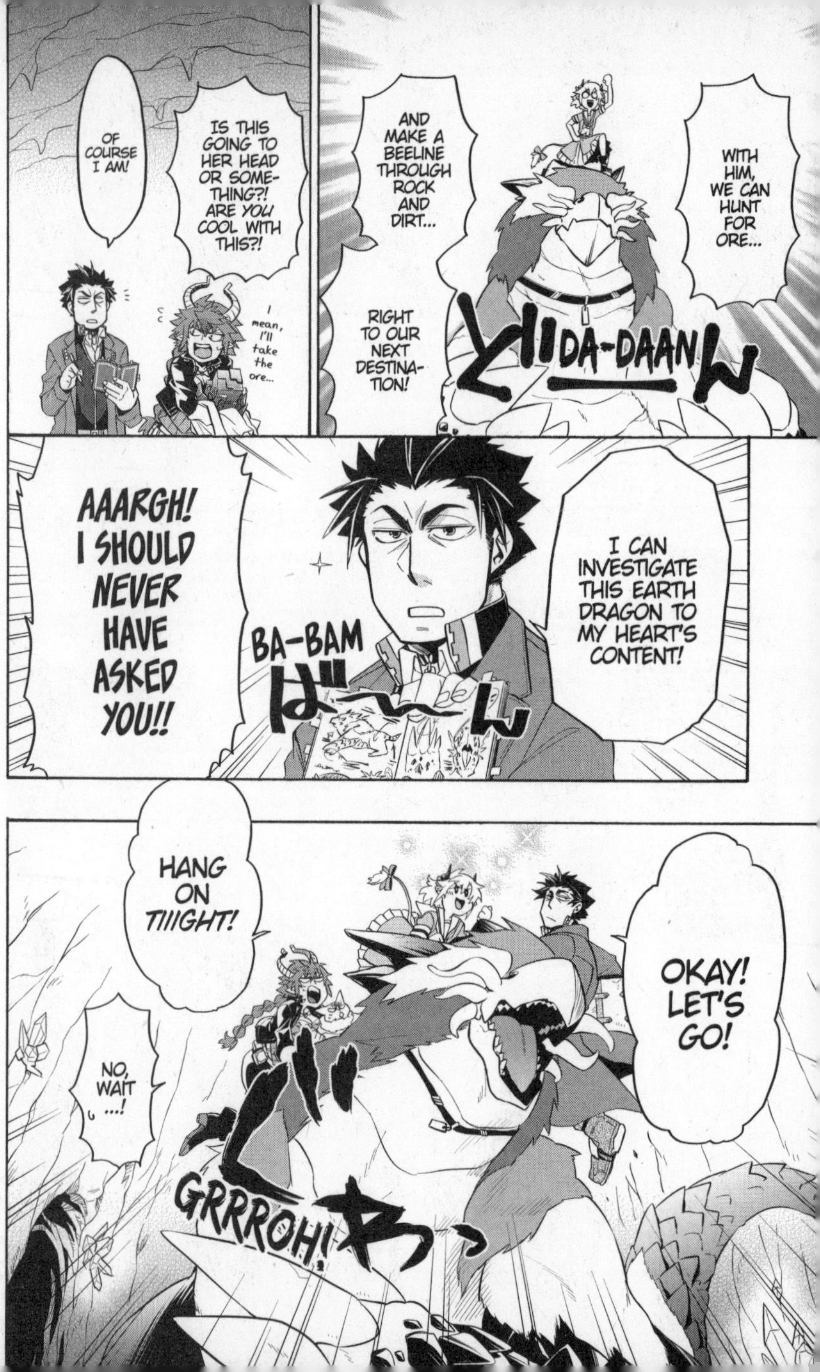
WITH HIM, WE CAN HUNT FOR ORE...
AND MAKE A BEELINE THROUGH ROCK AND DIRT...
RIGHT TO OUR NEXT DESTINATION!
DA-DAAN
IS THIS GOING TO HER HEAD OR SOME-THING?! ARE YOU COOL WITH THIS?!
OF COURSE I AM!
I mean, I'll take the ore...
I CAN INVESTIGATE THIS EARTH DRAGON TO MY HEART'S CONTENT!
BA-BAM
AAARGH! I SHOULD NEVER HAVE ASKED YOU!!
OKAY! LET'S GO!
HANG ON TIIIGHT!
NO, WAIT...!
GRRROH!

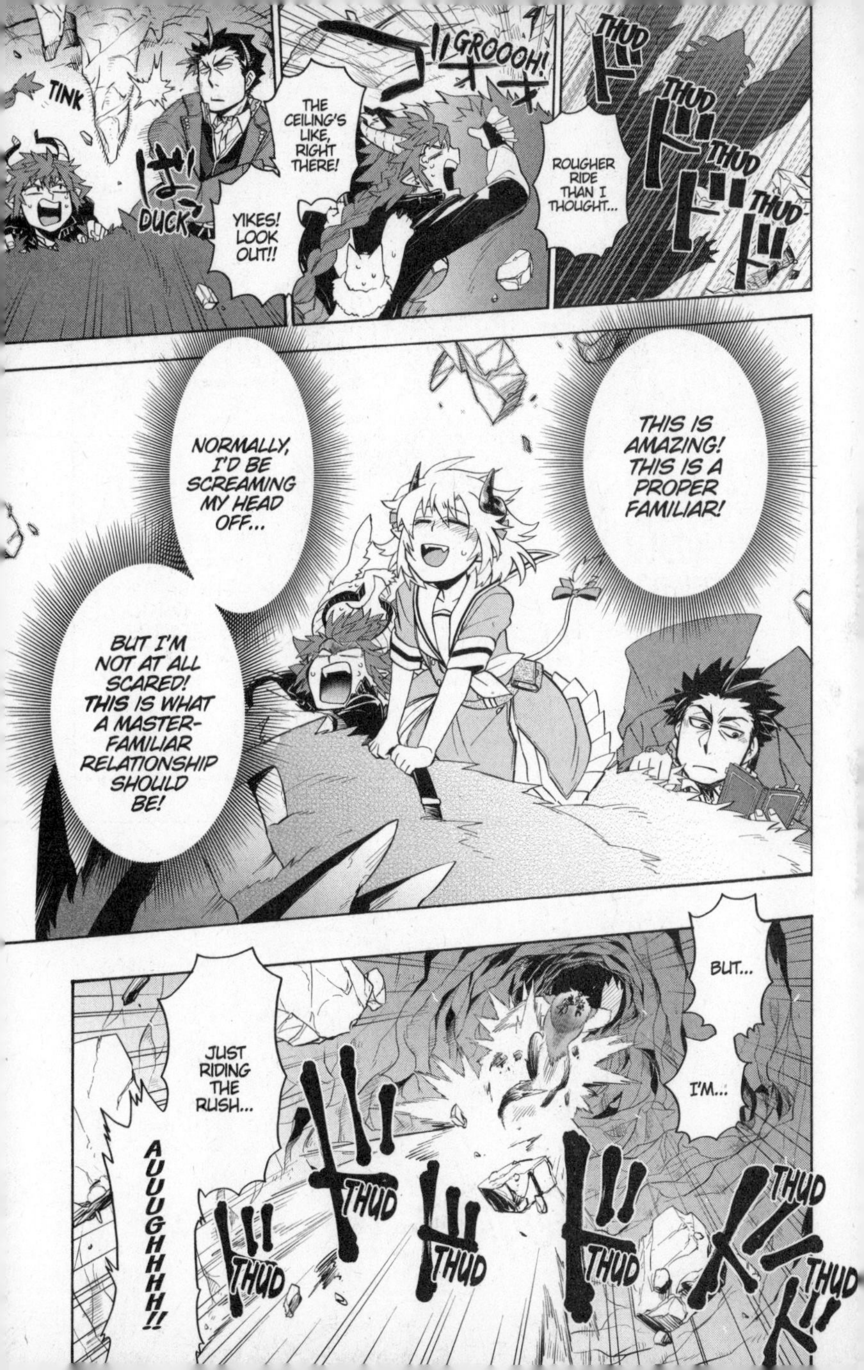
THUD
THUD
THUD
THUD
ROUGHER RIDE THAN I THOUGHT...
GROOOH!
THE CEILING'S LIKE, RIGHT THERE!
YIKES! LOOK OUT!!
TINK
DUCK
THIS IS AMAZING! THIS IS A PROPER FAMILIAR!
NORMALLY, I'D BE SCREAMING MY HEAD OFF...
BUT I'M NOT AT ALL SCARED! THIS IS WHAT A MASTER-FAMILIAR RELATIONSHIP SHOULD BE!
BUT...
I'M...
JUST RIDING THE RUSH...
AUUUGHHHH!!
THUD
THUD
THUD
THUD
THUD
THUD

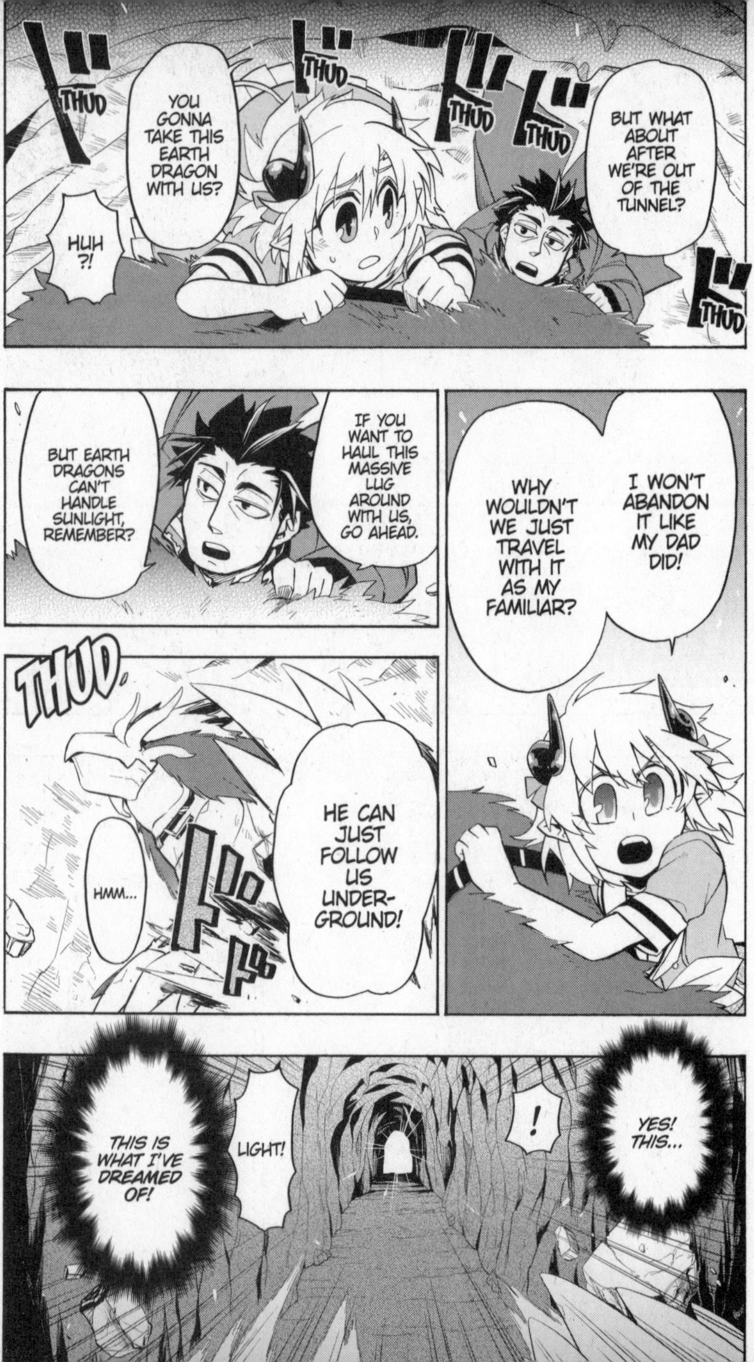
THUD
BUT WHAT ABOUT AFTER WE'RE OUT OF THE TUNNEL?
THUD
THUD
THUD
YOU GONNA TAKE THIS EARTH DRAGON WITH US?
THUD
HUH ?!
I WON'T ABANDON IT LIKE MY DAD DID!
WHY WOULDN'T WE JUST TRAVEL WITH IT AS MY FAMILIAR?
IF YOU WANT TO HAUL THIS MASSIVE LUG AROUND WITH US, GO AHEAD.
BUT EARTH DRAGONS CAN'T HANDLE SUNLIGHT, REMEMBER?
THUD.
HE CAN JUST FOLLOW US UNDER-GROUND!
HMM...
YES! THIS...
!
LIGHT!
THIS IS WHAT I'VE DREAMED OF!

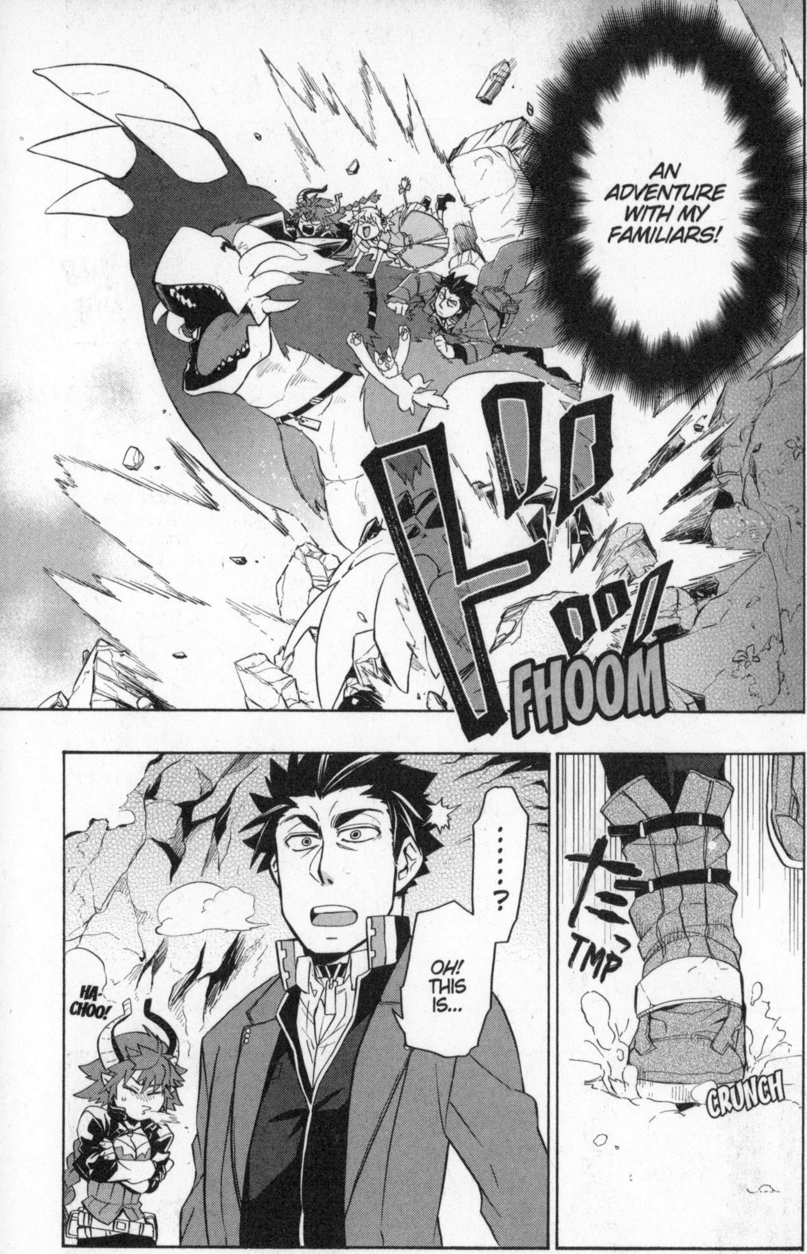
AN ADVENTURE WITH MY FAMILIARS!
FHOOM
TMP
CRUNCH
......?
OH! THIS IS...
HA-CHOO!

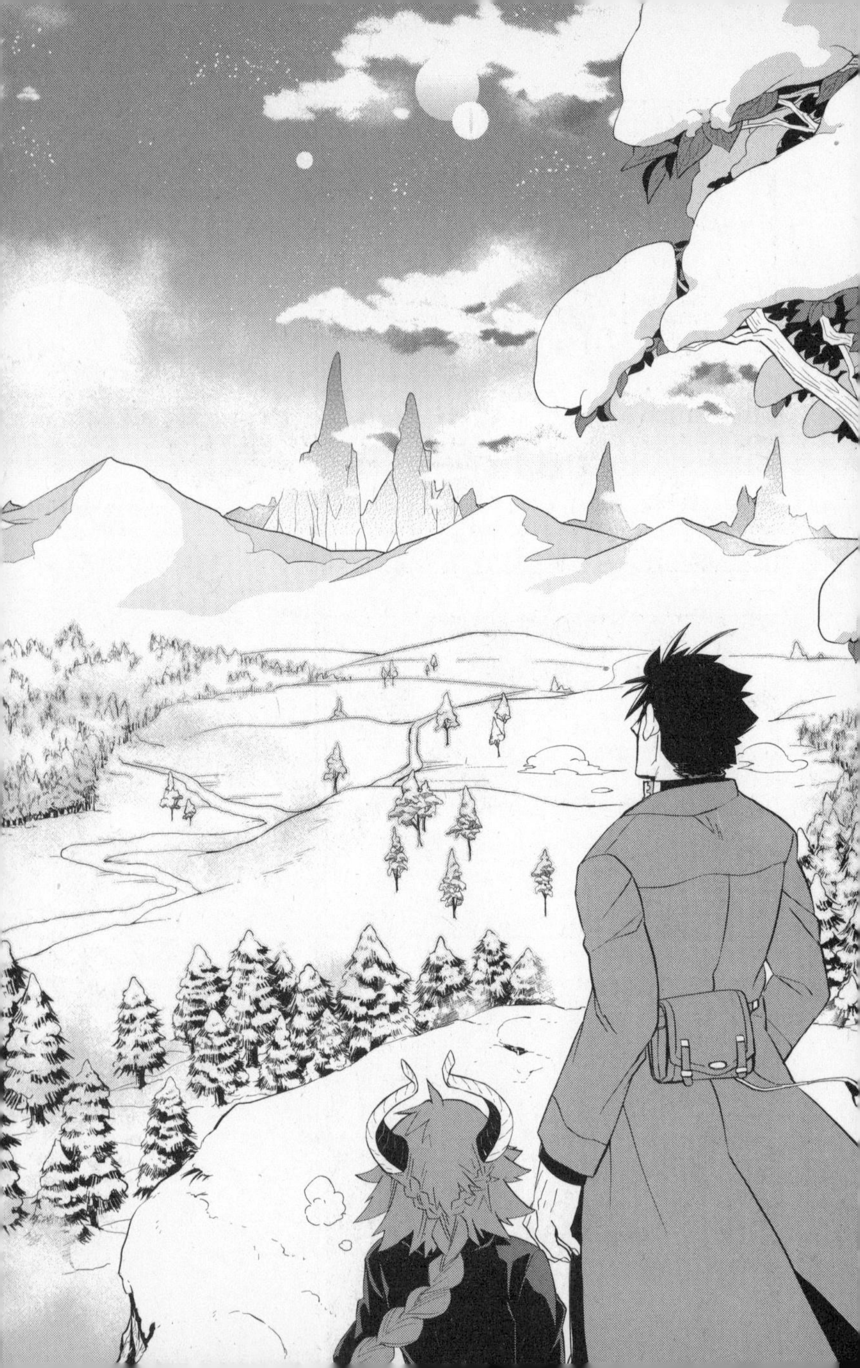

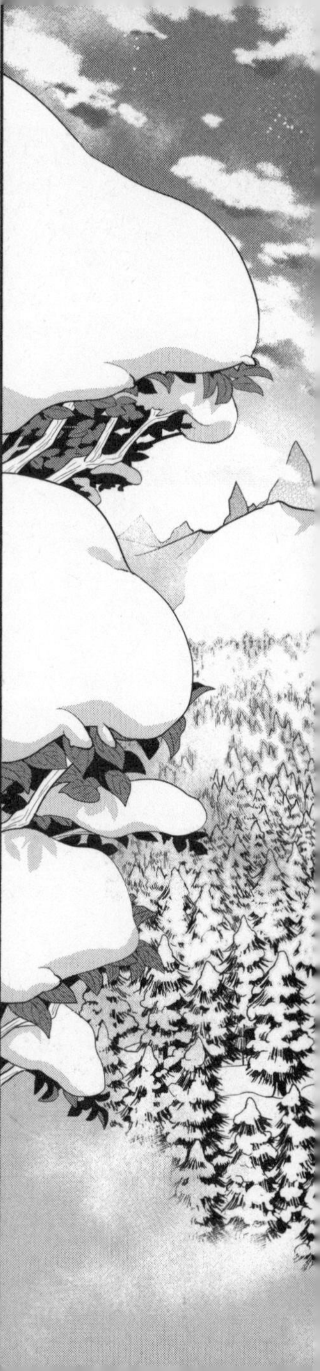
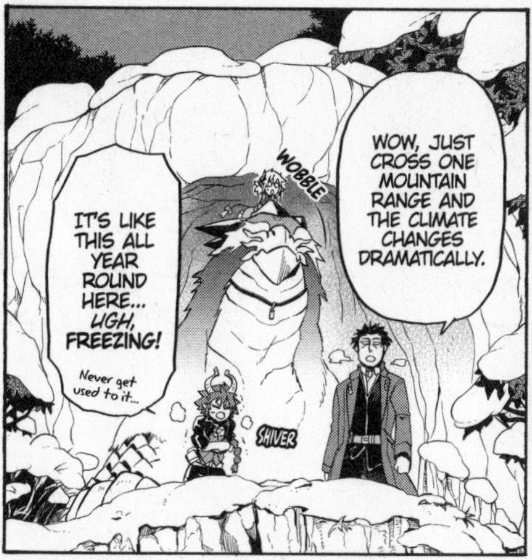
WOW, JUST CROSS ONE MOUNTAIN RANGE AND THE CLIMATE CHANGES DRAMATICALLY.
WOBBLE
IT'S LIKE THIS ALL YEAR ROUND HERE... UGH, FREEZING!
Never get used to it...
SHIVER
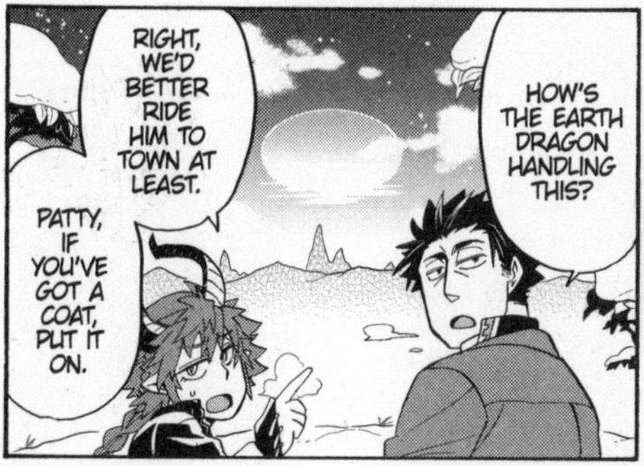
HOW'S THE EARTH DRAGON HANDLING THIS?
RIGHT, WE'D BETTER RIDE HIM TO TOWN AT LEAST.
PATTY, IF YOU'VE GOT A COAT, PUT IT ON.
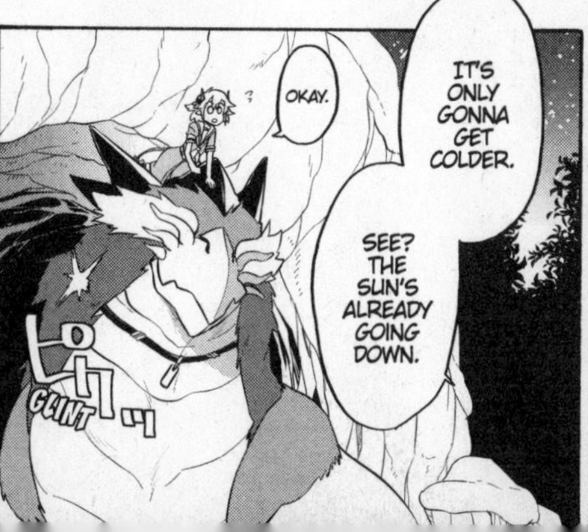
IT'S ONLY GONNA GET COLDER.
SEE? THE SUN'S ALREADY GOING DOWN.
OKAY.
GLINT

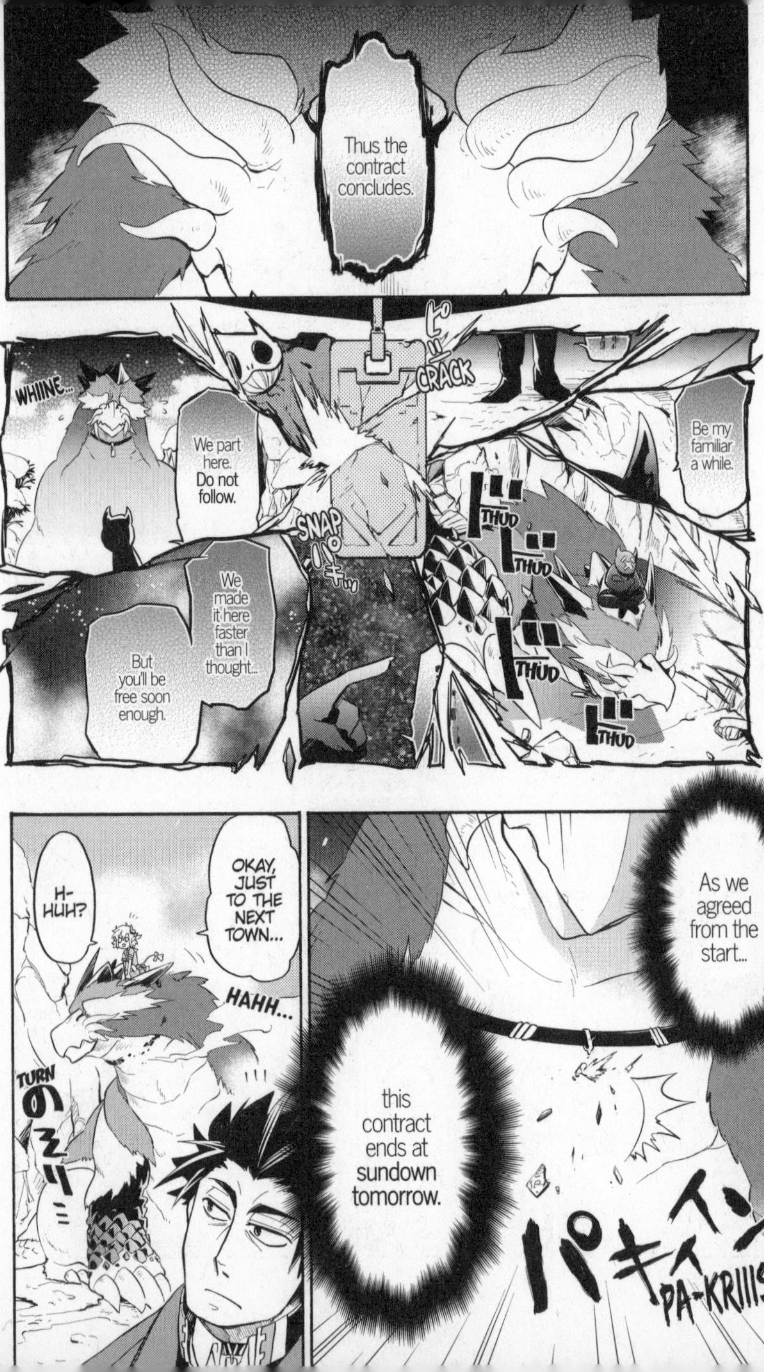
Thus the contract concludes.
CRACK
Be my familiar a while.
THUD
THUD
THUD
THUD
WHIINE...
We part here. Do not follow.
SNAP
We made it here faster than I thought...
But you'll be free soon enough.
As we agreed from the start...
this contract ends at sundown tomorrow.
PA-KRIIISH
OKAY, JUST TO THE NEXT TOWN...
H-HUH?
HAHH...
TURN

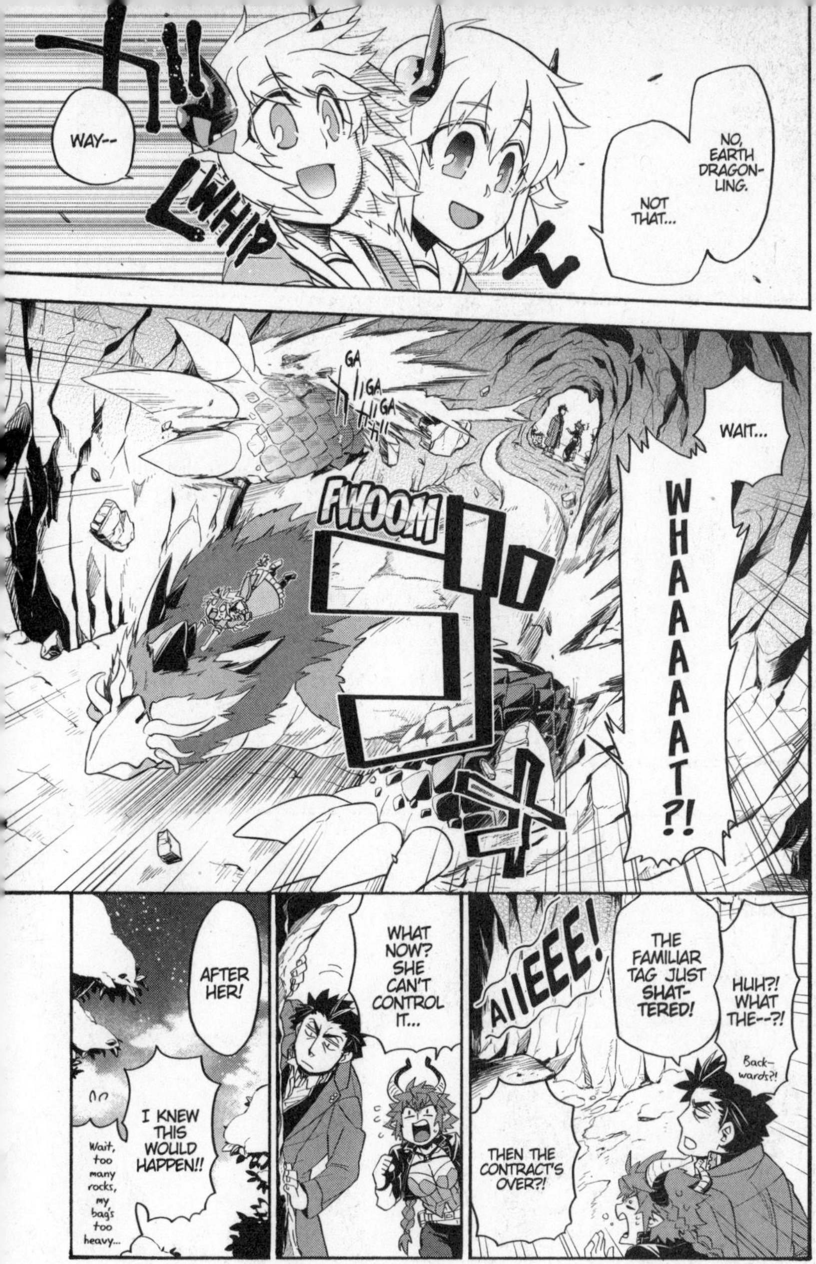
NO, EARTH DRAGON-LING.
NOT THAT...
WAY--
WHIP
WAIT...
WHAAAAAAT?!
GA GA GA!!
FWOOM
HUH?! WHAT THE--?!
Back-wards?!
THE FAMILIAR TAG JUST SHAT-TERED!
AIIEEE!
THEN THE CONTRACT'S OVER?!
WHAT NOW? SHE CAN'T CONTROL IT...
AFTER HER!
I KNEW THIS WOULD HAPPEN!!
Wait, too many rocks, my bag's too heavy...

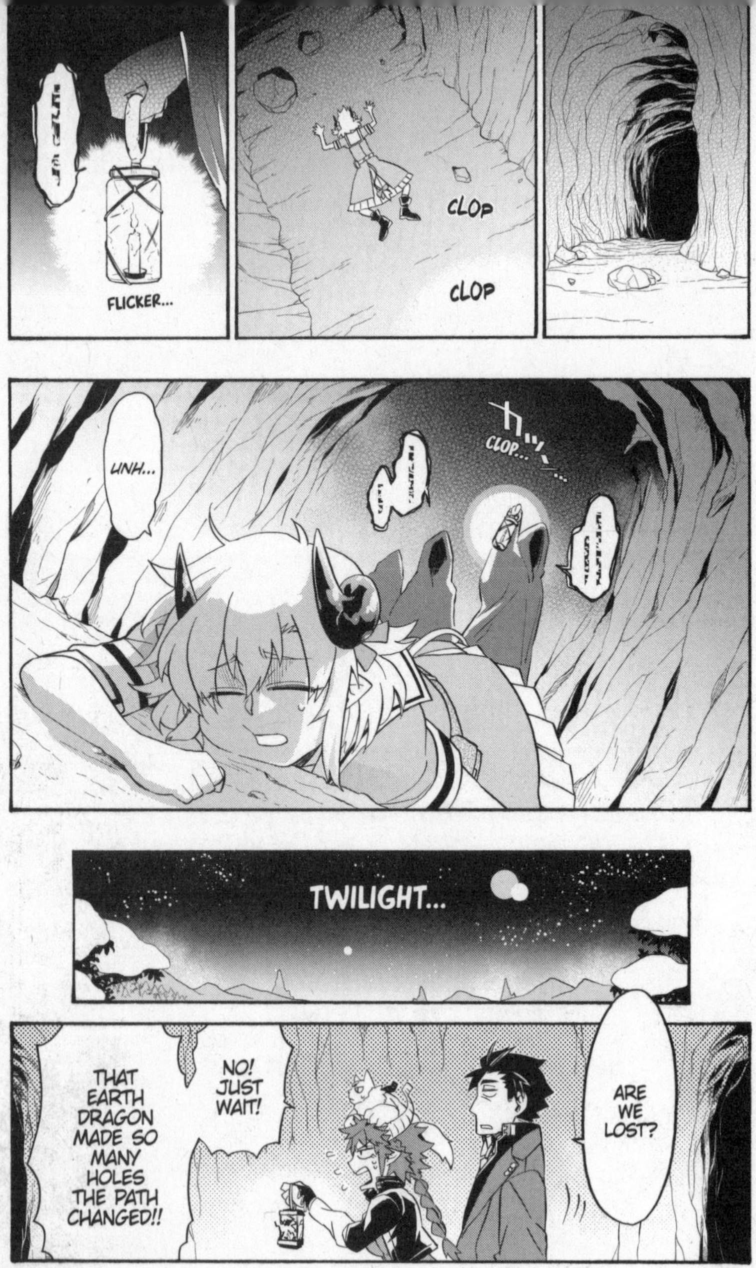
CLOP
CLOP
FLICKER...
カッ
CLOP...
UNH...
TWILIGHT...
ARE WE LOST?
NO! JUST WAIT!
THAT EARTH DRAGON MADE SO MANY HOLES THE PATH CHANGED!!

Sorry For My Familiar

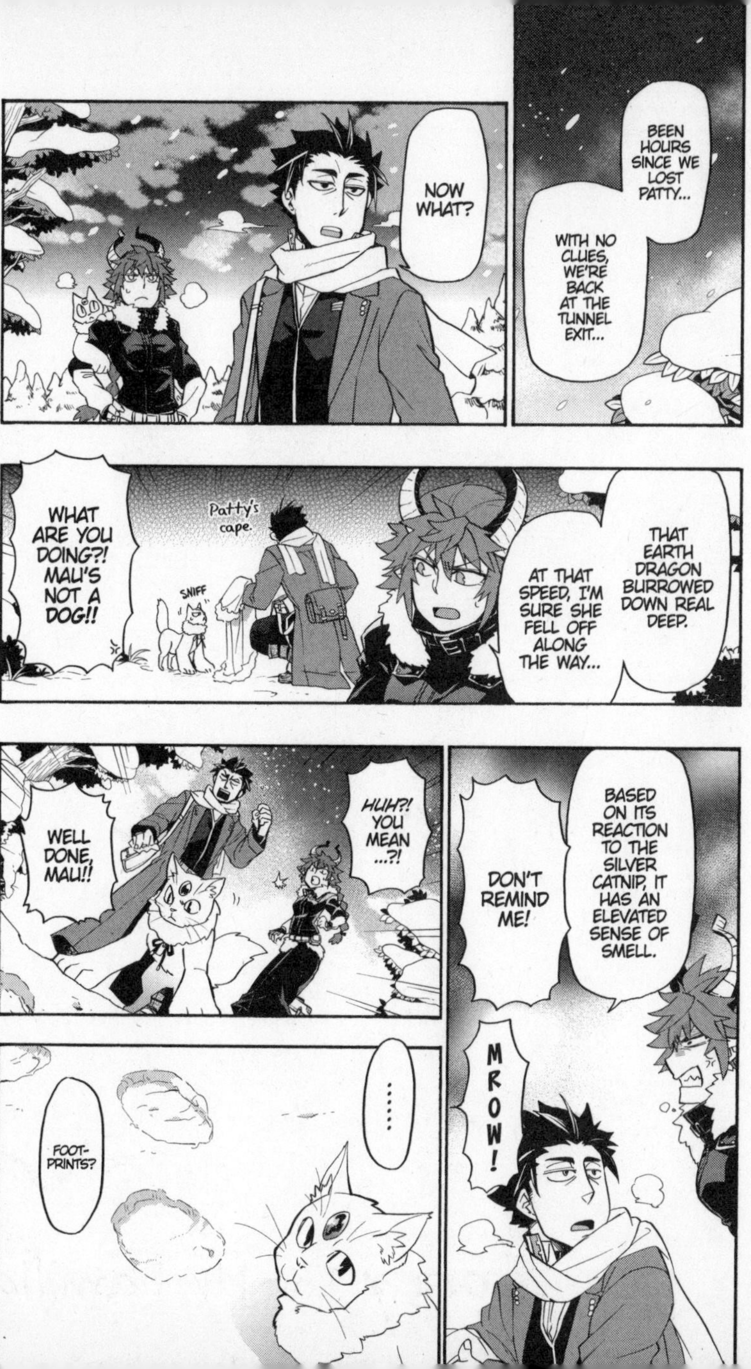
BEEN HOURS SINCE WE LOST PATTY...
WITH NO CLUES, WE'RE BACK AT THE TUNNEL EXIT...
NOW WHAT?
THAT EARTH DRAGON BURROWED DOWN REAL DEEP.
AT THAT SPEED, I'M SURE SHE FELL OFF ALONG THE WAY...
Patty's cape.
SNIFF
WHAT ARE YOU DOING?! MAU'S NOT A DOG!!
BASED ON ITS REACTION TO THE SILVER CATNIP, IT HAS AN ELEVATED SENSE OF SMELL.
DON'T REMIND ME!
MROW!
HUH?! YOU MEAN ...?!
WELL DONE, MAU!!
......
FOOT-PRINTS?

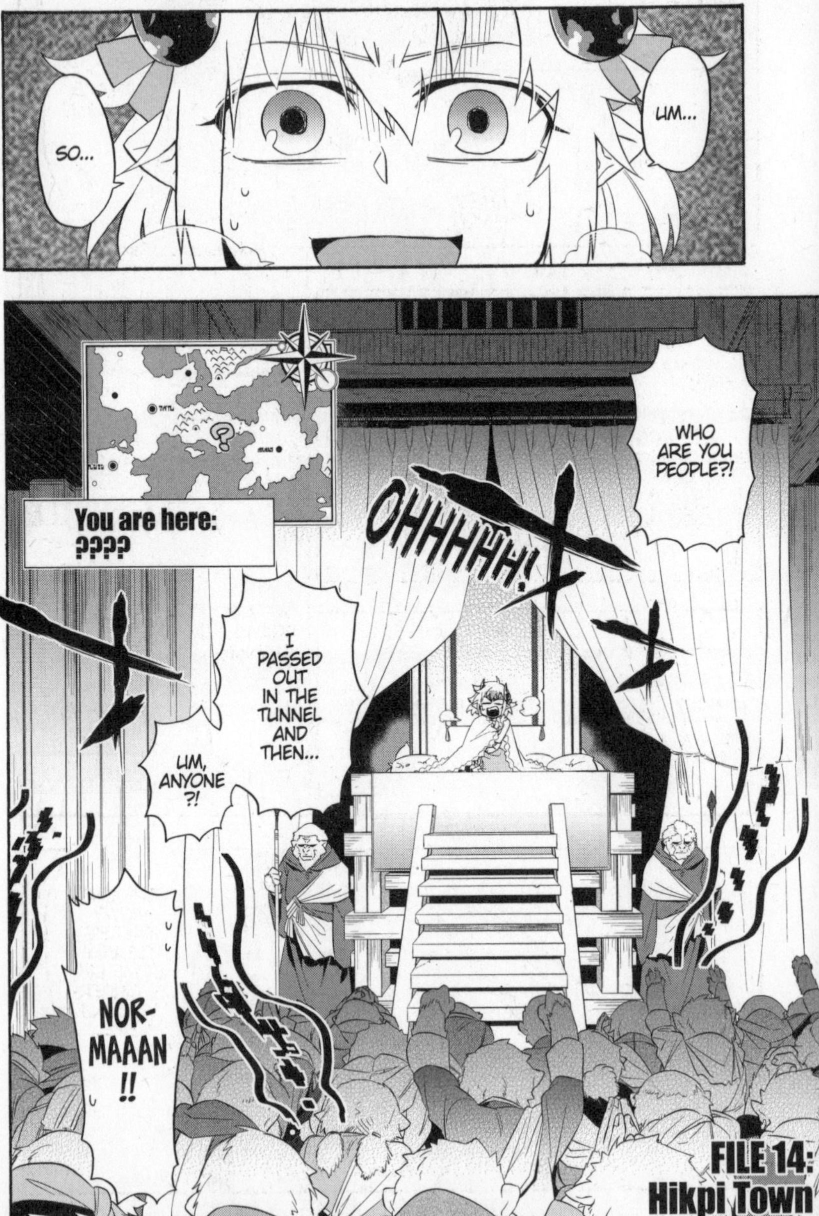
UM...
SO...
WHO ARE YOU PEOPLE?!
OHHHHHH!
You are here: ????
I PASSED OUT IN THE TUNNEL AND THEN...
UM, ANYONE?!
NOR-MAAAN!!

FILE 14: Hikpi Town

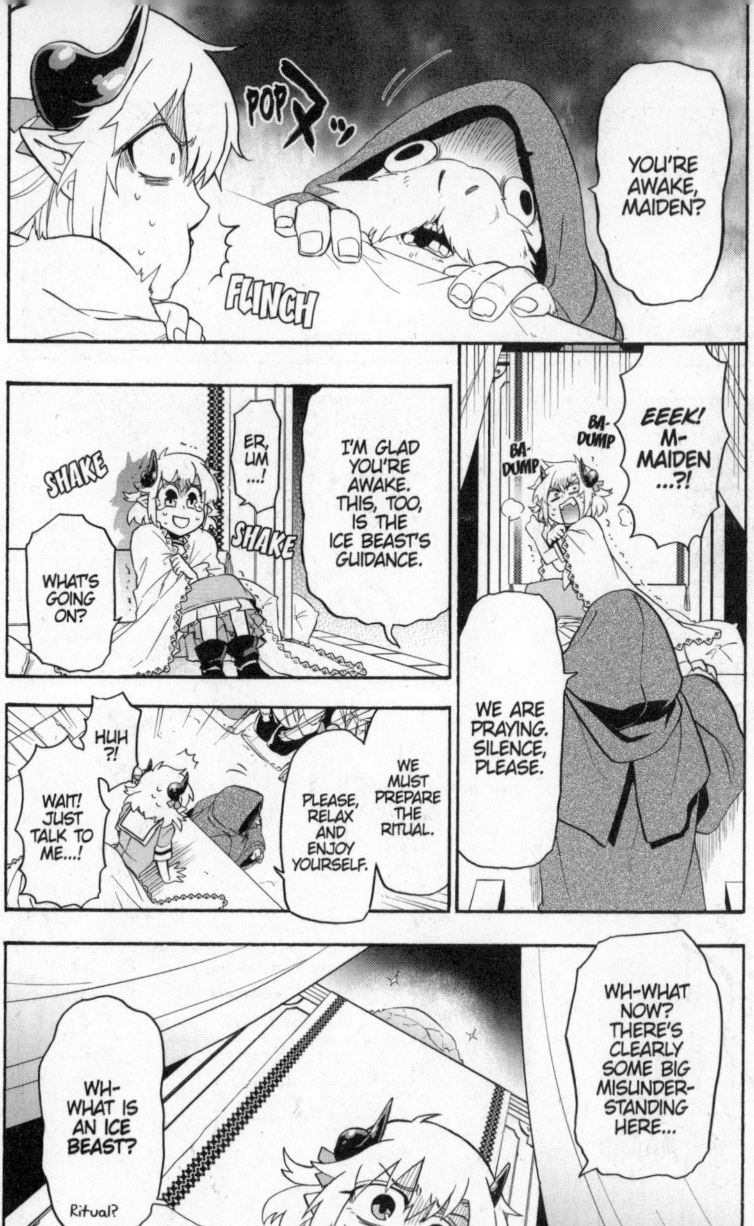
YOU'RE AWAKE, MAIDEN?
POP
FLINCH
EEEK! M-MAIDEN ...?!
BA-DUMP
BA-DUMP
WE ARE PRAYING. SILENCE, PLEASE.
I'M GLAD YOU'RE AWAKE. THIS, TOO, IS THE ICE BEAST'S GUIDANCE.
ER, UM ...!
SHAKE
SHAKE
WHAT'S GOING ON?
WE MUST PREPARE THE RITUAL.
PLEASE, RELAX AND ENJOY YOURSELF.
HUH ?!
WAIT! JUST TALK TO ME...!
WH-WHAT NOW? THERE'S CLEARLY SOME BIG MISUNDER-STANDING HERE...
WH-WHAT IS AN ICE BEAST?
Ritual?

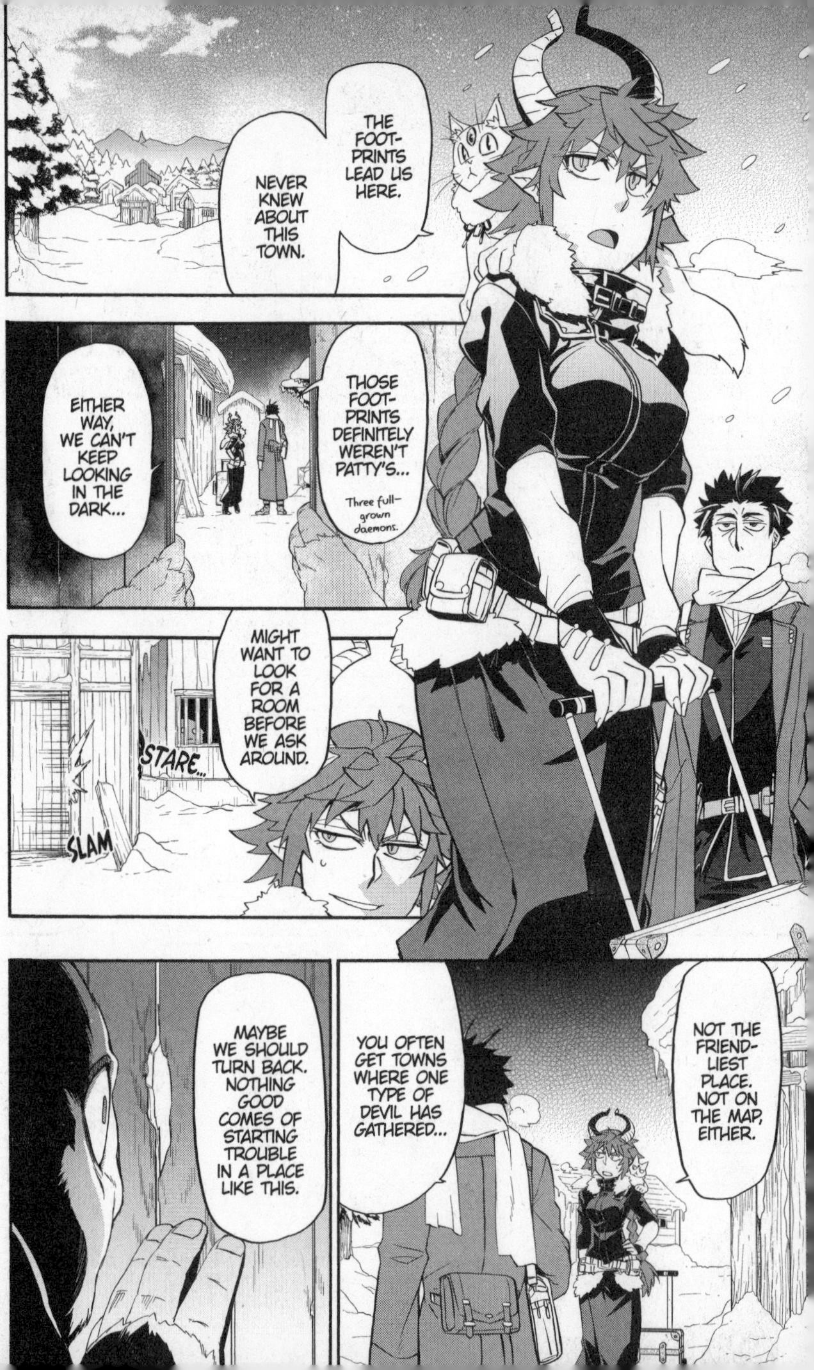
THE FOOT-PRINTS LEAD US HERE.
NEVER KNEW ABOUT THIS TOWN.
THOSE FOOT-PRINTS DEFINITELY WEREN'T PATTY'S...
Three full-grown daemons.
EITHER WAY, WE CAN'T KEEP LOOKING IN THE DARK...
MIGHT WANT TO LOOK FOR A ROOM BEFORE WE ASK AROUND.
STARE...
SLAM
NOT THE FRIEND-LIEST PLACE. NOT ON THE MAP, EITHER.
YOU OFTEN GET TOWNS WHERE ONE TYPE OF DEVIL HAS GATHERED...
MAYBE WE SHOULD TURN BACK. NOTHING GOOD COMES OF STARTING TROUBLE IN A PLACE LIKE THIS.

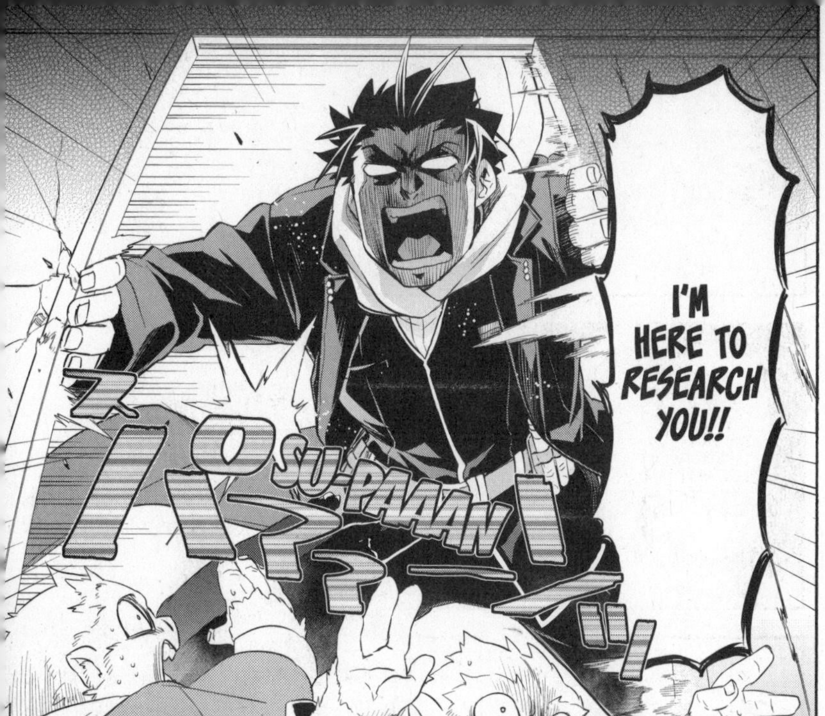
I'M HERE TO RESEARCH YOU!!
SU-PAAAAN!

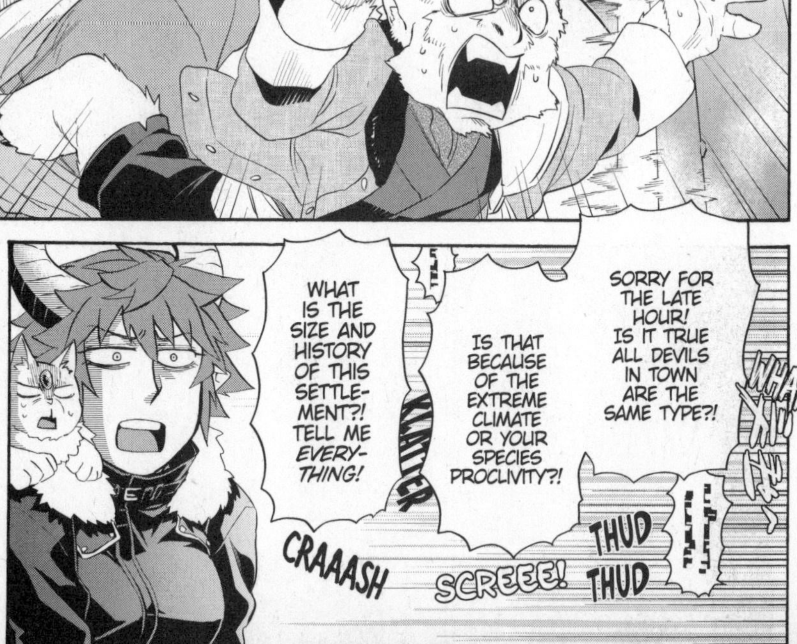
WHAM
THUD
THUD
SCREEE!
SORRY FOR THE LATE HOUR! IS IT TRUE ALL DEVILS IN TOWN ARE THE SAME TYPE?!
IS THAT BECAUSE OF THE EXTREME CLIMATE OR YOUR SPECIES PROCLIVITY?!
KLATTER
WHAT IS THE SIZE AND HISTORY OF THIS SETTLE-MENT?! TELL ME *EVERY-THING!*
CRAAASH

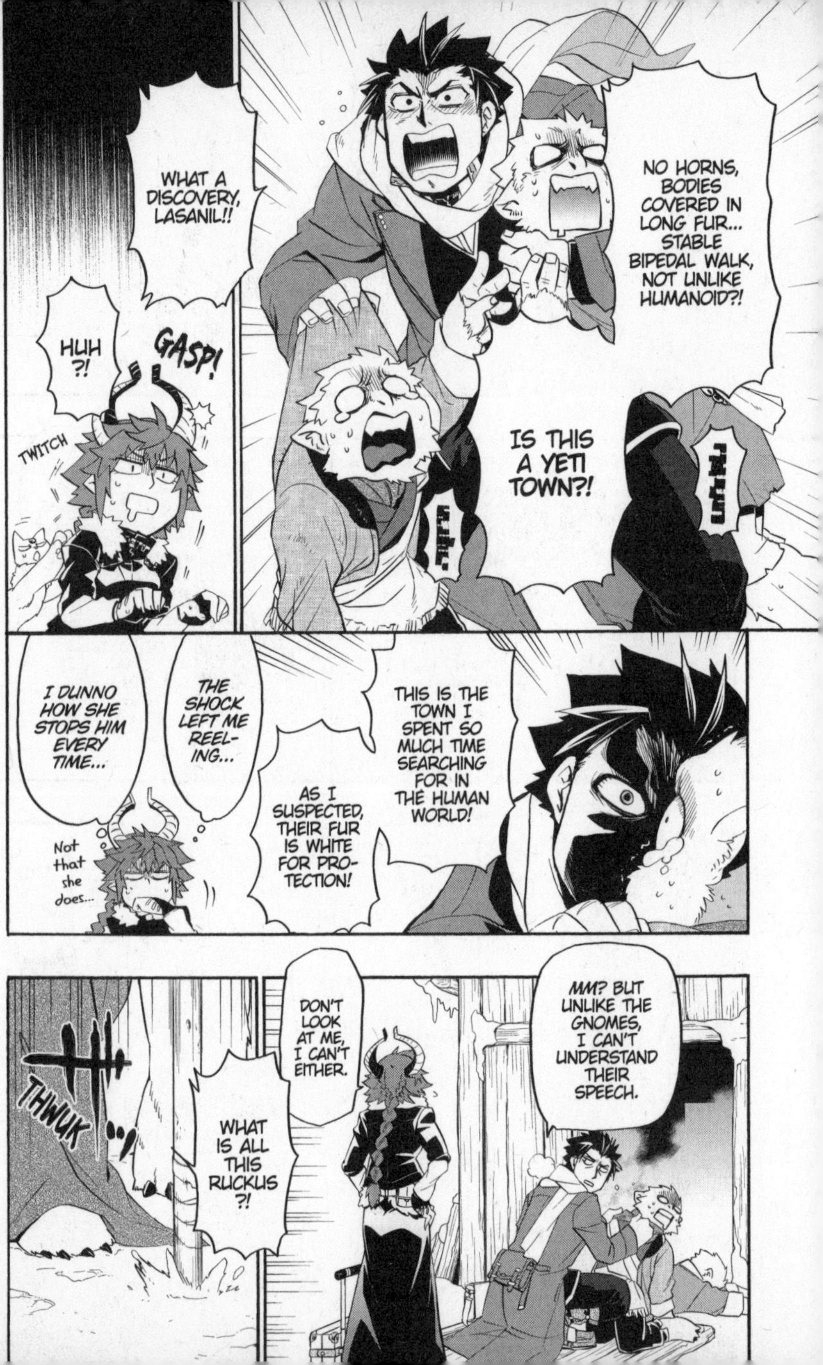
NO HORNS, BODIES COVERED IN LONG FUR... STABLE BIPEDAL WALK, NOT UNLIKE HUMANOID?!
IS THIS A YETI TOWN?!
WHAT A DISCOVERY, LASANIL!!
GASP!
HUH ?!
TWITCH
THIS IS THE TOWN I SPENT SO MUCH TIME SEARCHING FOR IN THE HUMAN WORLD!
AS I SUSPECTED, THEIR FUR IS WHITE FOR PRO-TECTION!
THE SHOCK LEFT ME REEL-ING...
I DUNNO HOW SHE STOPS HIM EVERY TIME...
Not that she does...
MM? BUT UNLIKE THE GNOMES, I CAN'T UNDERSTAND THEIR SPEECH.
DON'T LOOK AT ME, I CAN'T EITHER.
WHAT IS ALL THIS RUCKUS ?!
THWUK

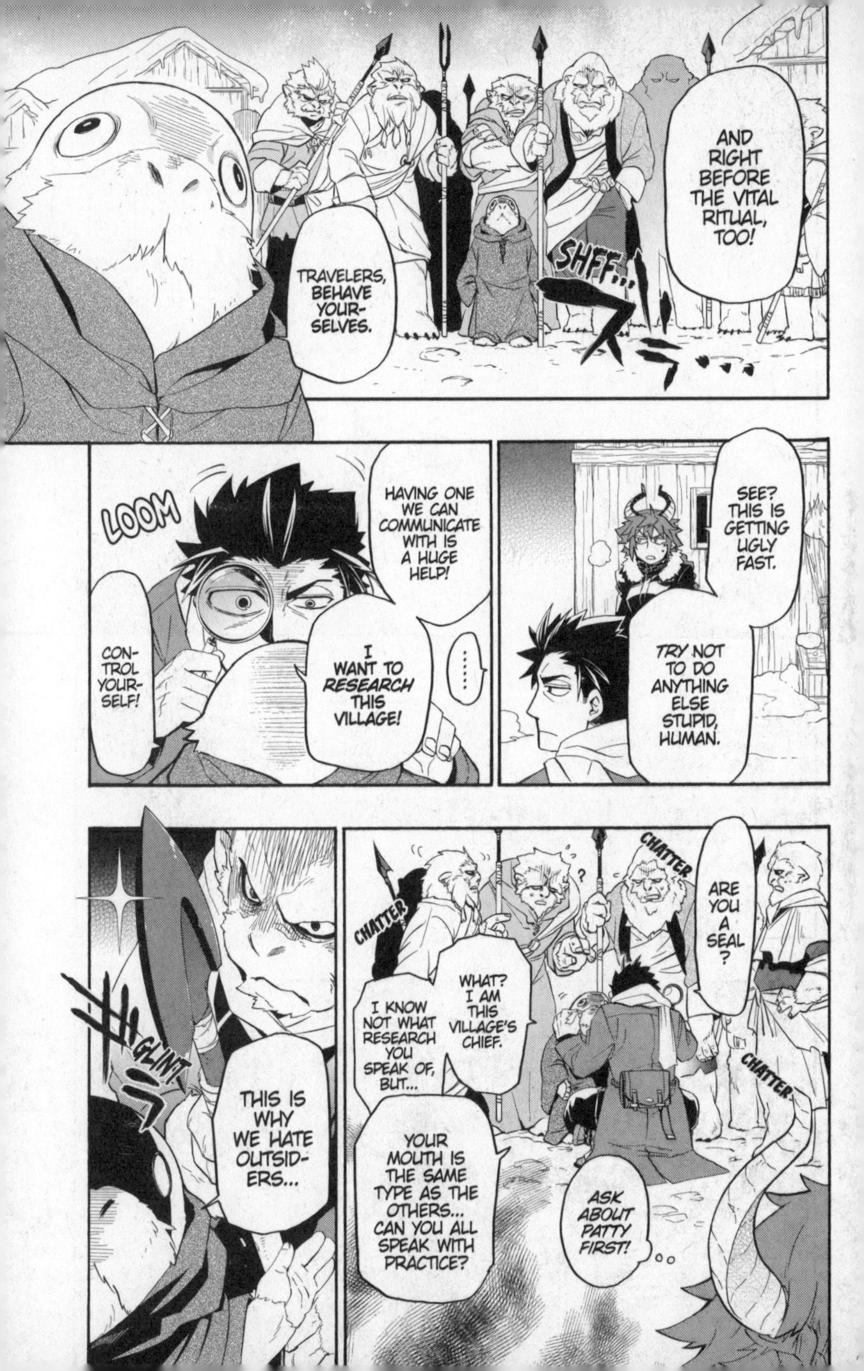
AND RIGHT BEFORE THE VITAL RITUAL, TOO!
SHFF...
TRAVELERS, BEHAVE YOURSELVES.
SEE? THIS IS GETTING UGLY FAST.
TRY NOT TO DO ANYTHING ELSE STUPID, HUMAN.
HAVING ONE WE CAN COMMUNICATE WITH IS A HUGE HELP!
LOOM
I WANT TO *RESEARCH* THIS VILLAGE!
......
CONTROL YOURSELF!
CHATTER
ARE YOU A SEAL?
WHAT? I AM THIS VILLAGE'S CHIEF.
CHATTER
I KNOW NOT WHAT RESEARCH YOU SPEAK OF, BUT...
CHATTER
YOUR MOUTH IS THE SAME TYPE AS THE OTHERS... CAN YOU ALL SPEAK WITH PRACTICE?
ASK ABOUT PATTY FIRST!
GLINT
THIS IS WHY WE HATE OUTSIDERS...

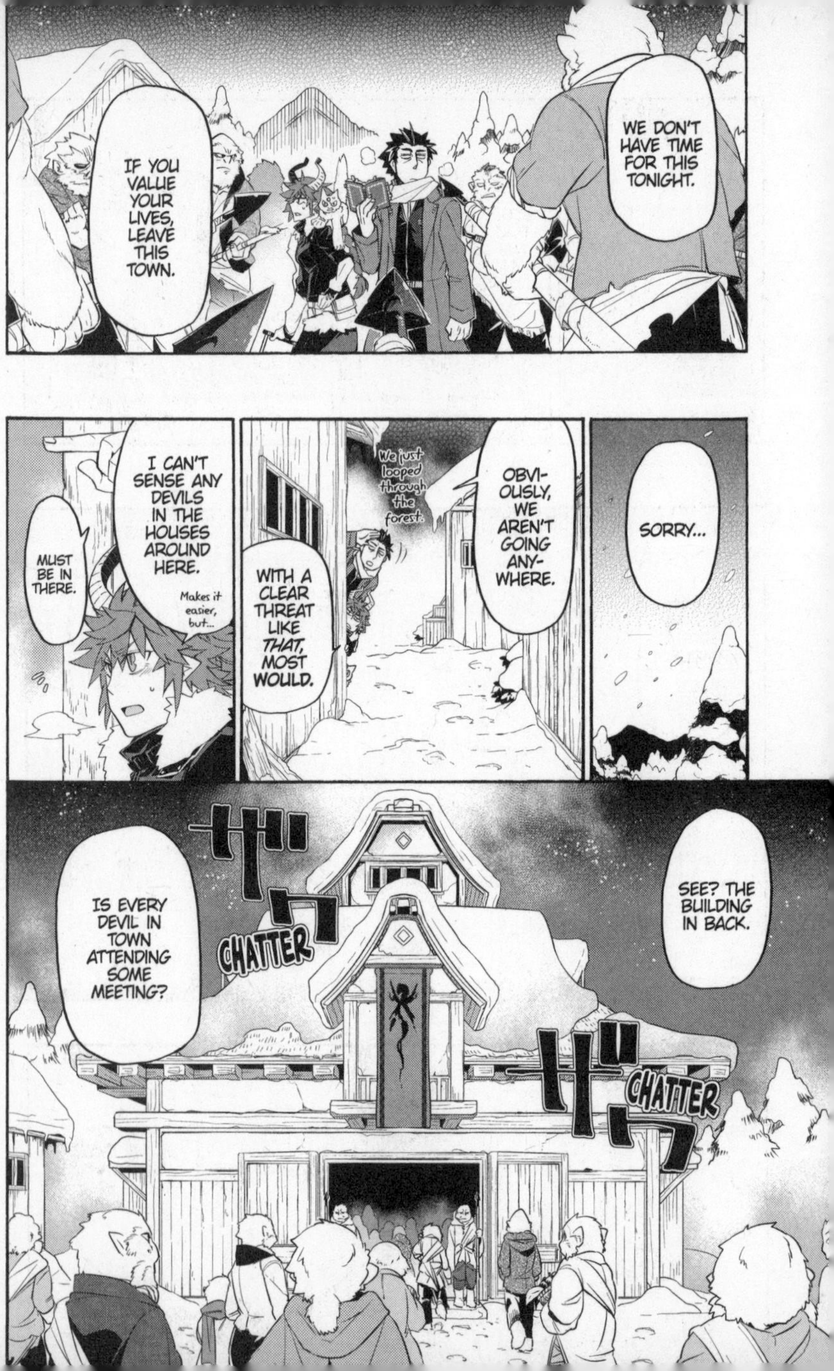

WE DON'T HAVE TIME FOR THIS TONIGHT.
IF YOU VALUE YOUR LIVES, LEAVE THIS TOWN.
SORRY...
OBVI-OUSLY, WE AREN'T GOING ANY-WHERE.
We just looped through the forest.
WITH A CLEAR THREAT LIKE THAT, MOST WOULD.
I CAN'T SENSE ANY DEVILS IN THE HOUSES AROUND HERE.
Makes it easier, but...
MUST BE IN THERE.
SEE? THE BUILDING IN BACK.
CHATTER
CHATTER
IS EVERY DEVIL IN TOWN ATTENDING SOME MEETING?

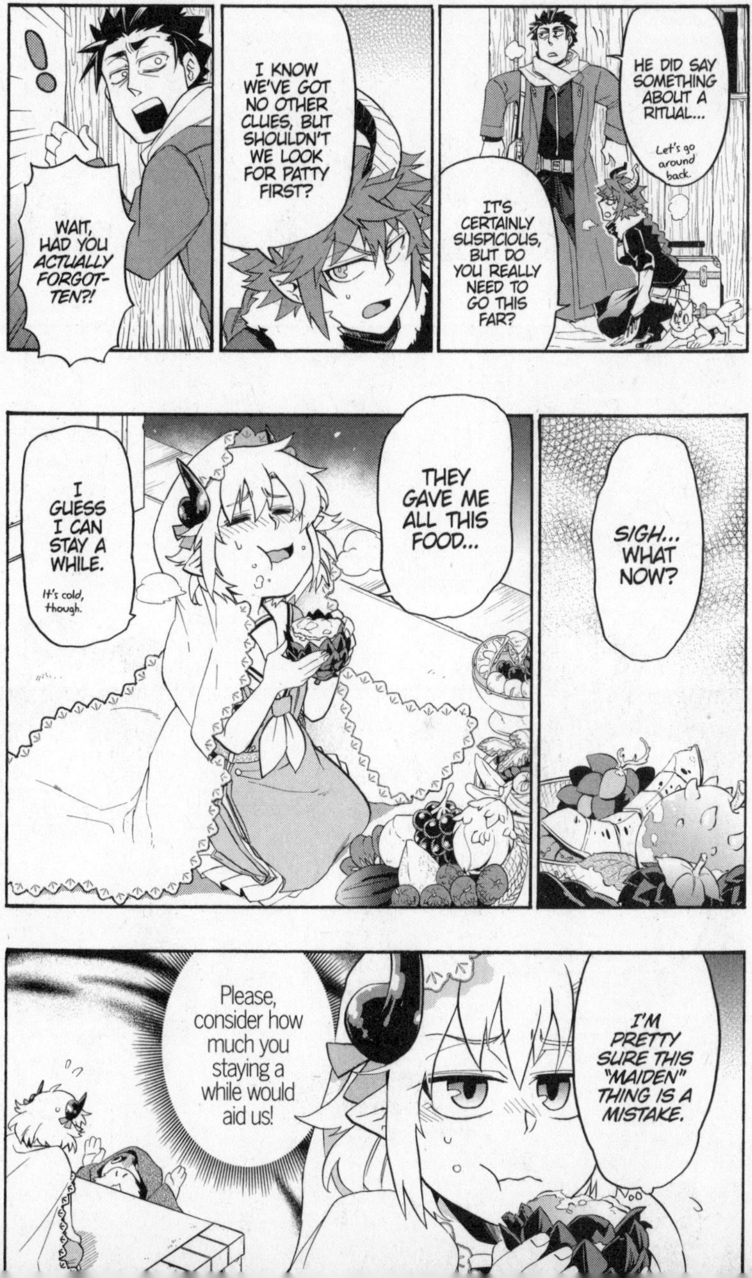
HE DID SAY SOMETHING ABOUT A RITUAL...
Let's go around back.
IT'S CERTAINLY SUSPICIOUS, BUT DO YOU REALLY NEED TO GO THIS FAR?
I KNOW WE'VE GOT NO OTHER CLUES, BUT SHOULDN'T WE LOOK FOR PATTY FIRST?
!
WAIT, HAD YOU ACTUALLY FORGOT-TEN?!
SIGH... WHAT NOW?
THEY GAVE ME ALL THIS FOOD...
I GUESS I CAN STAY A WHILE.
It's cold, though.
I'M PRETTY SURE THIS "MAIDEN" THING IS A MISTAKE.
Please, consider how much you staying a while would aid us!

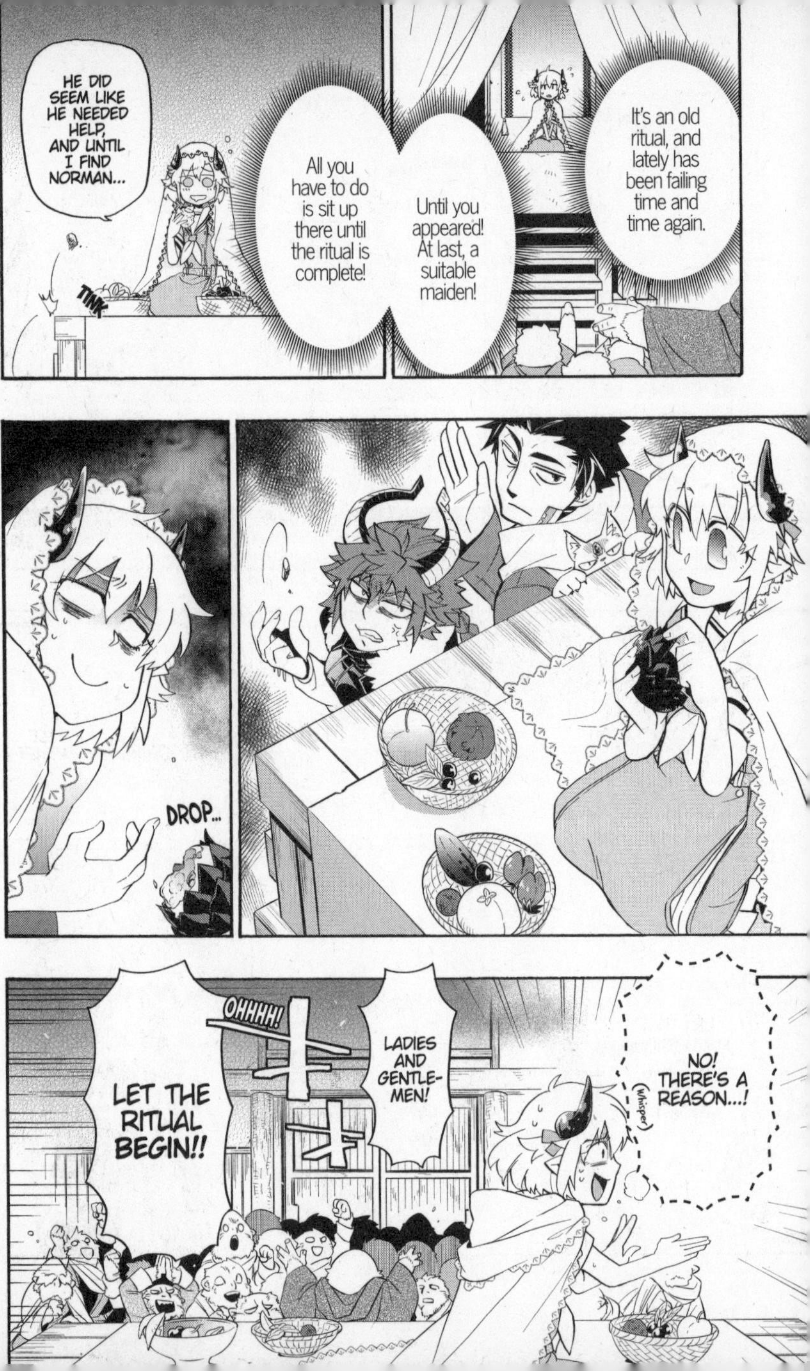
It's an old ritual, and lately has been failing time and time again.
Until you appeared! At last, a suitable maiden!
All you have to do is sit up there until the ritual is complete!
HE DID SEEM LIKE HE NEEDED HELP, AND UNTIL I FIND NORMAN...
TINK
DROP...
NO! THERE'S A REASON...!
(Whisper)
LADIES AND GENTLEMEN!
OHHHH!
LET THE RITUAL BEGIN!!

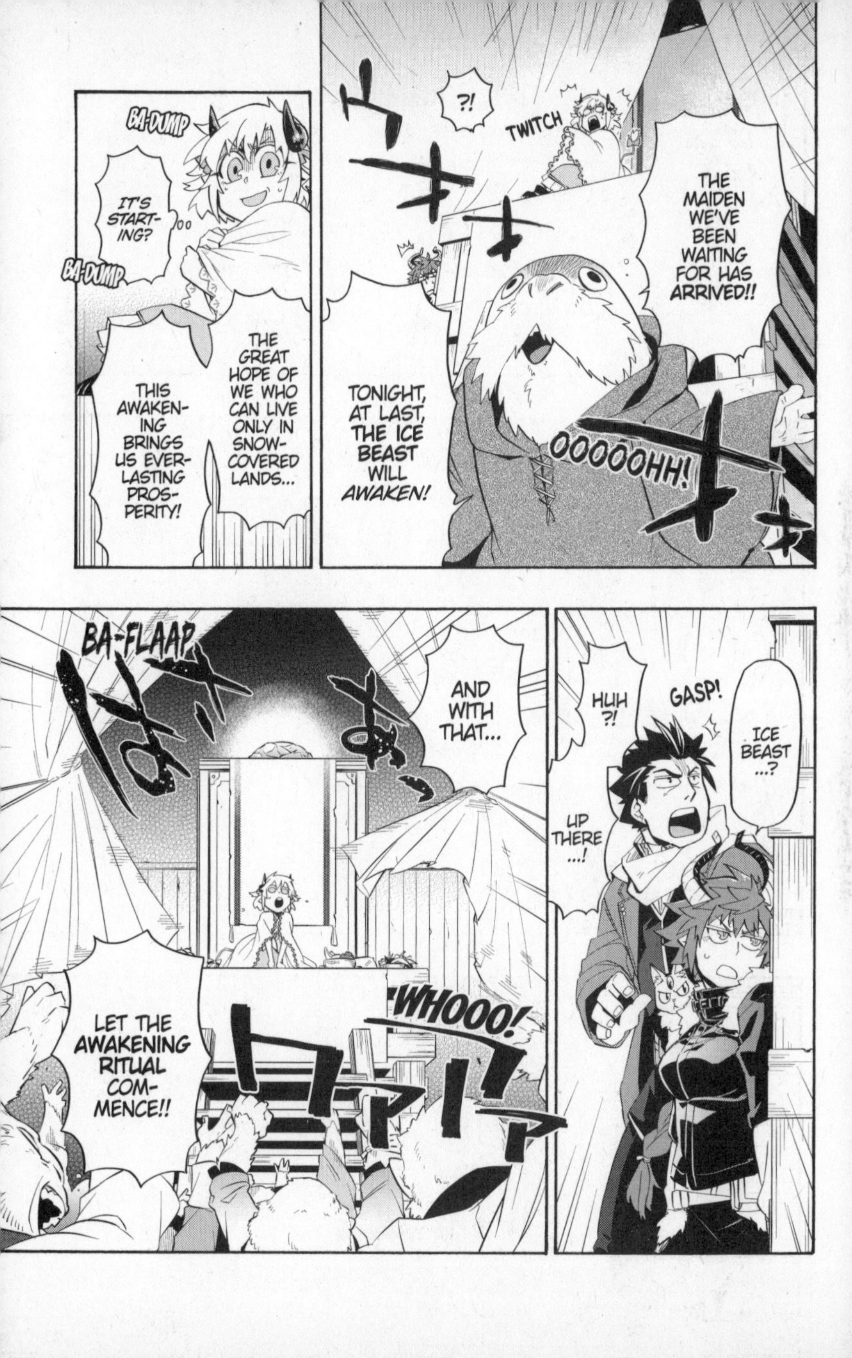
?!
TWITCH
THE MAIDEN WE'VE BEEN WAITING FOR HAS ARRIVED!!
OOOOOHH!
TONIGHT, AT LAST, THE ICE BEAST WILL AWAKEN!
BA-DUMP
IT'S STARTING?
BA-DUMP
THE GREAT HOPE OF WE WHO CAN LIVE ONLY IN SNOW-COVERED LANDS...
THIS AWAKENING BRINGS US EVERLASTING PROSPERITY!
GASP!
ICE BEAST ...?
HUH ?!
UP THERE ...!
AND WITH THAT...
BA-FLAAP
WHOOO!
LET THE AWAKENING RITUAL COMMENCE!!

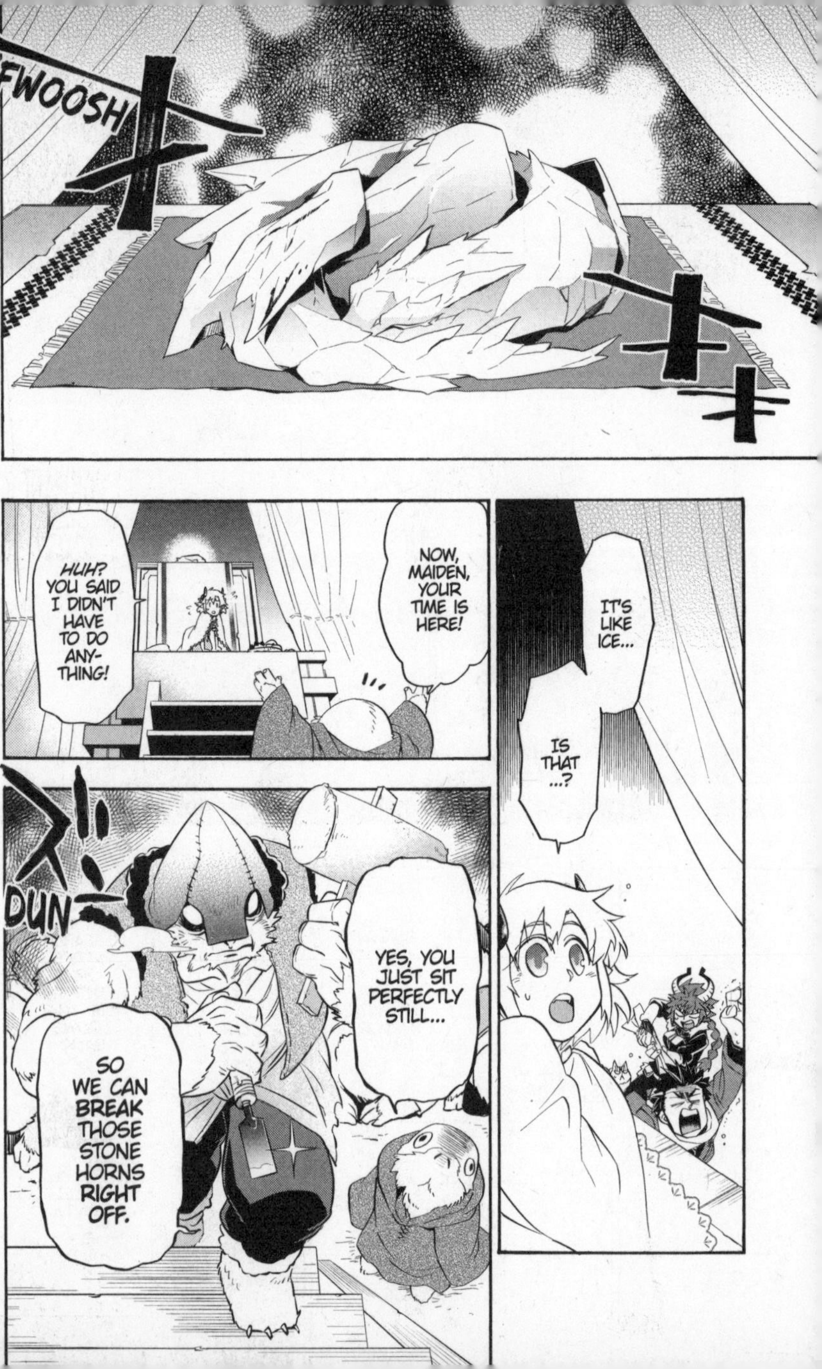
FWOOSH
IT'S LIKE ICE...
IS THAT ...?
NOW, MAIDEN, YOUR TIME IS HERE!
HUH? YOU SAID I DIDN'T HAVE TO DO ANY-THING!
YES, YOU JUST SIT PERFECTLY STILL...
SO WE CAN BREAK THOSE STONE HORNS RIGHT OFF.
DUN

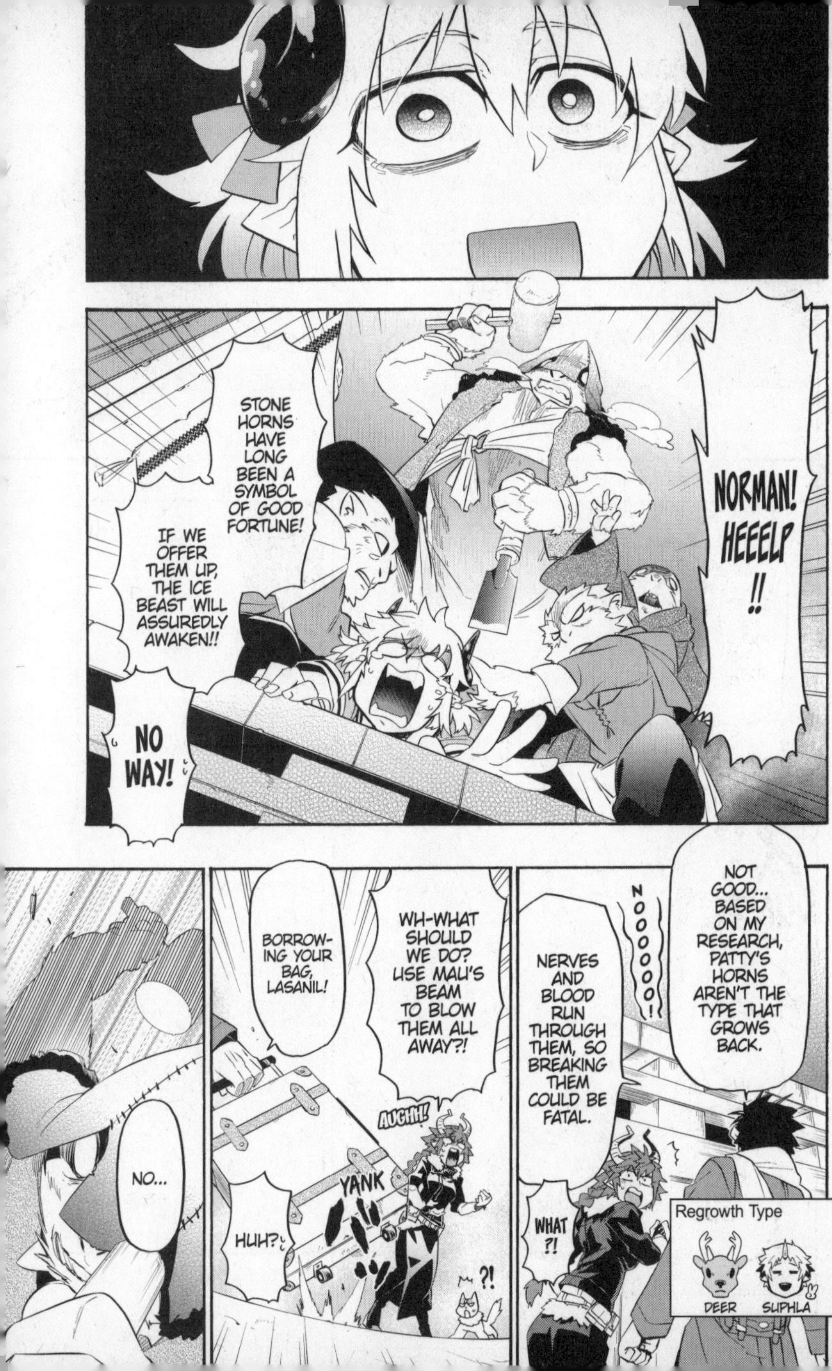
NORMAN! HEEELP!!
STONE HORNS HAVE LONG BEEN A SYMBOL OF GOOD FORTUNE!
IF WE OFFER THEM UP, THE ICE BEAST WILL ASSUREDLY AWAKEN!!
NO WAY!
NOT GOOD... BASED ON MY RESEARCH, PATTY'S HORNS AREN'T THE TYPE THAT GROWS BACK.
NOOOOOOO!
NERVES AND BLOOD RUN THROUGH THEM, SO BREAKING THEM COULD BE FATAL.
WHAT?!
Regrowth Type
DEER
SUPHLA
WH-WHAT SHOULD WE DO? USE MAU'S BEAM TO BLOW THEM ALL AWAY?!
BORROWING YOUR BAG, LASANIL!
AUGHH!
YANK
HUH?
?!
NO...

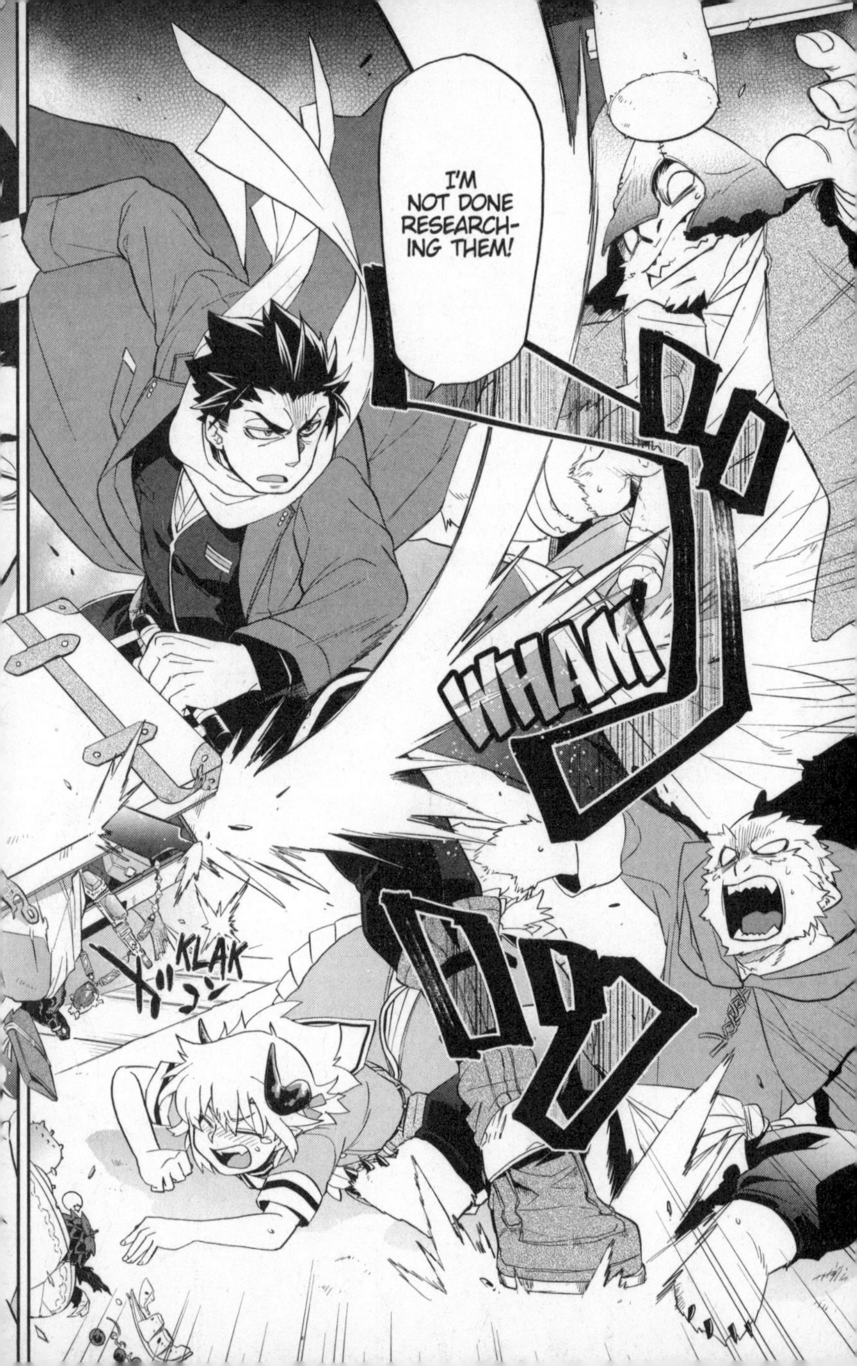
I'M NOT DONE RESEARCHING THEM!
WHAM
KLAK
ガコン

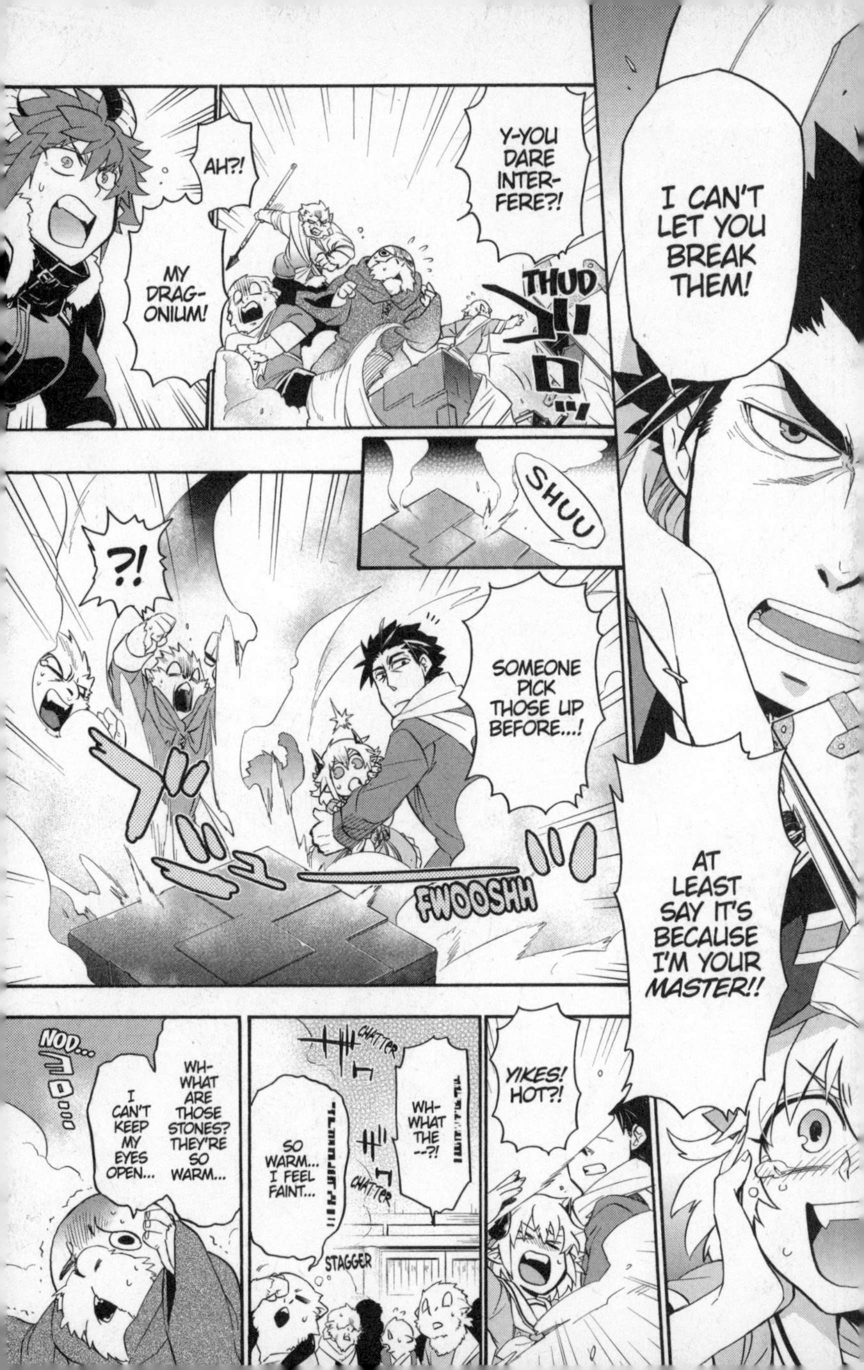
I CAN'T LET YOU BREAK THEM!
AT LEAST SAY IT'S BECAUSE I'M YOUR MASTER!!
Y-YOU DARE INTER-FERE?!
THUD
AH?!
MY DRAG-ONIUM!
SHUU
?!
SOMEONE PICK THOSE UP BEFORE...!
FWOOSHH
YIKES! HOT?!
CHATTER
WH-WHAT THE--?!
SO WARM... I FEEL FAINT...
CHATTER
STAGGER
WH-WHAT ARE THOSE STONES? THEY'RE SO WARM...
I CAN'T KEEP MY EYES OPEN...
NOD...

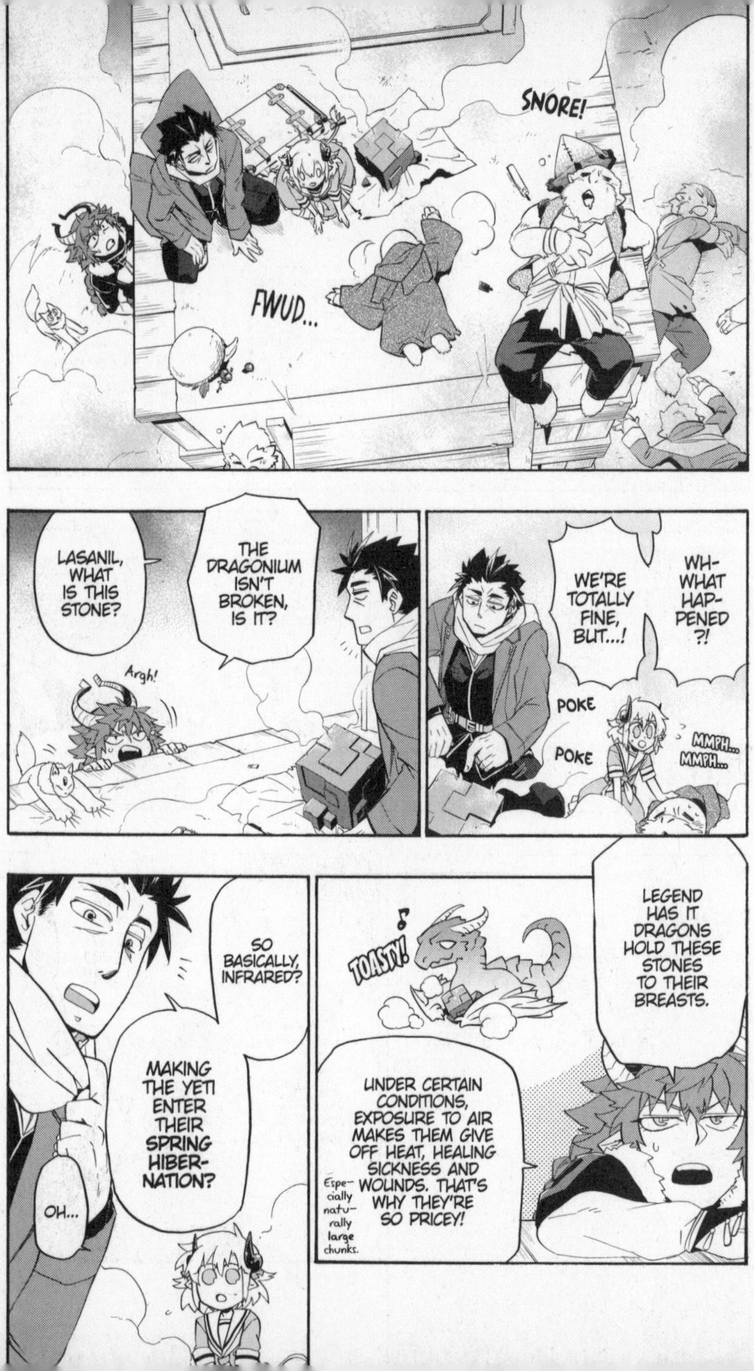
SNORE!
FWUD...
WH-WHAT HAPPENED?!
WE'RE TOTALLY FINE, BUT...!
POKE
POKE
MMPH... MMPH...
THE DRAGONIUM ISN'T BROKEN, IS IT?
LASANIL, WHAT IS THIS STONE?
Argh!
LEGEND HAS IT DRAGONS HOLD THESE STONES TO THEIR BREASTS.
TOASTY!
UNDER CERTAIN CONDITIONS, EXPOSURE TO AIR MAKES THEM GIVE OFF HEAT, HEALING SICKNESS AND WOUNDS. THAT'S WHY THEY'RE SO PRICEY!
Especially naturally large chunks.
SO BASICALLY, INFRARED?
MAKING THE YETI ENTER THEIR SPRING HIBERNATION?
OH...

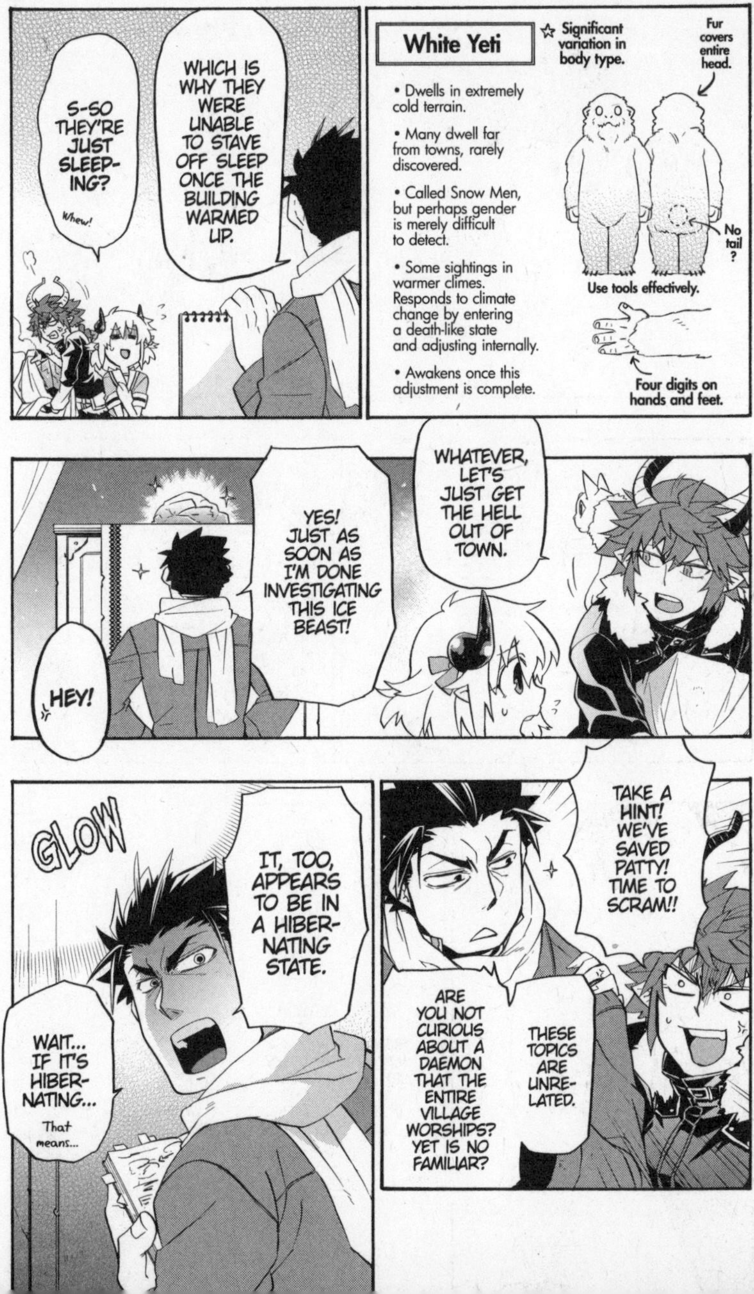
White Yeti
☆ Significant variation in body type.
Fur covers entire head.
• Dwells in extremely cold terrain.
• Many dwell far from towns, rarely discovered.
• Called Snow Men, but perhaps gender is merely difficult to detect.
• Some sightings in warmer climes. Responds to climate change by entering a death-like state and adjusting internally.
• Awakens once this adjustment is complete.
No tail?
Use tools effectively.
Four digits on hands and feet.
WHICH IS WHY THEY WERE UNABLE TO STAVE OFF SLEEP ONCE THE BUILDING WARMED UP.
S-SO THEY'RE JUST SLEEPING?
Whew!
WHATEVER, LET'S JUST GET THE HELL OUT OF TOWN.
YES! JUST AS SOON AS I'M DONE INVESTIGATING THIS ICE BEAST!
HEY!
TAKE A HINT! WE'VE SAVED PATTY! TIME TO SCRAM!!
THESE TOPICS ARE UNRELATED.
ARE YOU NOT CURIOUS ABOUT A DAEMON THAT THE ENTIRE VILLAGE WORSHIPS? YET IS NO FAMILIAR?
GLOW
IT, TOO, APPEARS TO BE IN A HIBERNATING STATE.
WAIT... IF IT'S HIBERNATING...
That means...

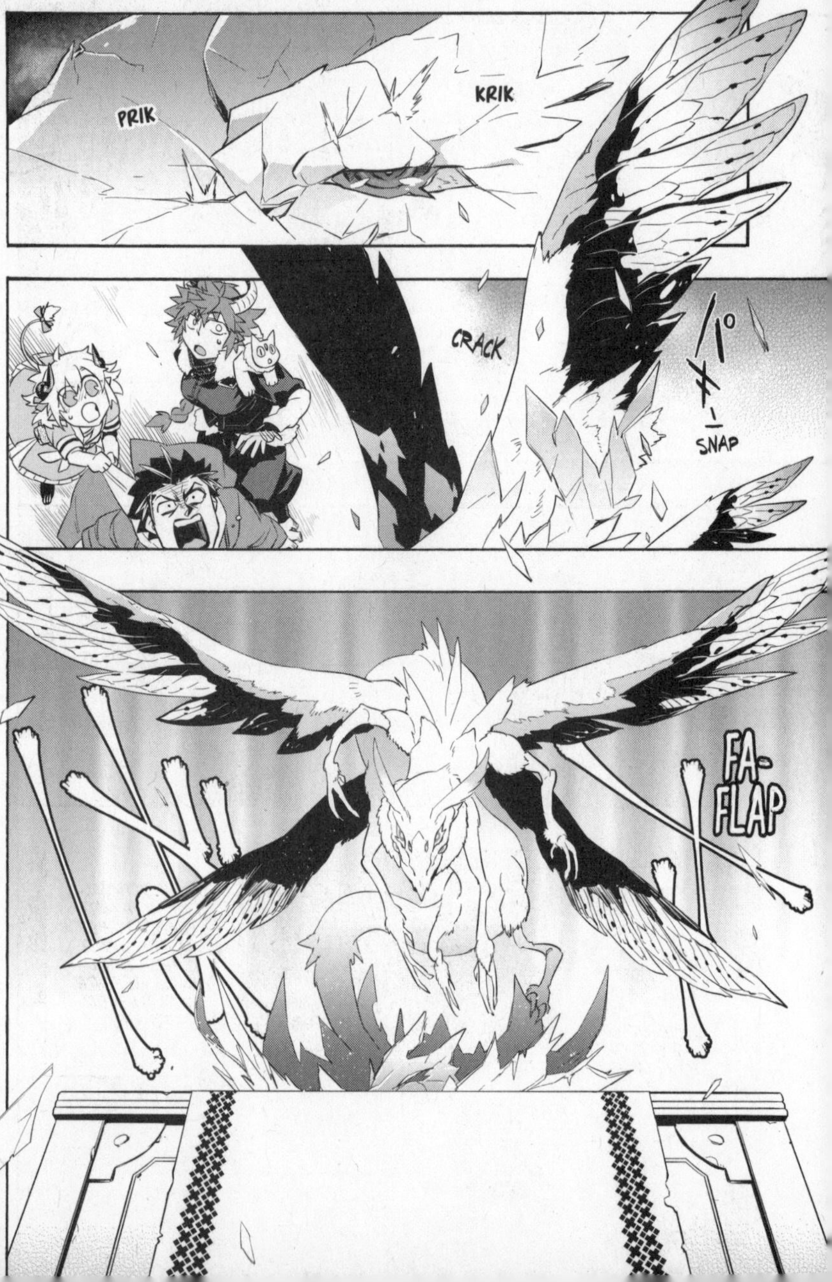
KRIK
PRIK
SNAP
CRACK
FA-FLAP

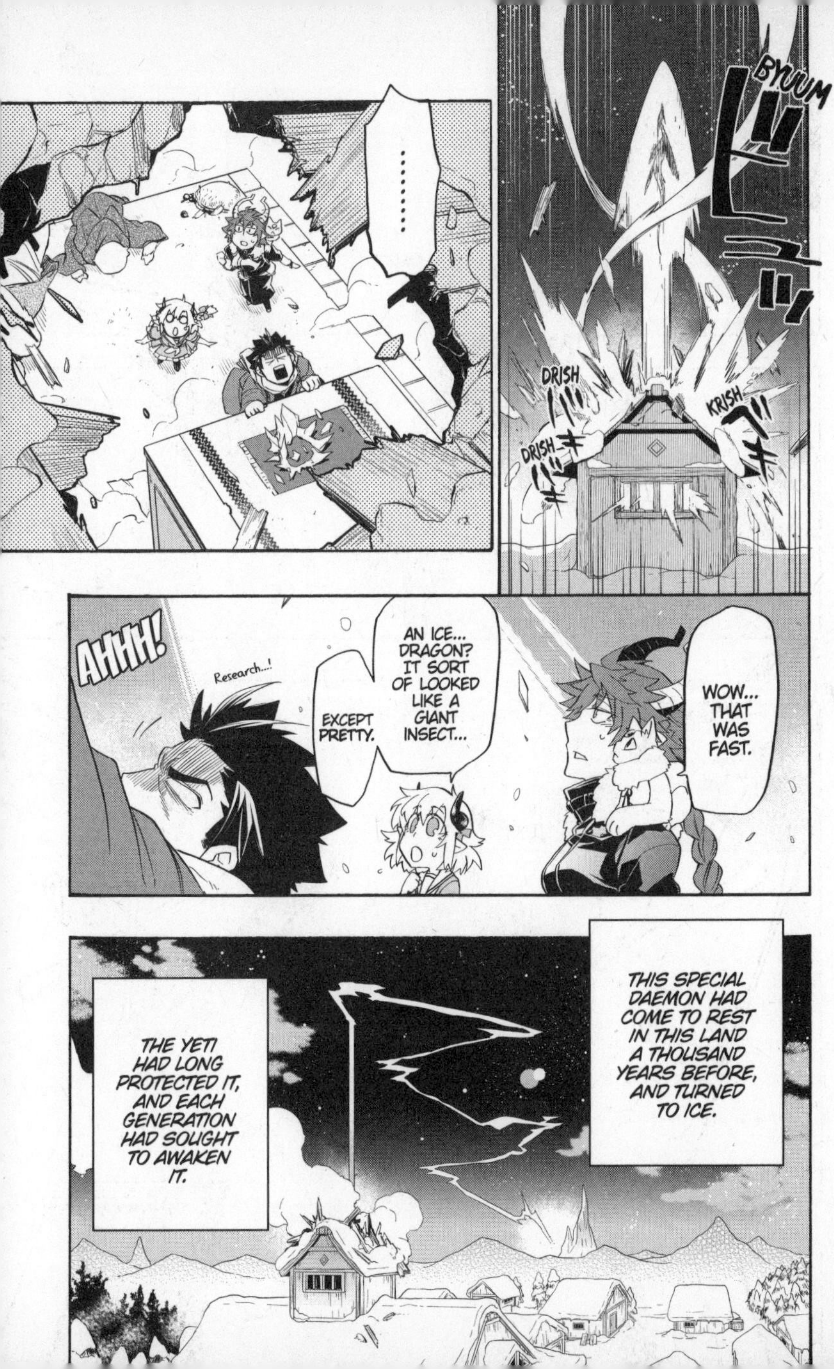
BYUUM
KRISH
DRISH
DRISH
......
WOW... THAT WAS FAST.
AN ICE... DRAGON? IT SORT OF LOOKED LIKE A GIANT INSECT...
EXCEPT PRETTY.
Research...!
AHHH!
THIS SPECIAL DAEMON HAD COME TO REST IN THIS LAND A THOUSAND YEARS BEFORE, AND TURNED TO ICE.
THE YETI HAD LONG PROTECTED IT, AND EACH GENERATION HAD SOUGHT TO AWAKEN IT.

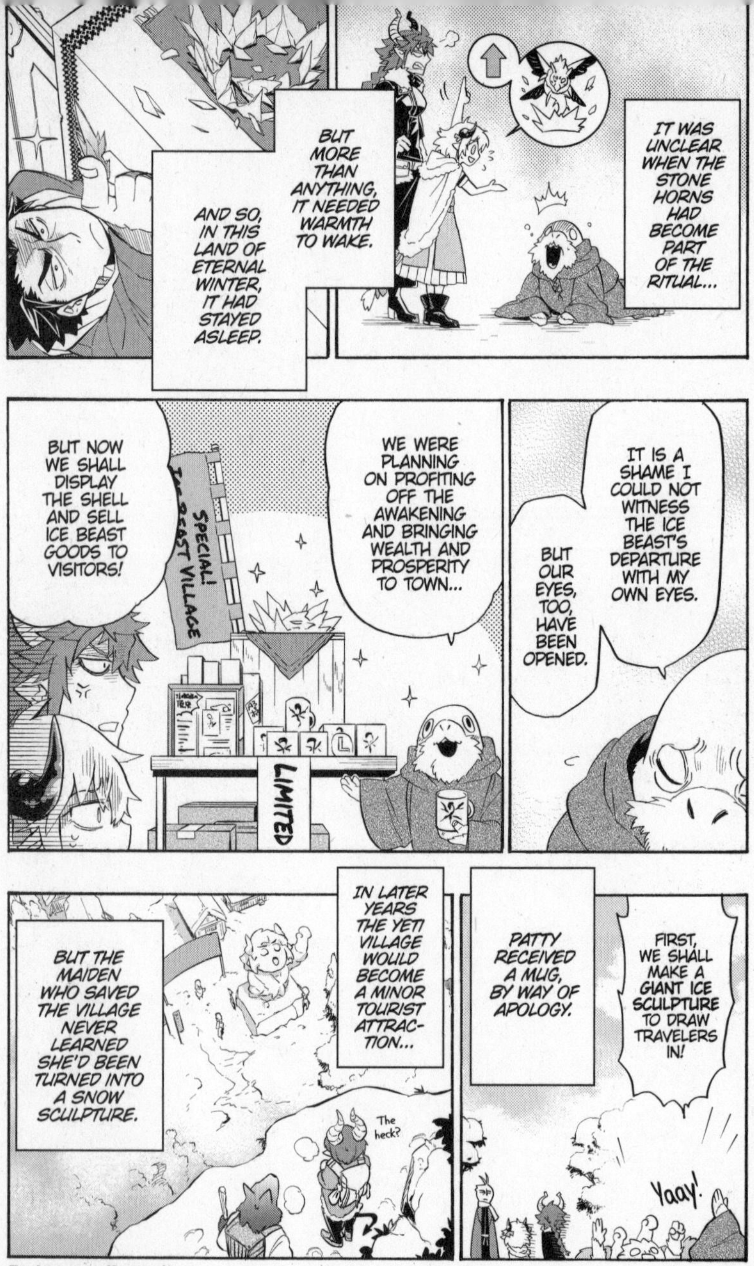
IT WAS UNCLEAR WHEN THE STONE HORNS HAD BECOME PART OF THE RITUAL...
BUT MORE THAN ANYTHING, IT NEEDED WARMTH TO WAKE.
AND SO, IN THIS LAND OF ETERNAL WINTER, IT HAD STAYED ASLEEP.
IT IS A SHAME I COULD NOT WITNESS THE ICE BEAST'S DEPARTURE WITH MY OWN EYES.
BUT OUR EYES, TOO, HAVE BEEN OPENED.
WE WERE PLANNING ON PROFITING OFF THE AWAKENING AND BRINGING WEALTH AND PROSPERITY TO TOWN...
BUT NOW WE SHALL DISPLAY THE SHELL AND SELL ICE BEAST GOODS TO VISITORS!
SPECIAL! ICE BEAST VILLAGE
LIMITED
FIRST, WE SHALL MAKE A GIANT ICE SCULPTURE TO DRAW TRAVELERS IN!
PATTY RECEIVED A MUG, BY WAY OF APOLOGY.
Yaay!
IN LATER YEARS THE YETI VILLAGE WOULD BECOME A MINOR TOURIST ATTRAC-TION...
BUT THE MAIDEN WHO SAVED THE VILLAGE NEVER LEARNED SHE'D BEEN TURNED INTO A SNOW SCULPTURE.
The heck?

To be continued!

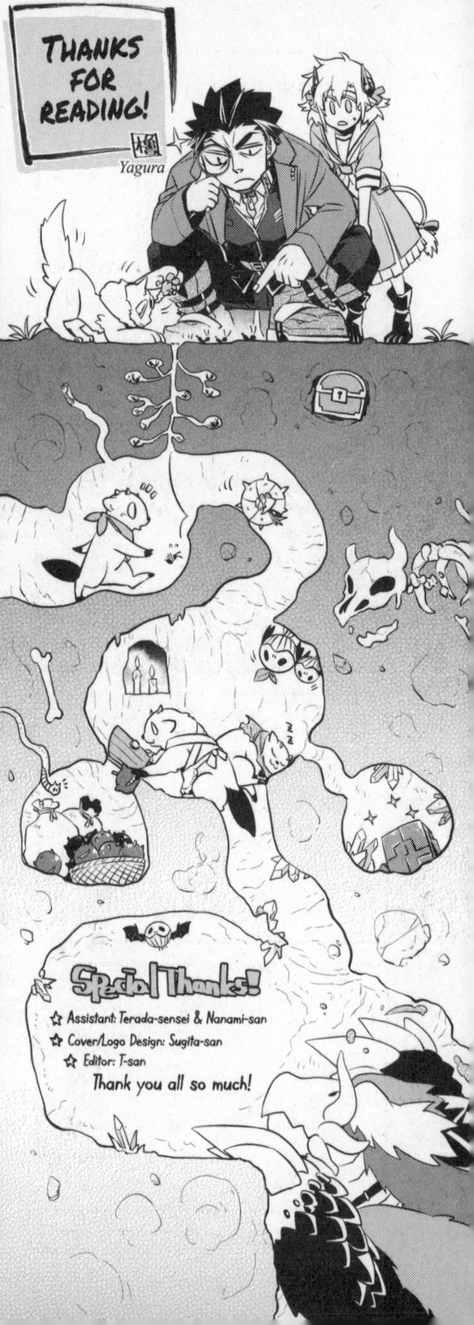
THANKS FOR READING!
Yagura
Special Thanks!
☆ Assistant: Terada-sensei & Nanami-san
☆ Cover/Logo Design: Sugita-san
☆ Editor: T-san
Thank you all so much!

IN THE HOSPITAL WITH UNCLE

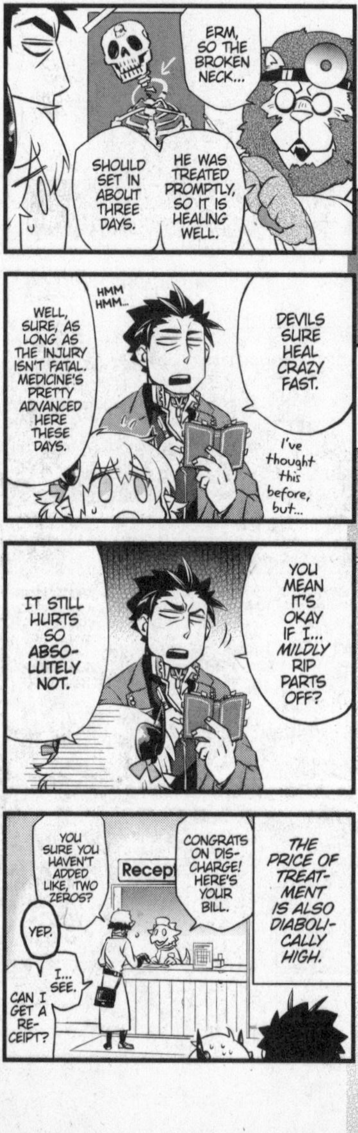
ERM, SO THE BROKEN NECK...
HE WAS TREATED PROMPTLY, SO IT IS HEALING WELL.
SHOULD SET IN ABOUT THREE DAYS.
I've thought this before, but...
DEVILS SURE HEAL CRAZY FAST.
HMM HMM...
WELL, SURE, AS LONG AS THE INJURY ISN'T FATAL. MEDICINE'S PRETTY ADVANCED HERE THESE DAYS.
YOU MEAN IT'S OKAY IF I... MILDLY RIP PARTS OFF?
IT STILL HURTS SO ABSOLUTELY NOT.
THE PRICE OF TREATMENT IS ALSO DIABOLICALLY HIGH.
CONGRATS ON DISCHARGE! HERE'S YOUR BILL.
YOU SURE YOU HAVEN'T ADDED LIKE, TWO ZEROS?
YEP.
I... SEE.
CAN I GET A RECEIPT?

ENTER LASANIL

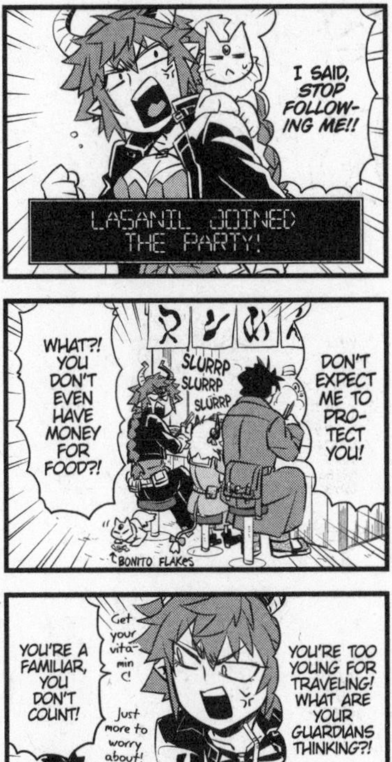
I SAID, STOP FOLLOW-ING ME!!
LASANIL JOINED THE PARTY!
DON'T EXPECT ME TO PRO-TECT YOU!
SLURRP
SLURRP
SLURRP
WHAT?! YOU DON'T EVEN HAVE MONEY FOR FOOD?!
BONITO FLAKES
YOU'RE TOO YOUNG FOR TRAVELING! WHAT ARE YOUR GUARDIANS THINKING?!
Get your vita-min C!
Just more to worry about!
YOU'RE A FAMILIAR, YOU DON'T COUNT!
SLURRP
IT'S SLIPPERY THERE, WATCH OUT!
...
SHE'D BE A GOOD MOTHER ...
FOR A DEVIL, SHE'S WAY TOO NICE...
SHE JUST MADE PATTY FEEL GUILTY.

(DEVILS) IN THE DESIGN

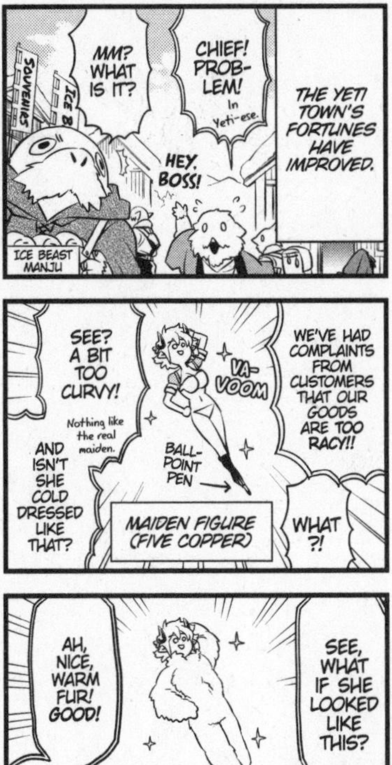
THE YETI TOWN'S FORTUNES HAVE IMPROVED.
CHIEF! PROB-LEM!
In Yeti-ese.
MM? WHAT IS IT?
HEY, BOSS!
SOUVENIRS
ICE BEAST MANJU
WE'VE HAD COMPLAINTS FROM CUSTOMERS THAT OUR GOODS ARE TOO RACY!!
WHAT?!
VA-VOOM
SEE? A BIT TOO CURVY!
Nothing like the real maiden.
AND ISN'T SHE COLD DRESSED LIKE THAT?
BALL-POINT PEN
MAIDEN FIGURE (FIVE COPPER)
SEE, WHAT IF SHE LOOKED LIKE THIS?
AH, NICE, WARM FUR! GOOD!
MUCH BETTER!
But pricey...
MAIDEN FIGURE (YETI VERSION)
THEY ONLY SOLD TWO, AND THE REST LAN-GUISHED IN THE WARE-HOUSE.
So many left...
We made too many...
BUT RARITY DROVE THE PRICE UP AFTER A FEW DECADES.

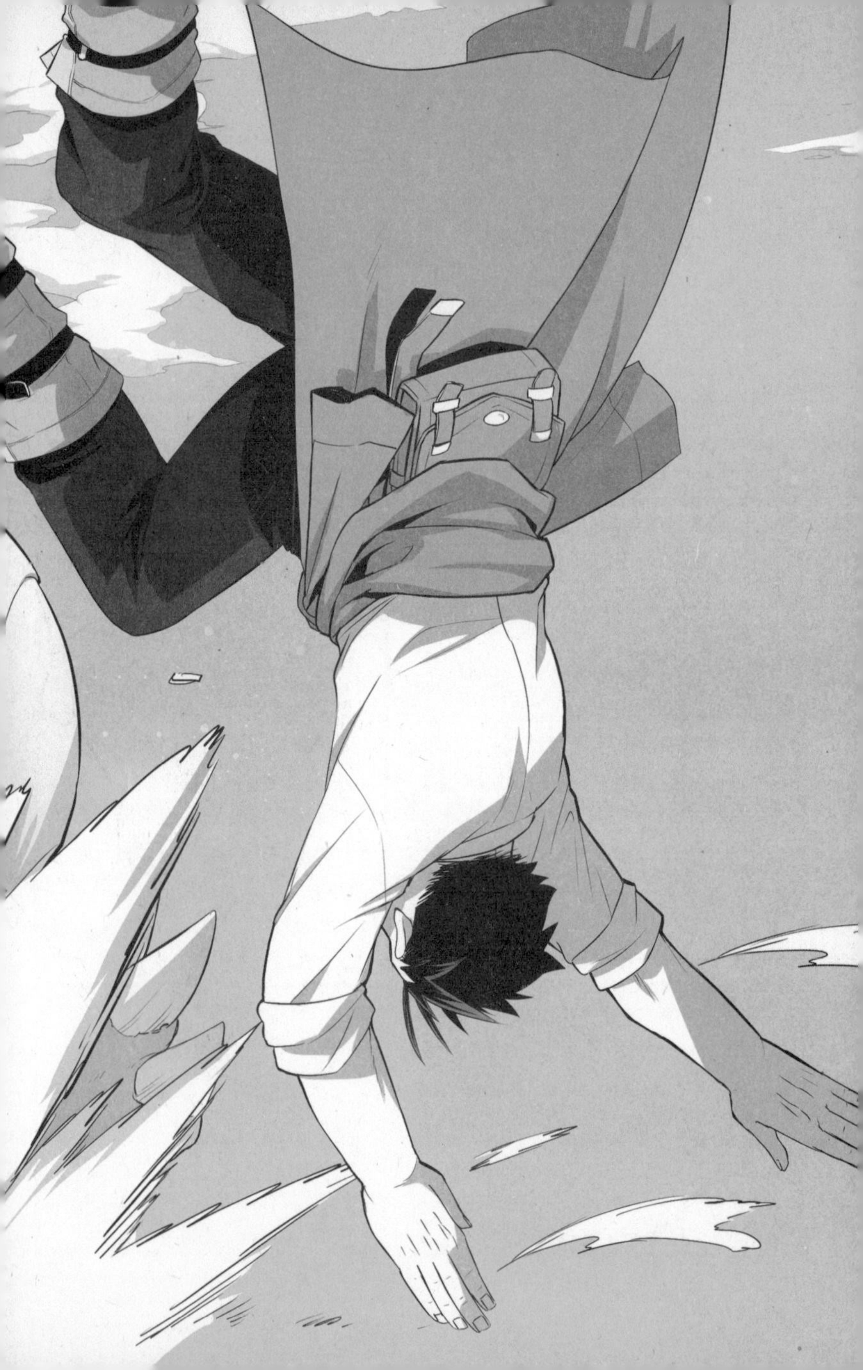

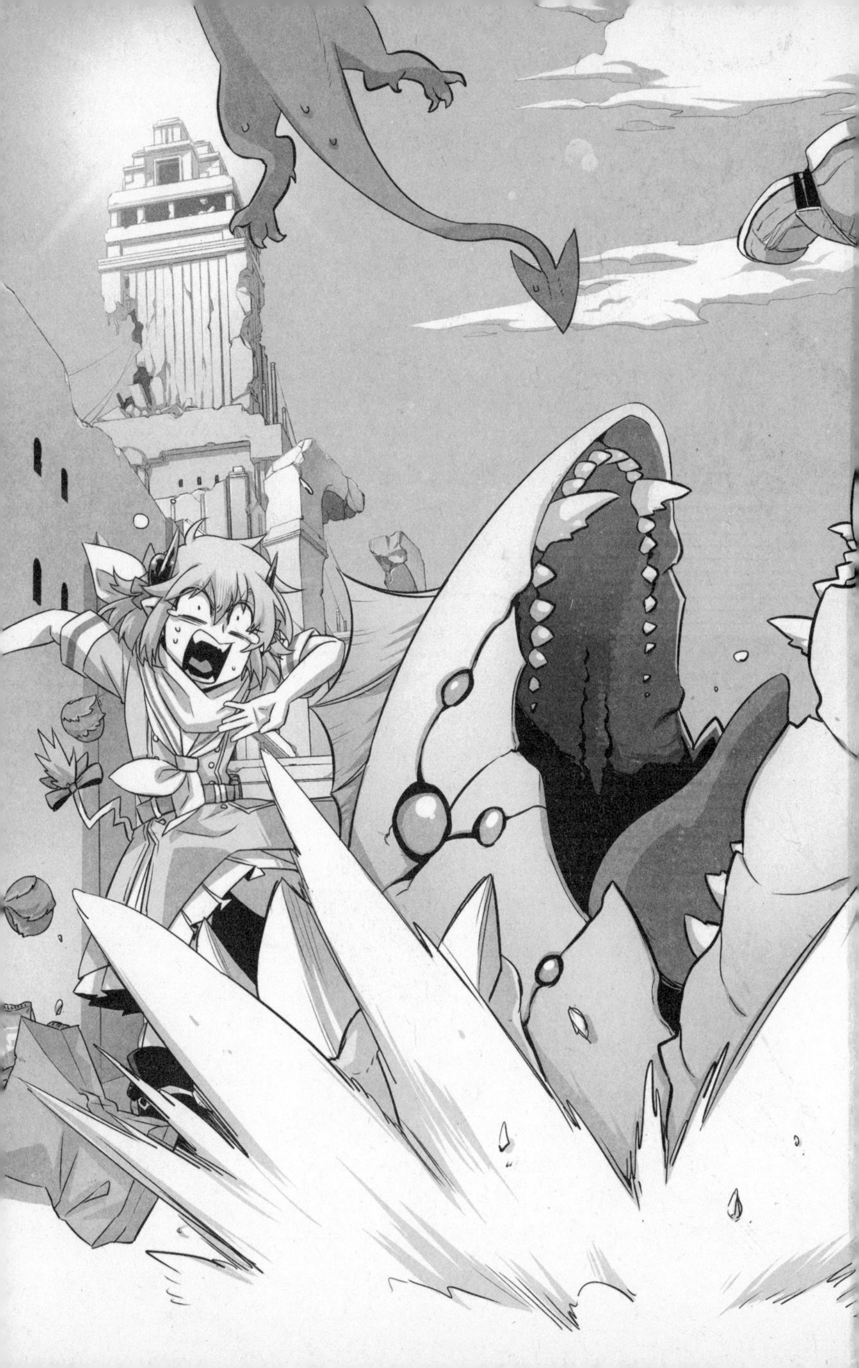

SEVEN SEAS ENTERTAINMENT PRESENTS

Sorry For My Familiar

story and art by TEKKA YAGURABA

VOLUME 2

TRANSLATION
Andrew Cunningham

ADAPTATION
Betsy Aoki

LETTERING AND RETOUCH
Kaitlyn Wiley

COVER DESIGN
KC Fabellon

PROOFREADER
Stephanie Cohen

EDITOR
Shannon Fay

PRODUCTION ASSISTANT
CK Russell

PRODUCTION MANAGER
Lissa Pattillo

EDITOR-IN-CHIEF
Adam Arnold

PUBLISHER
Jason DeAngelis

SORRY FOR MY FAMILIAR VOLUME 2
© Tekka Yaguraba 2017
All rights reserved.
First published in Japan in 2017 by Kodansha Ltd., Tokyo.
Publication rights for this English edition arranged through Kodansha Ltd., Tokyo.

Seven Seas books may be purchased in bulk for promotional, educational, or business use. Please contact your local bookseller or the Macmillan Corporate and Premium Sales Department at 1-800-221-7945, extension 5442, or by e-mail at MacmillanSpecialMarkets@macmillan.com.

Seven Seas and the Seven Seas logo are trademarks of Seven Seas Entertainment, LLC. All rights reserved.

ISBN: 978-1-626928-39-8

Printed in Canada

First Printing: July 2018

10 9 8 7 6 5 4 3 2 1

FOLLOW US ONLINE: www.sevenseasentertainment.com

READING DIRECTIONS

This book reads from *right to left*, Japanese style. If this is your first time reading manga, you start reading from the top right panel on each page and take it from there. If you get lost, just follow the numbered diagram here. It may seem backwards at first, but you'll get the hang of it! Have fun!!

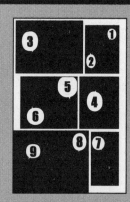